LEFT IN THE
DUST

LEFT IN THE DUST

How Race and Politics Created a Human and Environmental Tragedy in L.A.

KAREN PIPER

LEFT IN THE DUST
Copyright © Karen Piper, 2006.

First published 2006 by
PALGRAVE MACMILLAN™
175 Fifth Avenue, New York, N.Y. 10010 and
Houndmills, Basingstoke, Hampshire, England RG21 6XS.
Companies and representatives throughout the world.

PALGRAVE MACMILLAN IS THE GLOBAL ACADEMIC IMPRINT OF THE PALGRAVE MACMILLAN division of St. Martin's Press, LLC and of Palgrave Macmillan Ltd. Macmillan® is a registered trademark in the United States, United Kingdom and other countries. Palgrave is a registered trademark in the European Union and other countries.

ISBN-13: 978-1-4039-6931-6
ISBN-10: 1-4039-6931-0

Library of Congress Cataloging-in-Publication Data
Piper, Karen Lynnea, 1965–
   Left in the dust : how race and politics created a human and environmental tragedy / Karen Piper.
      p.   cm.
   Includes bibliographical references and index.
   ISBN 1-4039-6931-0
   1. Dust control—California—Los Angeles.   2. Water supply—California—Los Angeles.   3. Water diversion—Environmental aspects—California—Owens Lake Region (Inyo County)   4. Paiute Indians—California—Owens Lake Region (Inyo County)—Government relations.   5. California—Race relations.   I. Title.
TD884.5.P53 2006
333.91'137'0979488—dc22

                                                                    2005051253

A catalogue record for this book is available from the British Library.

Design by Letra Libre, Inc.

10 9 8 7 6 5 4 3 2
Printed in the United States of America.

To my mom,
for the endless newspaper clippings
and hours of desert driving

To my dad,
for the memories

CONTENTS

LIST OF ILLUSTRATIONS

Introduction

Chapter One

Chapter Two

Chapter Three

Chapter Four

Chapter Five

Conclusion

ACKNOWLEDGMENTS

This book does not belong to me. It belongs to a community who trusted me enough to share, if only for a moment, the stories that they have lived. For this, I am grateful and can only hope that my book does justice to the shape of their lives. I knew I would fail to tell the story "right" for everyone. I decided I could only tell it as I lived it while writing. In Owens Valley, where so many different voices and lives compete for the same historic and territorial space, every word can seem contested. Also, this story is always changing, so keeping pace with it proved impossible.

I would especially like to thank Dorothy Alther and the Paiute Indian tribes for allowing me to bring their voices into this story. Another attorney, Robert Cellin, was the first to read my story and urged me to turn it into a book. He also made me see that stories like this one, sadly, are happening all across the United States—recently, most notably, in New Orleans. He was a kind mentor. I also want to thank Ellen Hardebeck, who read more than one draft of the sections on the dust mitigation project. She caught all my embarrassing mistakes and showed patience with my non-scientific way of thinking. Everyone at the Great Basin Air Pollution Control District was more than friendly to and open with me, even when I questioned or didn't understand their work. To me, they are the neglected heroes of this book, who have breathed in more dust than anyone should even while trying to stop the dust from blowing. I want to thank Bill Cox and Ted Schade especially for their input. Richard Knox was a constant source of faxes and was as dedicated as a man could be to activism against environmental pollution. Brian Lamb helped me to understand the legal dimensions of the problem. Julian Lukins is an amazing journalist and was always there to chase down the story; I relied on his stories from afar. The Eastern California Sierra Museum was another treasure trove of information, as was the curator himself.

In Los Angeles, at the Department of Water and Power, everyone in the library was very helpful. Though I could not get permission to use DWP illustrations, I was grateful for the people who helped me track down advertisements. The Center for Land Use Interpretation in Los Angeles has the best photographs of Owens Valley, as well as the friendliest staff imaginable. The Huntington Library in Pasadena hosted me while I wrote this book and provided a wealth of companionship and entertainment, both in the historians who worked there and the archival resources. Historian Andrew Harley was a source of support and inspired me with his own work on water in Mexico City and L.A. Mike Davis's work and kind words were invaluable to me.

Finally, my mother was the eyes for this book when I couldn't be in California. I sent her everywhere in Southern California, taking pictures. She wrote down quotes, drove in circles, kept me up on the news, and generally supplied the backbone of gossip for this book. She told me who got arrested, who died, and any other tidbits of information she could find. I had a hard time keeping up with all the newspaper clippings she sent me. For me, this is how history is revealed, through gossip and eavesdropping and clippings passed down from mother to daughter. So to all the people who shared their pieces of history, I am grateful for being allowed to participate.

There it is. Take it!
>   —William Mulholland on the opening
>   of the Los Angeles Aqueduct,
>   which brought Owens Valley
>   water to L.A., November 5, 1913

Hear me, Los Angeles:
There it is. Fix it!
>   —Michael Dorame on the dust pollution
>   problem in Owens Valley, caused by
>   the Los Angeles Aqueduct, July 2, 1997

LEFT IN THE
DUST

INTRODUCTION

I took an interest in Owens Lake because I grew up breathing its dust. This dust, which is fine and white as flour, covers my hometown when the wind blows. It comes from Owens Lake, which has been dry since 1920, when Los Angeles decided to drain it and send its water off to the city. It is currently the worst source of dust pollution in the nation. The lake, which is thirty miles long, is set at the base of the Eastern Sierras, two hundred miles north of Los Angeles. It is sometimes white from the salt, sometimes pink from algae, and sometimes a dirty gray. The surface of the lake grows "salt blooms," which are mushroom-shaped balls of crystal that seep up from the underground brine pool. When the wind blows, often up to sixty miles an hour, sand blows and knocks these fragile crystals off the surface. The cyclonic winds cause water spouts on Owens Lake—the wind was so strong that it once piled a group of rocks, four inches in diameter, on one side of the lake. Because of the strong wind conditions, the fine-grained dust travels unusually long distances. In a windstorm, the dust fills Owens Valley and spills over the 12,000 to 14,000–foot mountain peaks surrounding the valley to the west. To the south, the mountains are lower, so the valley acts as a funnel and easily pushes the dust through the first town south of Owens Lake, Ridgecrest, and on toward Los Angeles. Dust plumes have been tracked by satellite 150 miles south to the Los Angeles area, and high dust content in the Grand Canyon has been attributed to winds coming from Southern California.[1] (See figure I.1.)

I grew up in Ridgecrest (population 30,000), which is in the Indian Wells Valley, the next valley south of Owens Valley. Only fifty miles from the lake, Ridgecrest is the first town covered in dust when the wind blows from the north. In Ridgecrest, doctors have reported that emergency room visits go up ten times during dust storms. "When we see the white cloud

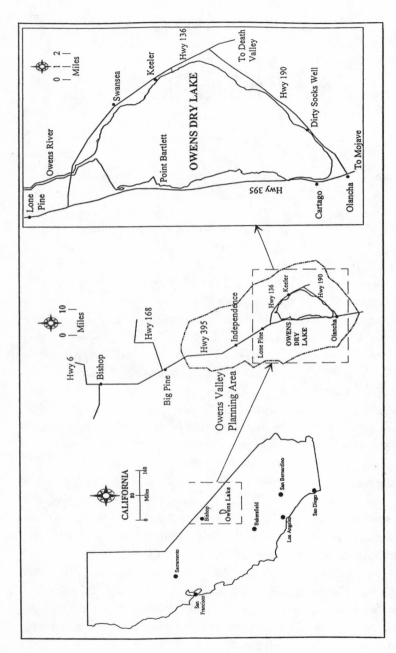

I.1. Map of the Owens Dry Lake. Courtesy Great Basin Air Pollution Control District, Bishop, CA.

headed down through the pass, the ER and doctors' offices fill up with people who suddenly got worse. It's a pretty straightforward cause and effect," explained Dr. Bruce Parker of Ridgecrest Community Hospital.[2] Locally, the dust is called "Keeler fog" after the town of Keeler on the shores of Owens Lake. As a child, I believed it really *was* fog—because it moved in like fog from over the mountains, blocking the sun. It hung in the air like fog even when there was no wind. There were days when the sun disappeared and it was hard to breathe—but no one ever explained to me what it was. No one knew, then, that it was dangerous. Now, they say, there are times when the dust is "worse than the highest concentrations when Mt. St. Helens blew."[3] (See figure I.2.)

The dust is called PM–10. The PM stands for "particulate matter." The 10 signifies that individual particles are smaller than 10 micrograms in diameter, which allows them to infiltrate lung tissue. You breathe this dust in, but you don't breathe it out. It remains permanently in your body, causing autoimmune reactions. Today, Harvard scientists have done a study showing that inhaling significant amounts of this kind of dust causes death rates

I.2. Dust Storm at Owens Lake. Photo by Karen Piper. Used with permission.

to rise by 26 percent.[4] The dust also contains a unique mix of toxic heavy metals such as arsenic, nickel, selenium, and cadmium.[5] Once naturally occurring in the brine lake, these metals became airborne after the lake was drained and disappeared. Thirty tons of arsenic and nine tons of cadmium, as well as nickel and other substances, are blown from the lake annually. Like asbestos, the dust can cause pulmonary fibrosis or other lung diseases, which are autoimmune responses to invasion by foreign bodies. The lungs scar and stiffen, causing decreased lung capacity over time. In some cases, the dust can cause pulmonary hypertension, or increased blood pressure in the pulmonary artery, eventually leading to failure of the left ventricle of the heart. According to a recent study on PM–10, "there may be no threshold below which health effects do not occur." These effects include absorption of the dust into the blood, allergic effects, fibrosis, cancer, and long-term decrease in lung function.[6] My sister now has a form of lupus, and three other girls in my neighborhood were also diagnosed with this disease; two have since died. My childhood friend from church now has acute respiratory distress syndrome, as do four babies from the same church—they are currently all in the hospital. And my mother's neighbor was just diagnosed with rheumatoid arthritis of the lungs and is on oxygen. I have suffered from bouts of pneumonia and asthma my entire life, as well as life-threatening allergies. The town is full of cancer, too, and my mother often calls to read me the obituaries. "So many people in their forties," she once commented. I took an interest in Owens Lake because of eighteen years' worth of dust embedded in my lungs. It was only as I began studying the history of Owens Lake that I found another—subterranean—story of racial oppression that led me back to the City of Los Angeles.

Owens Lake is not like other dry lakes. Most dry lakes were created by the recession of glaciers over thousands of years, which gave the lakebeds time to stabilize as they were shrinking. The surface of these dry lakes gradually became compacted and hardened after being exposed to hundreds of years of rainfall. Owens Lake, in contrast, is like a giant bowl of fresh talcum powder (see figure I.3). It was not completely dry until the mid-1920s, making it one of the youngest dry lakes in the world. In the 1800s, it had daily steamboat crossings and measured 110 square miles (see figure I.4). But in 1913, the Owens River was diverted away from the lake by the City of Los Angeles, and it slowly dried up. Ted Schade, who is an officer for the

I.3. Owens Dry Lake today. Photo by Karen Piper. Used with permission.

I.4. Owens Lake, circa 1920, Eastern California Museum.

Great Basin Air Pollution Control District, explained, "Owens Lake has been dry for less than a century; it is still in a very dynamic state. Given time, perhaps hundreds of years, Owens Lake would stabilize; we see signs of natural stabilization processes occurring. However, we cannot wait for hundreds of years."[7] Today, Owens Lake produces 10 to 100 times more dust than other dry lakes in southern California and Nevada and, by some estimates, about 8 percent of all the fine dust in the United States. By conservative estimates, Owens Lake emits 300,000–400,000 metric tons of dust per year. During a severe storm, 50 tons of dust per second comes off the lakebed.[8] (See figures I.5 and I.6.)

The U.S. Navy, which owns a weapons testing facility in the area, began to study the health effects of the dust long before the Environmental Protection Agency (EPA). Capt. William Ostag of the Naval Air Weapons Station complained: "Local public health officials have stated that compared to the rest of Kern County and California as a whole, an unusually high percentage of deaths that occur in the Ridgecrest area are the result of acute respiratory conditions." The U.S. Navy, concerned with these findings, solicited e-mail descriptions of illnesses associated with the dust.

I.5. Aerial View of Owens Dry Lake on a Clear Day, Mono Lake Committee. Reproduced with permission.

I.6. Aerial View of Owens Lake Dust, Mono Lake Committee. Reproduced with permission.

Hundreds of replies came in immediately, complaining of "allergy-like symptoms, sinus infections, migraine headaches, asthma attacks, and other respiratory ailments." Ostag commented, "We were especially distressed to learn of the asthma and other impacts on the thousands of children of our civilian employees."[9] These respiratory illnesses are only the immediate effect of the dust—many longer term illnesses either have not yet presented themselves or have not been associated with the dust.

In Owens Valley in Inyo County, 18,000 people live. There are several Paiute Indian reservations in the path of the dust, and the Paiutes have long been complaining of dust-related health problems. Tribal leader Sandra Jefferson Yonge, from the Lone Pine Paiute tribe, is tired of waiting for a solution to her health problems. In 1997, she said, "I think it's very criminal because I'm slowly dying. Once it was so bad I ended up in the hospital because I couldn't breathe."[10] Harry Williams of the Bishop Paiute tribe concurred: "We are being forced to live in a hazmat area every time we get a little bit of wind. Last Saturday I drove through Lone Pine and could taste the metallic taste in my mouth. . . . All the way along, the wind was blowing from the south, you see this big brown cloud above you. If people don't think that is a problem, I don't know what is a problem."[11] There are about 2,200 Paiutes living in Inyo County, as well as 290 Shoshone. This is the largest remaining Paiute population in the United States.

Besides those impacted by the dust in Ridgecrest and Owens Valley, there are also those from Los Angeles who receive the occasional dust storm—especially those living in L.A.'s Inland Empire. Eileen Jensen described walking outside with her husband one day in San Bernardino, east of Los Angeles, and finding the ground covered in "ash." She said, "When we went out to get the morning paper, we discovered our car was an ashtray. It was covered in gray ash. It was on the morning news: 'Where did it come from? Outer space? What was it?' By the time the evening news came on, it was discovered that it came from Owens Valley."[12] Eileen Jensen and her husband later moved to Owens Valley, but her husband had to return to Los Angeles because he developed chronic bronchitis. She said, "If he had stayed here [in Owens Valley], he would have been dead. He has the bronchitis now, but he is alive."[13] There are 1,700,000 people living in San Bernardino County, which is the first densely populated area that the dust hits. According to the 2000 Census, 39 to 40 percent of the residents are Hispanic.

Besides people, the dust also impacts sensitive ecosystems in several National Parks and wilderness areas surrounding Owens Lake, including the John Muir Wilderness and Ansel Adams Wilderness. The vegetation and soils of these areas are not adapted to saline conditions because, by some estimates, the lake held water continuously for at least the past 800,000 years.[14] Today, the Bristlecone Pine Forest, which contains trees up to 4,500 years old, has been found coated with alkali dust after a storm. Harry Williams of the Bishop Paiute tribe commented: "There is every year three hundred thousand tons of dust and it goes someplace. . . . We are talking eighty years of three hundred thousand tons. I don't know what that adds up to, but it's landing someplace. It's landing on wetlands. It's landing on animals. Things are being affected. The Forest Service is telling you the oldest things in the world, it's up that high."[15] In the early 1900s, horticulturalists noticed that the "Owens Lake Fog" that hung around the lake was an effective pesticide for local fruit trees. They also noticed that it killed unwanted plants in gardens and along roadsides. Owens Lake dust was briefly marketed as a pesticide or herbicide and even carried in cans across the

Sierras to clear grass and shrubs along the railroad in San Joaquin Valley.[16] Today, it is strangling National Parks.

Despite the obvious dessication of Owens Valley, the Department of Water and Power once proposed that all remaining shrubs and trees in the valley be destroyed because they used water that could go to the city. In 1959, a DWP report proposed that (a) the ground water be pumped to a level that would no longer support the growth of plants in the valley, and (b) "a program of removal" be used on any remaining plants in the valley.[17] In 1970, the Department of Water and Power began pumping groundwater, lowering the water table from 9.5 to 15 feet in Owens Valley. The woodlands and tule reed marshes completely disappeared, leaving only alkali scrubland. By 1974, the Grand Jury described Owens Valley: "The land is essentially barren, the pheasant population is zero, planted birds are shot in a few hours on two or three designated days. Quail may be seen principally around population centers. . . . Ducks and geese rarely use the area, once a major flyway, since food and water are no longer available."[18] In contrast, the owner of the Cerro Gordo mine described the days when the lake was full: "When the ducks took off on Owens Lake, you could hear them at Cerro Gordo [several thousand feet above the lake]." He remembered the days when ducks were hauled out by the wagonload to feed the miners at Cerro Gordo.

Navy scientists at the China Lake Naval Weapons Center first identified Owens Lake as a source of large dust storms in 1975. In 1979, after receiving a large number of complaints from the public, the Inyo County (Owens Valley) Board of Supervisors passed Resolution 79–43 requesting the district to "take whatever steps are necessary to abate said hazard."[19] Legally, it fell under the mandate of the Great Basin Unified Air Pollution Control District (APCD) to abate such problems. So in 1982, the Great Basin APCD demanded that because the Los Angeles Aqueduct had caused the dust problem, the Los Angeles Department of Water and Power must apply for an air quality permit in order to continue diverting water from Owens Lake. This decision by the APCD was nothing more than an attempt to do its job and protect air quality, but for the Department of Water and Power, the decision was seen as a threat to the livelihood of Los Angeles and the millions of people who lived there. The DWP repeatedly petitioned but failed to get action, so finally it reached an agreement with the Great Basin APCD to fund studies to stop the dust. In return, the Great Basin APCD agreed not to divert water from the City of Los Angeles.[20]

In 1987, the dust problem was recognized by the EPA as being in violation of the Clean Air Act (later its status would be raised to "serious")—air quality violations were found to reach twenty-six times the federal standards set by the Clean Air Act.[21] In accordance with the laws of the Clean Air Act, the EPA established February 8, 1997 as the deadline for a State Implementation Plan (SIP) to fix the problem. The EPA mandated that the Department of Water and Power clean up the problem, which the EPA called a major health risk. Even though the dust problem had existed since the 1920s, it took the administration over sixty years to even declare it a problem. Initially, this was due to ignorance about the danger of this kind of dust. But even after the EPA officially recognized the danger in 1987, the Department of Water and Power still took another fourteen years to start implementing a solution—for reasons that were largely political.

During this time, the Department of Water and Power continued to deny that the dust *was* a problem, claiming that it only affected visibility "a little." Controversy over the significance of Owens Lake dust swirled for decades. But the denial of risk may have been a strategic way for the Department of Water and Power to deny or postpone responsibility. In *Ecopopulism,* sociologist Andrew Sasz claims that denial is a common response by industry to the environmental problems it creates: "The firms or industrial sectors blamed for the problem are likely to respond with counterclaims—that there is no problem, or that it is exaggerated, or that the data are too poor for anyone to say anything certain about the purported risk."[22] Anecdotal, community, or physical evidence was downplayed by both the government and the Department of Water and Power in deferment to "scientific" knowledge—which did not yet exist. So there was a vacuum in "legitimate" knowledge, which is not uncommon in hazardous waste situations.

In Owens Valley, part of the problem was that there had been no epidemiological health studies; the health impact from the dust is still historically unknown. Although scientists agree that the dust poses a significant health risk, there are no statistics on how many have died or become ill from the dust. Some have suggested that the Department of Water and

Power has discouraged these kinds of studies, whether openly or covertly. The District Attorney of Inyo County, LaJoie Herald Gibbons, Jr., for instance, said that he approached a doctor in Lone Pine twenty-five years ago and asked for help in getting autopsies of people who died in the area so he could determine the health hazard. The doctor's response was, "I don't think I can do that. I do physicals for the [Los Angeles] Department of Water and Power."[23] Since the Department of Water and Power is the landlord in Owens Valley, as well as a major employer and provider of services, people are often afraid to challenge it.

For this reason, many Owens Valley locals, as well as Navy employees, took it upon themselves to try to sort out the extent of the problem. After finding fish in his lake "belly up," one Owens Valley rancher decided to conduct his own study of the dust's toxicity, concerned that his water was also full of the arsenic that was coating the soil. He said, "I did my own experiment by putting ground from my flower bed (where I could no longer get flowers to grow) into two pots along with green onion seeds and watered one with well water and the other with bottled water. The one I watered with bottled water grew to about four inches in a week and a half, and the other never did grow."[24] He believed that his well was contaminated with Owens Lake dust. In 2000, the Ridgecrest *Daily Independent* also reported that dangerous levels of arsenic had been found in Ridgecrest's underground aquifer.[25] The arsenic level has since been found to be as high as 48 parts per billion (ppb). The allowable level of arsenic in drinking water, set by the EPA, is 10 ppb. Studies have shown that long-term doses larger than 10 ppb may cause cancer of the bladder, kidney, liver, lung, nasal passages, prostate, and skin. In addition, arsenic has been linked to cardiovascular, hormonal, immunological, neurological, and pulmonary diseases. In Ridgecrest, besides the 48 ppb of arsenic in the water, there is the additional problem of arsenic that blows off the dry lakebed. Arsenic, which naturally occurs in the area, becomes a problem only when it is unnaturally concentrated in certain areas. Owens Lake dust is spreading arsenic all over Owens Valley and Ridgecrest. Today, the number-one health concern among people in Ridgecrest is putting water back in Owens Lake.[26]

I began this book as an experiment to discover the connection between disease and dust, and to find out why it was so difficult to thrive in Ridgecrest. There are several approaches to the story of Owens Lake. On the one hand, there is the federal or legal story, which is largely framed by the EPA. On the other hand, there is the city story, which is about the threat to Los Angeles's water. But I wanted to tell the other, largely unheard, stories of those who breathed the dust from Owens Lake, including the Paiutes on reservations created by the Department of Water and Power, the Japanese interned at Manzanar during World War II, and the local populations in Ridgecrest and Owens Valley. These stories are not difficult to find. Because the dust has been blowing since the 1920s, there has been a great deal of publicity about it, even before anyone knew the dust was toxic. In the 1970s, for instance, photographs from Ridgecrest's *Daily Independent* show dust storms in which there was no visibility from one side of the road to the other. Lou Parrachia of Ridgecrest described those bad storms: "The wind came up, and there would be a white out. It would come in through the tiniest cracks of your house. You could rub your hand over any flat surface and there would be a fine coating of white dust."[27] In Manzanar, near Owens Lake, the Japanese internees during World War II said it was like having a barrel of flour dumped on them. By recovering these anecdotal dust stories, I hope to revise the "official" narrative that has been circulated by the Department of Water and Power. These stories, oral and written, have not previously been gathered. They create a picture of a place and people deeply impacted, to this day, by the City of Los Angeles. In Lone Pine, which is even closer to the lake, resident Lois Wilson said, "There's lots of talk about shooting out the transformers or blowing up the aqueduct like they did in the old days. But that's just talk. Nobody wants to go to prison."[28]

I am interested in weaving together federal, scientific, legal, and local histories because I believe that Owens Lake itself provides a forum for all these different discourses to intermingle, fight, and forge a new, interdisciplinary language. Besides merging and molding the languages that surround it, Owens Lake is now also reshaping the City of Los Angeles as well as threatening to expose the subtext of racism behind the distribution of risks in L.A. Ulrich Beck in *Risk Society: Towards a New Modernity* argues that today cities are forced to deal with the negative effects of modernization, whereas in the early twentieth century, the immediate effects were often positive. Beck describes risk society as an "epoch in which the dark sides of progress increasingly come to dominate social debate."[29] The Department of Water and Power, for instance, has to choose between the lesser of two evils: the effects of toxic dust or not enough clean water for Los Angeles. In a risk society, the institutions themselves are forced to change because of the adverse effects of their working. The risks or negative side effects of urbanization and industrialization may have grown so great that the business of shuffling risks has overtaken the business of providing services. Across the nation, cities are finding themselves in financial crises as they deal with aging infrastructures and the environmental consequences of their development.

Los Angeles finds itself in a growing double bind because of Owens Lake. Returning water to Owens Lake means increasing water shortages and expense for the City of Los Angeles. For this reason, the City has long tried to avoid this possibility. But hanging on to the water for Los Angeles means sacrificing the health of those outside the city, particularly the Indians of Owens Valley. Ultimately, the EPA will not allow this to happen, even if the City argues that it is the responsible thing to do. Besides telling the stories of those who have breathed the dust, *Left in the Dust* examines how Los Angeles has dealt with this issue—which is ironically contributing to the argument to privatize water in L.A. The City of Los Angeles is saying that it simply cannot afford to solve the problem. This book explains why the Department of Water and Power held on to its water so tightly for so long, forcing the Great Basin Air Pollution Control District (APCD) to try to stop the dust without using water. Ultimately, after twenty years of trying to solve the dust problem in this way, the Department of Water and Power is being forced to return some water to Owens Lake. Today, as the Department of Water and Power contemplates the possibility of permanently returning water to the lake, it is also being forced to revise drastically its ideas about serving the "public good." It is also increasingly contemplating bankruptcy, as studies have shown that the expense of fixing Owens Lake may bankrupt the City. In this sense, the Department of Water and Power may now be losing out not only to Owens Lake but also to private water and electric companies that are ready to move in if it collapses. *Left in the Dust* looks first at the history of the battle between Owens Valley and Los Angeles at the beginning of the twentieth century and examines the DWP's financial crisis at the end of the century—when it was confronted with competitors like Enron and Poseidon. In both instances, with help from the government, the real benefactors have been corporate enterprises, venture capitalists, and real estate speculators. Those who have been sacrificed on both ends of the aqueduct are people of color and working-class people.

The Censored City

Though descriptions of the dust have long peppered the local news, knowledge of the dust's health hazard has remained abysmally low in Indian Wells and Owens Valley. This knowledge has been limited, in part, because the Department of Water and Power has long censored any problems with the aqueduct. From the start, dissenters against the aqueduct plans were seen as a threat to the growth of Los Angeles. They were combated with lawsuits and publicity campaigns by the Department of Water and Power. In 1914, for instance, bacteriologist Dr. Ethel Leonard filed suit to keep the City from supplying aqueduct water to its residents. She suggested that the water in Owens Valley was polluted by the remains of animals found floating in the aqueduct, as well as runoff from slaughterhouses and dumps.[30] (Years later, Father John J. Crowley said that the only bighorn sheep he could find in Owens Valley were those that had "fallen into the aqueduct."[31]) Los Angeles countered with a publicity campaign to prove the water's purity, narrowly averting a closure of the aqueduct. Publicity battles such as this one were common in DWP history—the Department of Water and Power often described itself as a victim of people threatening its water supply. It saw itself as the city's protector, definer, and instigator of growth. Those who disagreed with the policies of the Department of Water and Power were labeled early on as naysayers.

Before the aqueduct opened, some people were concerned about the water's purity while others believed that the aqueduct engineering was not sound—largely because its designer, William Mulholland, was a self-trained engineer. Finally, many believed that the aqueduct was unnecessary and merely a corrupt moneymaking scheme. (Out of the 20,000 cubic inches that the aqueduct supplied, the City said it could use only 2,000—the City also admitted that it had not looked into developing its own underground water source.)[32] In general, early critics questioned the soundness of the aqueduct plan, the purity of the aqueduct water, and the integrity of the water board. Labeled the aqueduct naysayers, these critics were often mocked or silenced by the *Los Angeles Times*, whose owner had a financial stake in the success of the aqueduct. The naysayers were commonly depicted as buffoons in cartoons by the *Los Angeles Times* and the Department of Water and Power. (One cartoon, for instance, depicts a naysayer being swept away in a flood of approaching aqueduct water.)

While "boosters" hyped the values of Los Angeles in order to sell land, extolling its wonders in endless ad campaigns and newspapers articles, those who depicted Los Angeles as a bleak or corrupt place were at first called naysayers and later called *noir*. Interestingly, the connection between naysayer and *noir* has never been studied. Roman Polanski's *Chinatown* (1974) is the most well-known *noir* narrative of the history of the Los Angeles Aqueduct. *Chinatown*'s writer, Robert Towne, came up with the script after studying the Los Angeles–Owens Valley conflict: "I started with Carey McWilliams' book on Southern California, *An Island on the Land* (1946) and then went to Morrow Mayo's *Los Angeles* (1933) and several tracts. I read some of the Department of Water and Power's own accounts which rationalised and justified what happened."[33] *Chinatown* tells the story of a corrupt scheme to acquire power for a handful of men by acquiring water when water was not even needed by the city. In order to use Department of Water and Power land for filming, Towne claimed, "We just told them we were doing a detective story set many years ago, so they had no idea what was going on."[34] In *Chinatown*, the corruption in Los Angeles is so entrenched that there seems to be no way of combating it—those in power own the media and the police as well as the water and land.

Originally, Roman Polanski wanted to call the film *Water and Power*, but, fearing lawsuits from the Department of Water and Power, he ultimately cut the Owens Valley story from his narrative and renamed the movie *Chinatown*. Robert Towne says that he and Polanski thought of the original title "because water *was* power. . . . You could see it running through the movie. It was a river of greed."[35] Interestingly, though critics repeatedly claim this film is about the "rape" of Owens Valley, *Chinatown* does not once mention Owens Valley, though there is one scene in the film in which an irate farmer from "the valley" interrupts a water board meeting by herding his sheep down the aisle. The farmer complains, "You steal water from the valley. Ruin their grazing. Starve the livestock. Who's paying you to do that, Mr. Mulwray? That's what I want to know." Mr. Mulwray looks down and says nothing. Polanski knew that dealing with the Department of Water and Power would be difficult, which may be why there is no mention of Owens Valley, and evil becomes Chinatown. Still, DWP employees and relatives are notorious for proclaiming that the movie is "completely fictional" and has nothing to do with them. William Mulholland's granddaughter, Catherine Mulholland, said simply, "It's literally not true"—which is the same thing Gerald Gewe, the assistant general manager of water at the DWP, told me when I went to visit him at the Department of Water and Power.

Because of the change in title from *Water and Power* to *Chinatown*, the issue of corruption also gets deflected from the Department of Water and Power to the Chinese. Polanski said that after the title was changed, he had to "set at least one scene in L.A.'s real-life Chinatown," and so Chinatown came to represent all that is ugly and unbeatable about Los Angeles. At the end of *Chinatown*, a policeman says to Jake, in reference to the impossibility of fighting corruption in Los Angeles, "Forget it, Jake, it's Chinatown." He continues, "You may think you know what you're dealing with, but you don't." Though Jake is supposed to "forget it" or push it out of his mind in order to survive in the city, it is Chinatown that haunts the narrative for its refusal to adjust to the rationality of the West. Sadly, fear of censorship from the Department of Water and Power may have contributed to the racist component of this film.

In order to understand why the title of *Chinatown* was changed, it may be helpful to look at another film that was also originally called *Water and Power*. This 1984 television movie made for ABC attempted to tell the history of Owens Valley's resistance (including the bombings of the aqueduct) to the Department of Water and Power. But the DWP forbade filming on its land because, representatives said, "the movie might have triggered copycat bombings of the aqueduct by unbalanced viewers." Subsequently, ABC changed the name "Owens Valley" to "Paiute Valley" and did not name the DWP. When the movie ultimately aired, it was a watered-down work called *Ghost Dancing*, filmed in St. George, Utah—called "Paiute Valley" in the movie—with no reference to the California issue. After intensive dealings with the Department of Water and Power about filming on its land, producer Robert Berger deleted all references to the DWP to avoid lawsuits. He explained the situation: "It would be foolhardy to rub those people the wrong way if you could avoid it." Claiming he was "unnerved" by the fact that the DWP had obtained a copy of the script before he even approached them, Berger decided to foreclose any dealings with the DWP.

Residents of Owens Valley, however, were outraged that the film would not be filmed in their valley. They claimed the DWP had "intimidated" ABC into changing the script and urged ABC to film in the valley despite DWP refusal. Six hundred people signed a petition stating, "The Department of Water and Power has asserted its power again. . . . The DWP has bullied ABC." Inyo County district attorney Buck Gibbons said, "There's a name for the place where this kind of censorship occurs, and none of us wants to live there." Even Steve Hinder, the director of DWP's public affairs, concurred that the department simply did not want the film to be made. "Frankly, we would prefer that the film not be produced at all," he said, "but that's not within our power, and we weren't suggesting that." And Paul Lane, DWP's chief engineer, said, "We need good movies that portray the beauty of the valley, not some kook trying to blow up the aqueduct."

In *Ghost Dancing*, an old woman does in fact blow up the aqueduct in order to draw attention to the plight of the valley, but the incident is covered up by a powerful water board intent on keeping the valley's problems quiet. Screenwriter Philip Penningroth said he was saddened by the changes that had been made. He commented: "The whole controversy is a rather striking case of life mirroring art. My story was made up. There was no situation I knew of where the DWP tried to systematically block publicity. Lo and behold, the producers are flatly blocked from filming and the DWP wants the names changed. . . . Their exercise of power in this case is scary. *Real* scary." DWP representative James Wickser scoffed at the idea that DWP was censoring ABC. He said, "It's a big fuss over nothing. We simply felt that since the work was fiction, the names of the facilities should not be used. It's a little like *Chinatown*. There's a brief web of truth mingled with mostly fiction. No wells have dried up. And there are no little old ladies sitting in the middle of a dust bowl. . . . The real tragedy is that in the county's efforts to gain publicity, they've lost tourism by painting such a bleak picture." But Mary Gorman, a "little old lady" living in Owens Valley (she was ninety-three when the movie came out) said she might have been the model for the character in *Ghost Dancing.* "I wanted to do it [blow up the aqueduct] a few times myself," she explained.[36]

Besides causing problems for ABC, the DWP has, at least on one occasion, intimidated local reporters covering water issues. Benett Kessler received a Gulf Oil Conservation Award for her "fearless reporting" on the Owens Valley issue in 1982. But Gulf claimed that she had been forced to deal with "intimidation tactics that cost her a job at one radio station." These intimidation tactics were later confirmed when, in a taped phone conversation, the wife of the station's owner admitted that Kessler was let go after the DWP threatened to revoke the lease on their land. John Heston, the station owner's partner, said of their efforts, "The DWP has been trying to run us out of town for years. But harassing a small-time news service is one thing; when they get so big they can scare ABC, they're too damn big."[37]

Given a hundred-year history of suppressing aqueduct naysayers, it is no wonder that the Owens Lake dust issue took a long time to surface. The Department of Water and Power has been able to influence the media in two ways: (1) by lawsuits or threats of lawsuits and (2) by control over property. Besides its historical connection to the owner of the *Los Angeles Times,* the Department of Water and Power now owns much of the desirable land for filmmaking around Los Angeles—including Owens Valley. Because of this, the DWP had (and still has) a say in what kind of movies were made on its land. This has strongly influenced how the history of the Department of Water and Power has been portrayed. Also, since most Owens Valley residents live on DWP land, they have been afraid of retaliation from their landlord if they speak out. Mary Gorman once complained that the dust issue never got the publicity it deserved because "Everyone's always been afraid to express themselves because they are worried about their land leases."[38]

In Owens Valley, until recently, knowledge of the dust problem was also abysmally vague. Many did not even know that the problem existed. Recently, I visited a grocery store, which had been opened by a newly arrived Mexican American family on the shore of the dry lake. It was a simple all-purpose restaurant, fruit stand, and convenience store that served the local population of Olancha, population 120. I asked the owner how he felt about living on Owens Lake, directly in the line of dust. He replied in broken English, "Owens Lake, what's that?" To me, this type of ignorance was not surprising. I never saw a dust mask worn during a dust storm. I once asked a local doctor about the health hazard, and he merely laughed. "I'm seventy years old," he said, "lived here all my life, and I'm still standing. Go over there and breathe that Los Angeles smog, that's what will make you sick." In reality, however, the dust hazard is far worse than Los Angeles's smog. On a day of only faint dust, the material deposited in the human body is 18 micrograms (per cubic meter of air) versus 3.40 mg from a day of heavy smog in Los Angeles. On a day of severe dust, the level is up to 89 mg.[39] This kind of denial or ignorance, I propose, has been shaped by the very polarized nature of the battle between Owens Valley and Los Angeles. Ultimately, censorship in Los Angeles does not occur in outright ways. It takes place insidiously, from suggestions of retaliation, control over land, lawsuits and threats of lawsuits, and endless propaganda about the wonders of the aqueduct.

Rethinking L.A.

In 1997, I went to the main office of the Los Angeles Department of Water and Power to hear its side of the story. Richard Knox, who heard I was going to the Department of Water and Power, asked if I would bring a box of Owens Valley dust and a portable fan to blow the dust around the office. Knox, a DWP-employee-turned-activist in Owens Valley, believes in "simulating the effects of an Owens Lake dust storm" for the people responsible for the problem. He tried this earlier at the California Air Resources Board but claimed, "they were not willing to experience, even for a brief period, the conditions experienced by Keeler residents on a regular basis."[40] In *Erin Brockovich*, there is a similar scene in which Brockovich tells the PG&E employees that she has had toxic "water brought in especially for you." I decided not to bring the box of dust, however, because I wanted to hear Jerry Gewe's perspective on things. I decided that blowing dust in his face would not help.

When I arrived at the DWP main office in downtown Los Angeles, I was amazed by how fortress-like it seemed. Surrounding this modernist skyscraper is a 1.2 million-gallon "moat" of water that travels 233 miles

I.7. Main Office of the Department of Water and Power. Photo by Karen Piper. Used with permission.

down the Los Angeles Aqueduct from Owens Valley. The building seems to combine modernism with medievalism, as if the one bridge to the main entrance could be pulled up at the first sign of trouble. Built in the mid-1960s, it was supposed to reflect the theme of "water and power," and cost more to build than the Los Angeles Aqueduct. Surrounded by fountains, moats, and flags, this building indeed projects an intimidating authority (see figure I.7). Walking through the front doors, I was immediately faced with a life-sized cutout photograph of William Mulholland. Behind him, the walls were covered with mural-sized historical photographs of aqueduct construction, and there was a large sign that read, "All packages must be searched."

Jerry Gewe greeted me from his fourteenth-floor office, which looked out over the Los Angeles skyline. I told Gewe that I was a professor from Missouri and didn't know much about the issue, hoping that he would relax and give me his real opinion. It worked. Gewe said there was some dust, but that it was not a problem—and that it had not been caused by the City of Los Angeles. He told me that there was no real health problem in Ridgecrest, either, explaining that the issue had been taken too far: "Ridgecrest isn't really significantly impacted. It's far enough away in terms of health impacts. . . . It affects their visibility a little bit, but it's not a health impact. I'm not downplaying that there is a problem there, but again those people . . . they either knew or should have known the problem at the time they moved in there. It was there long before any of these people were there. So I mean, they're making choices. They like the isolation of that location. . . . There's tradeoffs."[41]

Gewe did not know that I was from Ridgecrest or that I was sick. He didn't know that I had moved to Ridgecrest when I was seven and did not see myself as having a "choice"—and that my parents hadn't known the dust was toxic. But I did not tell Jerry Gewe this. He told me Owens Valley residents should be blamed for the dust, because they drank water that could have gone to the lake. He had said earlier to the press that the dust could be caused by dune buggies in the area.[42]

Ultimately, Gewe tried to convince me that Owens Valley was "better off" for having been colonized by Los Angeles. If Owens Valley had received its federal reclamation project, he said that it would look like Bakersfield in the San Joaquin Valley. Its residents would probably be growing alfalfa to feed cattle today, or rice, another important California field crop, which loses more water to evaporation that the City of Los Angeles uses every year.[43] Owens Valley would be polluted and crowded, he said—with the same drainage issues, pesticide buildup, and ozone pollution problems of the San Joaquin Valley. He explained this position: "The only thing worse than the DWP in the Owens Valley would be no DWP. If we weren't there, what would they look like? They'd have air pollution problems that are much more severe than what they have now. They'd have traffic problems. And so because we're there and have the watershed, they've got that pristine environment."[44]

Of course, Gewe is certainly right that Owens Valley *looks* better today because it remained relatively undeveloped. But it is very hard to argue that Owens Valley is "pristine." It is one of the most dangerously polluted areas in the nation—even if it looks pretty when the wind isn't blowing. But Gewe sat in his blue suit and talked about the beautiful "high desert valley" while he had one of his three secretaries make me coffee. I concurred ("It is beautiful") and drank my coffee and tried not to cough. I was still fighting my latest bout of pneumonia, which I had picked up during the last big storm. But I smiled the way a perfectly healthy woman should smile and commented on the lovely view of the skyline. "This is beautiful, too," I said.

The Department of Water and Power at the time was trying to claim that it was not "feasible" to stop Owens Lake dust from blowing. State law, according to former California Senator Tom Hayden, allows officials "to take into account economic and technical feasibility issues" when dealing with human health problems resulting from pollution.[45] Policymakers call this "cost-benefit analysis," which means that any regulation (for example, to stop the dust) must be subject to an examination of whether the economic benefits (in this case, restoring human health) outweigh the costs (in this case, the loss of clean water and money spent on the project). If not, the theory goes, human health must be sacrificed. This policy became law under Ronald Reagan with Executive Order 12291, which required that all new regulations be methodically examined by this method. In some ways, it is simply a recent version of the "greatest good for the greatest number"— with the main difference that *dollars* are now read as the greatest good. The dust problem, in short, did not have to be solved if doing so was found to be "unfeasible." So I asked Gewe what was "feasible" at Owens Lake. He replied, "We really need to take a step back and do the research necessary to support whatever can be done to solve the problem, assuming we can solve it. If not, we need to be intellectually honest and say there really is not a feasible solution. . . . We really need the sound basis of science before we get into it."[46] This was after thirteen years of study. The Department of Water and Power, at that time, did not seem interested in finding a solution and offered none. It was not even convinced that there was a problem.

Both sides seemed to be losing in this battle over dust. The Paiutes of Owens Valley complained that they did not have the "technical or financial resources" to fight the Department of Water and Power. Their attorney, Dorothy Alther, explained, "One of the problems that we encountered was that I'm an attorney, not a technical person—hydrologist—and a lot of information is technical. You go to the DWP and you've got five technical staffs." Tom Hayden claimed that the Department of Water and Power intentionally used technical language to mask the problems it created. In "Risk and Social Learning," B. Wynne claims this is a common strategy of public or corporate institutions. Wynne explains that technical or scientific discourse tends to claim objectivity while at the same time telling the public how "stupid and irrational they are."[47] This technical language then serves to obfuscate the issues for communities that may be lacking in scientific education.

Areas like Owens Valley rather than wealthy neighborhoods may be forced to deal with pollution problems precisely because of their lack of education. This is the case in many communities receiving hazardous waste throughout the nation. In 1984, the California Waste Management Board recommended that communities be targeted for waste disposal that have fewer than 25,000 residents who: (a) have low incomes, (b) have a demonstrated "lack of concern with issues," and (c) have lived there for twenty-plus years. It also suggested that ranchers, farmers, or those in exploitive industries would be most adaptable, as well as those with no more than a high school education, those older than middle age, Republican, and not concerned about the environment. The report explained: "All socioeconomic groupings tend to resent nearby sitings of major facilities, but middle and upper socioeconomic strata possess better resources to effectuate their opposition."[48] In Owens Valley, the population falls into this report's definition: all of the towns have fewer than 10,000 in population, they are largely poor, contain "old-timers" and ranchers, and have few resources to fight Los Angeles. Ellen Hardebeck of the Great Basin APCD stated the environmental justice issues involved in the dust problem: "Those that live close to the lakebed are suffering serious health impacts, and many of these people are poor, or members of a minority group. There are several Indian tribes that have reservations near the lake."[49] The Paiute attorney, Dorothy Alther, has since notified the air resources board of her intention to take action on civil rights violations. The Department of Water and Power—along with the EPA—is potentially in violation of the Civil Rights Act for creating and allowing, in a discriminatory fashion, an environmental hazard affecting the Paiutes of Owens Valley to occur for so long.

Recently, the Department of Water and Power was also accused of inequitably distributing aqueduct water pollution *within* the city. After the release of *Erin Brockovich,* the real Erin Brockovich, who now lives in Los Angeles, discovered that the Department of Water and Power was mixing Owens River water with groundwater polluted with industrial solvents to provide to the lower income areas of the city. "It's disturbing," Brockovich

remarked, "that it was only after the movie *Erin Brockovich* was released . . .
that the water board fessed up that there were about 200 potential sources for
hex chrome [Chromium 6]. . . . The DWP knows that if you drink enough
Chromium 6, you are a dead person."[50] The Department of Water and Power
did not think it "feasible" to clean up that problem, which they did not address until Erin Brockovich brought national attention to it. Now they are
also dealing with the dust issue, due to a federal mandate, but their commitment to the health of Owens Valley is questionable. Historian Andrew Hurley writes, "Over time, the ability of cities like Los Angeles . . . to grow has
depended upon their ability to exploit social divisions and regional inequali-
ties in both the pursuit of remote resources and the allocation of newly-
created environmental hazards."[51] Both within and outside of Los Angeles,
these inequities in the distribution of waste have allowed the city to grow.
There is, for example, no Chromium 6 or toxic dust in Bel Air—although Bel
Air consumes more resources than any other part of Los Angeles.

Interestingly, the tendency to dump pollutants on nonwhite populations
is occurring worldwide. In 1991, chief economist of the World Bank,
Lawrence Summers, claimed that since Third World countries made less
money in terms of earning potential, they should take on more of the
world's pollution. In an internal memo, he wrote: "A given amount of
health impairing pollution should be done in the country . . . with the lowest wages. I think the economic logic behind dumping a load of toxic waste
in the lowest wage country is impeccable and we should face up to that. . . .
I've always thought that under-populated countries in Africa are vastly
UNDER-polluted."[52] In this memo, Summers explained that taking toxic
waste could be the contribution of "under-populated" or poor areas to the
world economy. It is important to remember that this is not some inadver-
tent remark—this has become standard economic policy regarding pollution. In fact, far from being reprimanded for this view when his memo was
leaked to the public, Lawrence Summers was appointed the U.S. Treasury
Secretary under Clinton. He is now the president of Harvard University.

In the United States, corporate interests have commonly been insepara-
ble from government interests. At the beginning of the twentieth century,
President Roosevelt helped men like Henry Huntington and Otis Chan-
dler become rich by diverting the Owens River. Though Roosevelt appeared to be the enemy of private power companies, he was actually

supported in his ruling by the Pacific Electric and Power Company. The reason was that its owner, Henry Huntington, stood to make more money from getting water to his real estate holdings than from selling electricity.[53] Recently, the administration helped men like Ken Lay of Enron and Dick Cheney of Halliburton gain wealth through the deregulation of electricity. Ken Lay wrote to congratulate Lawrence Summers on his appointment to U.S. Secretary of the Treasury. Summers responded: "I'll keep my eye on power deregulation and energy market infrastructure issues."[54] While dust and other pollutants are being transported to poor people, privatization of previously public utilities has made a fortune for a handful of corporations. (Though Enron declared bankruptcy, an international law—implemented by the Bush administration—allowed Ken Lay to keep his profits in the Cayman Islands.)

In essence, the two seemingly opposite actions of regulation and deregulation have had a similar effect on the poor by consolidating wealth through consolidating natural resources. For the poor, there is only the "economic logic behind dumping a load of toxic waste in the lowest wage country." There is the knowledge of and ultimately the indifference to the fact that certain people—usually poor or nonwhite—must be sacrificed for the logic of the "greater good." At Enron, recently released transcripts show traders joking about the money "stolen" from the poor and elderly of California. One Enron trader joked with another about the insider knowledge of "all the money you stole from those poor grandmothers in California." His friend responded, "Yeah, Grandma Millie, man. But she's the one who couldn't figure out how to fuckin' vote on the butterfly ballot." The first trader replied, "Yeah, now she wants her money back for all the power you've charged—jammed right up her ass for fuckin' 250 dollars a megawatt hour."[55] Buying and selling electricity in California demonstrated the abuses that can and do occur, yet the pressures of deregulation still remain.

Buying and selling pollution now seems to be the wave of the future—at least under the current administration. In July 2002, George W. Bush announced that he would make the buying and selling of "pollution credits" the official way of dealing with air quality issues in the future. Under Bush's "Clear Skies Initiative," those who violate the Clean Air Act could buy pollution credits, or the "right to pollute," rather than clean up the problem. The idea is that an overall cap on pollution credits will ultimately lower the nation's total air pollution—which will decrease even more over time. Unfortunately, from an environmental justice perspective, this program is flawed. For one thing, companies may find it cheaper to buy the right to pollute than to retrofit factories for better air quality. Also, localities without the infrastructure for industrial development may be eager to sell their credits to polluting companies as a means of generating revenue. Environmentalists are now arguing that "hotspots" of environmental pollution will occur when localities begin auctioning off their environments. For instance, Lynn Scarlett, executive director of Reason Public Policy Institute in Los Angeles, argued that "air-permit trading, for example, may shift pollution to certain 'hotspots,' thereby unevenly benefiting different populations."[56] In this sense, it may be cheaper for the City of Los Angeles to try to buy pollution credits than to fix Owens Lake. It remains to be seen whether correcting the problems of Owens Lake will be affordable or "feasible"—in the long run—for the Department of Water and Power. Owens Lake, in effect, remains the implosive center of a struggle that sometimes seems as if it will have no end. When pollution and water shortages become redefined as economic opportunities, the burden of waste tends to fall on the poor, who do not have enough money to buy clean air and water.

Left in the Dust, to use the words of an Enron trader, looks at what is being jammed up whose ass—by either corporate interests or the Department of Water and Power. Deregulation is a way for the current administration to find more wealth and thus supposedly "jump start" the economy by sacrificing more of the environment. In contrast, however, regulation based upon outmoded early industrial or New Deal technologies is not in the environment's best interest either. As I will demonstrate, the Department of Water and Power, which has long touted its role as looking out for the public good rather than private gain, has actually created and protected private gain while creating environmental disasters. One professor explained its confusing logic: "Water used to help achieve clean air, in the view of the DWP, can be classified [as] 'waste.' On the other hand, water which might end up fueling further poorly-planned and insupportable growth in the Los Angeles metropolitan area can be classified as nectar from the gods."[57] The problem, as demonstrated in this case study, lies not in "public versus private" control of utilities. The history of the DWP reveals that the notion of the public can be equally corrupt. Indeed, I will argue that the problem is corruption in both realms, which leads to overlooking damage done to the poor and nonwhites for the sake of someone else's "greater good." The DWP long ignored the costs to human health that its policies had created. Beginning in Los Angeles, and tracing the aqueduct back to its source, *Left in the Dust* looks at the larger implications of what Erin Brockovich meant when she said, "The DWP knows . . . you are a dead person." I ask, in particular, who that "you" may be. On the day I visited the DWP main office and talked to Jerry Gewe, I couldn't stop thinking about what Erin Brockovich had said. "They know you are a dead person," I whispered to myself. Jerry Gewe hardly ever looked at me when he talked, instead addressing my male photographer. But when he finally turned to me and looked me in the eyes, I could not help thinking that this "you" was me.

ONE

ESPRIT DE CORPS AT THE DEPARTMENT OF WATER AND POWER

In Owens Valley on Highway 395, I met a Department of Water and Power employee who offered to show me the aqueduct "intake," where Owens River is diverted into the Los Angeles Aqueduct. This is where the river mysteriously disappears as its journey to Los Angeles begins. It is a simple concrete barricade that funnels the river into the aqueduct channel. Strangely, the channel looks the same on both sides of the barricade, so I couldn't tell the difference between the river and the aqueduct. The DWP employee had greeted me with a growling Rottweiler at his side, but he quickly called off the dog and stretched out his hand to shake mine. "I always carry a gun and take my Rottweiler with me out here," he explained as we followed the aqueduct up to the intake reservoir. He didn't explain why he needed a gun, so I guessed. "Oh, do you have problems with mountain lions?" I asked. "Not so much down here, I guess," he replied. "But up in those hills, that's where they are. I can feel their eyes on the back of my head when I walk." He continued, "It's pretty isolated out here, and that can really get to you after a while. But someone's got to do it for the sake of the City, I guess . . . to keep the water coming."[1]

This man, I knew, was one in a long line of men whose job it was to "keep the water coming," security guards who had been stationed along the aqueduct since it was opened. Jubilant crowds once arrived to watch Owens River water cascade down the mountains into the City when it first arrived in Los Angeles on November 5, 1913 (see figure 1.1). "There it is, take it," William Mulholland, the aqueduct's chief engineer, called to the crowd at the aqueduct opening after unfurling an American flag. From its inception, the aqueduct was described as a patriotic enterprise of imperialist expansion—complete with its own army. Owens River had been "discovered" by Mulholland when he was scouting around for new sources of water for Los Angeles in 1904. Mulholland teamed up with J. B. Lippincott, an employee of the U.S. Reclamation Service, who came to Owens Valley in the early 1900s purportedly to help develop a federal irrigation project for Owens Valley residents called the Owens Valley Project. In order to acquire the water rights in Owens Valley, Mulholland hired Lippincott as a consulting engineer to surreptitiously buy up water rights for Los Angeles.

Believing they were selling their water rights for their own benefit to the Owens Valley Project, Owens Valley farmers instead found out that their water was going to Los Angeles. The City then bought out the farmers in a checkerboard fashion, forcing property values down and scaring people into selling early. Lippincott knew his actions were questionable even before accusations of corruption were leveled at him by residents of Owens Valley. He wrote to the head of the Reclamation Bureau that though he supported giving water to Los Angeles, he feared it would put the bureau in "rather an embarrassing position . . . with reference to the Owens Valley Project."[2] But he believed that the nation would ultimately support him for working in the best interest of Los Angeles.

He was right. The struggle between Owens Valley farmers and Los Angeles ultimately was resolved in Washington, D.C. In 1906, President Theodore Roosevelt decided, "It is a hundred or a thousand fold more important to state that this water is more valuable to the people as a whole if used by the city than if used by the people of the Owens Valley."[3] The oft-quoted motto of Roosevelt's Progressive party was "the greatest good for the greatest number." The greatest number, Roosevelt believed, lived in Los Angeles. The Reclamation Service's plans for setting up an irrigation system in Owens Valley were officially abandoned. As historian Abraham

1.1. Opening Ceremony for the Los Angeles Aqueduct, Eastern California Museum.

Hoffman notes, "Owens Valley fell victim to standards set not by the City of Los Angeles but by Washington, D.C., acting in accordance with the philosophy of the Progressive movement in the first decade of the twentieth century."[4]

Roosevelt's actions drastically impacted Owens Valley, yet Roosevelt himself was not really that concerned with its dilemma. Roosevelt saw the problems of the settlers in Owens Valley as incidental to the larger struggle between private and governmental enterprises over providing utilities. He wrote, "I am also impressed by the fact that the chief opposition to this bill, aside from the opposition of a few settlers in Owens Valley . . . comes from certain private power companies whose object evidently is for their own pecuniary interest to prevent the municipality from furnishing its own water." A private power company had already established itself in the Owens River gorge, and Roosevelt did not want to see Owens Valley taken over by private enterprises that would sell water and power to Los Angeles. The true enemies, in his mind, were monopolies that threatened to obstruct the public good—other complaints were treated as incidental. Roosevelt said of the private power companies, "Their opposition seems to me to afford one of the strongest arguments for passing the law, inasmuch as it ought not to be within the power of private individuals to control such a necessary of life as against the municipality itself."[5] Roosevelt chastised Lippincott for concealing his intentions, but Lippincott defended himself: "I firmly believe that I have acted for the greatest benefit of the greatest number, and for the best building up of this section of the country."[6] Lippincott was eventually absolved of all blame.

Roosevelt's decision to give the water to Los Angeles rather than to Owens Valley reflected his belief in the superiority of urban areas over rural areas, as well as public over private. J. B. Lippincott once argued, "The domestic use of water is the highest use to which it can be put." By this he meant that it was better to supply houses with water than to supply farms—that is, Owens Valley. The Progressives believed that the "highest use" for water, or its most "noble" purpose, was supplying residences rather than agriculture. But Roosevelt's belief in urbanization and the "public good" included underlying assumptions about imperialistic growth. The aqueduct would not only help the country expand and acquire new territories; it would also allow Los Angeles to abandon the older Mexican water system, the *acequias,* which were seen as dirty and inefficient. It would enable white flight to the suburbs of Los Angeles and end the so-called Indian problem in Owens Valley. In short, the Los Angeles aqueduct would bring with it a long story of inevitable "progress"—to meet the needs of the ever-growing white metropolitan populace.

Roosevelt, in fact, had several key political ideas that would have led him to support Los Angeles over Owens Valley:

1. Cities were seen as more *defendable* than rural areas against Native Americans. Theodore Roosevelt claimed that urbanization would force Native Americans to disappear from the "regions across which their sparse bands occasionally flitted." Native Americans were seen as having mutable and sparsely populated settlements that could not withstand large and permanent settlements. Densely settled populations, it was believed, would simply push out Indians. Roosevelt believed that "mere savages, whose type of life was so

primitive as to be absolutely incompatible with the existence of civilization" would inevitably "die out" from areas that were densely settled.[7] In Owens Valley, the so-called Indian wars had plagued the settlers since the 1860s— requiring military forts and soldiers to be permanently established in the area. This was not only a drain on government funding but also an embarrassment to the military. In many ways, the decision to send water to Los Angeles could be seen as a solution to the Indian "problem" in Owens Valley.

2. Cities were also seen as more "civilized" than rural areas. Many saw creating great cities in remote or inhospitable areas as a sign of colonial power and authority, as well as an inevitable sign of civilization and progress. In 1909, geographer Isaiah Bowman claimed that "one could build a city of a hundred thousand at the South Pole and provide electric lights and opera. Civilization could stand the cost."[8] Supplying electricity and water to the desert city of Los Angeles presented a similar challenge—but with the same "noble" goal of extending civilization. Los Angeles, it was believed, would be a great imperial center that demonstrated America's successful colonization. Cities, in short, were a *symbol* of successful conquest in the colonies, representing the pinnacle of Anglo-American civilization.

3. Port cities were seen as sites for further imperialist expansion. Roosevelt claimed that Los Angeles was an important port city for his expansionistic goals in the Pacific. Roosevelt claimed: "Our interests are as great in the Pacific as in the Atlantic. . . . The awakening of the Orient means very much to all the nations of Christendom, commercially no less than politically; and it would be short-sighted statesmanship on our part to refuse to take the necessary steps for securing a proper share to our people of this commercial future."[9] Like the British, Roosevelt believed that naval supremacy was key to military and commercial success. He had already acquired Hawaii, Puerto Rico, and the Philippines by 1898. In 1904, he paid Panama $10 million for rights to build the Panama Canal, which would make Los Angeles a major port city on the West Coast. Roosevelt openly modeled his ideas for expansion on the British Empire. In "Expansion and Peace," he wrote, "It is the great expanding peoples which bequeath to future ages the great memories and material results of their achievements . . . England standing as the archetype and best exemplar of all such mighty nations. But the peoples that do not expand leave, and can leave, nothing behind them."[10]

Finally, the aqueduct would help to keep the city safely segregated by allowing white people to move away from the already polluted inner city and drawing white immigrants from around the nation. By 1922, Pastor Bob Shuler commented, "Los Angeles is the only Anglo-Saxon city of a million population left in America. It is the only such city that is not dominated by foreigners. It remains in a class to itself as the one city of the nation in which the white, American, Christian idealism still predominates."[11] William Mulholland was also repeatedly lauded for single-handedly saving the city from what was then described as a backward Mexican water system. So while the water was supposed to be for everyone, it ultimately benefited white people.

In fact, it was mainly a *handful* of white men who benefited most from the aqueduct. These were the men who knew about the aqueduct plans before it was announced to the public, including water commissioner Moses Sherman, railroad baron Henry Huntington, and *Los Angeles Times* publisher Harrison Gray Otis. They bought up land around the proposed aqueduct terminus in the San Fernando Valley and subdivided it for an enormous profit after the water arrived. In this sense, the water was not for the public good but for the benefit of land speculators.[12]

There was a great deal of controversy at the time over whether Los Angeles even needed more water. In its defense, the water board argued that "while the existing water supply may be sufficient to meet the present demands of Los Angeles, the future development and prosperity of the city is dependent not only on an adequate domestic supply to meet its growing need but also for those of neighboring municipalities and agricultural lands."[13] The theory advocated by the water board was that developing agricultural properties around an urban core would ultimately lead to the subdivision of those properties into housing plots. Essentially, the water board decided to *move* agriculture from Owens Valley to Los Angeles to develop the neighboring San Fernando Valley—with the idea that eventually the San Fernando farms would turn into suburbs, thus justifying this move. It was an ideology of the inherent worth of urban expansionism. The board stated, "Doubtless these lands if irrigated, would soon become densely populated suburban additions to a Greater Los Angeles."[14] In fact, the board was right, though the benefits of this suburban sprawl are now no longer self-evident. But bringing water to Los Angeles to develop the San Fernando Valley was extremely controversial, because it seemed to confirm that the aqueduct was *really* intended to make a few men rich rather than to benefit the public.

Meanwhile, in Owens Valley, the "public" was even more inflamed. In *Los Angeles,* Morrow Mayo wrote, "the City of Angeles moved through this valley [Owens Valley] like a devastating plague. It was ruthless, stupid, cruel, and crooked."[15] Farms began to dry up, and farmers fought back in the only way they could, by blasting the aqueduct. As they watched the lake drying up in the 1920s, Owens Valley residents responded by sabotaging the aqueduct. Violence on both sides became so regular that the *Los Angeles Times* dubbed this period "California's Little Civil War." William Mulholland gave "shoot to kill" orders for anyone who interfered with the aqueduct.[16] He notoriously complained that there were not enough trees left in Owens Valley on which to hang all the troublemakers.[17] Confronted with a losing war and no water, most Owens Valley residents eventually left.

The aqueduct was called "The Big Ditch" by employees who guarded it, such as Jess Ramsey, who worked at Sand Canyon Station from 1933 to 1938. Lois Ramsey Carr, his daughter, described his job: "He had to what we'd call 'ride ditch.' He did it on horseback, eight miles one way, eleven miles the other . . . that was to guard the aqueduct from any thievery or bombing or anything like that that went on."[18] In 1930, a Department of Water and Power advertisement entitled "Vigilance" honored the men who monitored the length of the aqueduct. The advertisement described the aqueduct itself as the "jugular vein" of the city, which must be defended at all costs. "Department engineers go forth each day from isolated mountain stations to scale a hundred storm swept passes," the advertisement extolled. It continued, "With 1,300,000 persons dependent upon this Aqueduct for their daily water there must be no interruption in its operation."[19]

The Department of Water and Power, from its inception, claimed that its motto was "Esprit de corps" and compared its guards and other personnel to a military regiment. In 1924, the Department of Water and Power used the term esprit de corps to headline its first magazine, *The Intake*, claiming: "By this military phrase is meant the common spirit that does or should prevail among a group of persons, such as the men of a regiment, a body of officials or the employees of a concern. It implies a common sympathy, devotion and enthusiasm, and a jealous regard for the whole. It has an equivalent expression in just one word, one of the biggest words in the dictionary—loyalty."[20] Militarily protecting an imperialistic enterprise was viewed as a "public good" at the time. The DWP was expanding civilization, creating a country with a band of men who were sacrificing themselves for this greater good. The Los Angeles Aqueduct was a *manly* project—

and, indeed, the great length of its canal (with its spouting end) could be said to emblemize masculinity. William Mulholland saw himself as the military leader of this regiment, as he explained to *Los Angeles Times* editor Allen Kelly: "I'm going into this as a man in the army goes into war, because it would be cowardly to quit." According to his granddaughter, Catherine Mulholland, "Nor was his military analogy inapt as the organization needed to achieve this mighty task resembled a military campaign."[21] In 1907, the bureau of the Los Angeles Aqueduct explained, "The construction of the Aqueduct resembles somewhat a military campaign. Men have to be quickly ordered to remote portions of the line and from one point to another, as the exigencies of the work require."[22] Those who were involved in this "campaign" often also held military ranks: Gen. Harrison Gray Otis, editor of the *Los Angeles Times,* served in the Spanish-American War; Lt. Gen. Adna Romanza Chaffee, chairman of the board of Public Works, had a long and distinguished military career in the Indian wars, the Spanish-American War, and the Boxer Rebellion; Moses H. Sherman of the first Water Commission just liked to call himself "General."

The building of the aqueduct was described in terms of a military campaign; the protection of the aqueduct was seen as a military duty. Disloyalty to the aqueduct—as to the U.S. Army—was viewed as treasonous. This military campaign had specific homosocial rules, which were said to reflect the beliefs of the city and even the nation. In 1928, a Department of Water and Power advertisement explained this position: "Anything less than full support of the City's water and electric investment by any citizen is disloyalty to the deliberately established policy and purpose of Los Angeles."[23] A 1934 advertisement for the Department of Water and Power, called "On Guard," claimed, "It is a simple operation to press an electric button in your home, office or factory. . . . Behind that button is a highly trained organization of engineers and craftsmen constantly on duty and on guard."[24] The man in this advertisement has an electrical wire in one hand and a shotgun at his hip, though there is no explanation why an electrician would need a shotgun. Instead, the advertisement associates the electrician with the cowboy, making the frontier safe for settlement.

The Los Angeles Aqueduct was modeled after the Roman aqueduct system, in which clean water was channeled to the city from outlying areas. Like the imperial Roman aqueduct system, the Los Angeles Aqueduct would similarly have to be guarded in its remote frontiers, where residents did not share the vision of the city-state (see figure 1.2). In *William Mulholland*, Catherine Mulholland wrote: "Just as Caesar . . . anticipated as a model a kind of city-state existing in Rome's own peripheries and provinces, so the leaders of an expanding Los Angeles looked to extend boundaries in order to create a new kind of city."[25] At the Los Angeles Aqueduct's opening, former California governor George C. Pardee compared the aqueduct builders to the ancient Romans. Pardee suggested that the aqueduct "ranks higher than the bloody accomplishments of all the Caesars; sets high among the great men of the world those whose genius has made it possible, and records among the great people of the earth the Californians who commanded that it should be built."[26] The reference to Romans, Caesars, and gladiators is fairly constant in the rhetoric surrounding the construction of the aqueduct. In *Material Dreams,* Kevin Starr wrote, "Like the ancient Romans to whom it frequently compared itself, the Los Angeles oligarchy employed two essentials to human life, land and

1.2. The Los Angeles Aqueduct. Photo by Mary Piper. Used with permission.

water, to transform the City of Angels within three decades into an imperial American metropolis."[27]

Interestingly, as urbanization and industrialization became a global phenomenon, so did the uniformity of water control schemes. Historian Norman Smith writes, "Dam-building has to a large degree been standardized, and twentieth-century dams in many ways lack the individuality of the works of earlier centuries."[28] Dam-building and large-scale irrigation projects were seen around the world at the end of the nineteenth century as noble pursuits and ways of extending civilization. In *Rivers of Empire*, Donald Worster explains that there was an international camaraderie among hydraulic engineers at that time: "They understood that they were engaged in a mission of conquest that was going on in all parts of the world—in India, Egypt, the Sahara, Australia. A great and noble work it was."[29] American engineers often traveled to India or otherwise modeled their work on Indian efforts, whose large-scale irrigation projects had been developed a good thirty years before those in the American West.[30] During construction of the aqueduct, Mulholland consulted Sir William Willcocks, the builder of Egypt's Aswan Dam.[31] In the 1880s, George Chaffey started a planned community, with the help of irrigation, in the Los Angeles area; then he went on to establish an irrigation-based development in Australia.[32] These men were thought to be doing the work of extending civilization around the world through large-scale water projects.

The new pharaohs and caesars of the modern era of water works were the chief engineers. The Department of Water and Power regularly describes the aqueduct as the singular achievement of William Mulholland. In a pamphlet for the aqueduct, they advertise: "Water is the life blood of every community. The man who did more than any other to furnish that vital element to Los Angeles was William Mulholland."[33] The image of Mulholland supplying blood to bring life to Los Angeles suggests, in a Christlike narrative, that the city emerged because of one man's sacrifice and devotion. The Department of Water and Power writes, "The courses of Los Angeles, the city, and William Mulholland, the man, were singularly parallel."[34] Los Angeles and Mulholland were seen as predestined to grow, mature, and realize their true potential together. They became, in the end, each other. Mulholland, at the aqueduct opening, called his podium "an altar, and on it we are consecrating this water supply and dedicating this aqueduct to you."[35] The water came down the chute, and Mulholland said simply, "It is finished." In this statement, the man who was called "Saint Mulholland" by some chose Christ's last words to end his own saga.

The "public" for which Mulholland supposedly sacrificed himself was required only to "share the vision" or the faith of Mulholland. In sharing this vision, the public could literally share the body of Mulholland, drinking the water that is his blood. In a 1929 advertisement by for the Department of Water and Power, the iconic image of Mulholland with his surveying equipment is positioned next to the caption, "Vision." It reads, "Civic vision and engineering genius have transformed Los Angeles from a small Western city to the Metropolis of the Pacific." Mulholland's contemporaries, particularly men, would most likely idealize this colonial image of frontiersman-explorer and engineering genius. The Department of Water and Power demanded nothing less than loyalty to this vision. The DWP book, *Sharing the Vision,* described this dream: "In 1913, the City of Los Angeles completed construction of the Los Angeles Aqueduct. It began as a dream of dedicated men of vision and its completion was a monument to perseverance, technology, and skill. The Los Angeles Aqueduct stands today as a reminder of what we are capable of when we push forward boldly to meet a challenging future."[36] In pledging loyalty to Mulholland as general and chief engineer, other men could vicariously partake in his "genius" and dedicate themselves to the utopian "vision" of development.

Through the blood of Mulholland, men could be associated with the homosocial militaristic operation of the aqueduct; the role of woman, in contrast, was that of consumer, "home manager," organizer of servants. In the 1920s, Los Angeles began aggressively marketing the free electricity that was generated as the gravity-fed aqueduct flowed downhill to the City of Los Angeles. In a 1928 advertisement, women were described as consumers of electricity who would benefit from *"rates so low as to make electricity the home manager's most economical household servant."*[37] The Department of Water and Power sponsored cooking classes, appliance exhibits, and radio programs promoting home electricity. *The Intake* remarked, "Electric appliances made kids get better grades, freed women from household drudgery, and saved marriages—woe to the husband who kept his wife in the gas age."[38] A 1939 advertisement bragged, "Your Electricity Travels 300 Miles to Broil Your Steak!" and depicted a suburban husband's barbecue hooked up directly to the Owens Gorge power plant. The Department of Water and Power hired consultants to help young couples set up their new homes. It distributed a booklet called "The How and Why of Home Modernization" free of charge to its rate-payers, with ideas on updating kitchens, adding rooms, and remodeling the bath with "well planned, up-to-date" ideas. The Department of Water and Power put out a slew of advertisements, actively promoting the concept of the "modern homemaker" and suburban enclave in the 1930s.

Beginning a national trend that people usually associate with the 1950s, Los Angeles started to sell "suburbia" long before World War II. Women were encouraged to make their homes into "showplaces" for aqueduct water and electricity. The Department of Water and Power sponsored a "plant a tree" campaign to use aqueduct water and began encouraging homeowners to put lights on their trees at Christmas. By 1940, the Department of Water and Power extolled the wonders of this "electric" city: "Nothing more clearly typifies the characteristic hospitality of Southern Californians than does the illuminated outdoor Christmas tree. Few places in the United States afford equal opportunity for open-hearted manifestation of 'good will toward men.' That, obviously, is one of the reasons why the lighting of Christmas trees has become one of Los Angeles' most cherished traditions. Another is that a progressive people are electrically minded."[39] Through their commitment to being both "progressive" and "hospitable," women could manifest loyalty to Los Angeles's "vision." The military conquest of the Californian desert by men established a safe domestic realm in the wilderness for women. As the preservers of domestic space, women needed only to manage the "servants" that the men brought home—that is, electricity and water.

The men who oversaw aqueduct construction and security are remembered in the history of the Los Angeles Aqueduct. The laborers who actually built the aqueduct are largely forgotten, as are the people who were displaced by the aqueduct and the women who consumed its goods. If the irrigation engineers sometimes saw themselves as Egyptian pharaohs, the history of their "slaves" has gone largely unrecorded. Over one hundred thousand men and women constructed the aqueduct; they worked in temporary shifts of up to four thousand at a time, building the entire aqueduct in five years. The construction of the Los Angeles aqueduct was described as nothing less than a military venture, requiring military camaraderie and machine guns. The builders of the aqueduct, it was boasted by the Department of Water and Power, were "100 percent American"—that is to say, anyone of Mexican, African, or Asian descent was excluded.[40] In discriminating against these groups, the City promoted a sense of national identity centered on whiteness. The 1882 Chinese Exclusion Act had prohibited Chinese immigrants from becoming naturalized Americans and halted further immigration, due to fears that the Chinese were taking American jobs. As a municipal enterprise, the aqueduct could legally employ only naturalized American citizens and non-Asians.[41] However, other nonwhite immigrants were also excluded in a xenophobic move to provide a sense of security and employment to Anglos settling in the West.

The question of who was considered "American" and who was not was complex. Dr. Raymond Taylor, who worked on the aqueduct line, recalled that the shift crews had "at least one Irishman on them and the rest were likely to be composed of Cornish Englishmen . . . very few straight Americans."[42] It seems that American citizenship was less important than whiteness for employment on the aqueduct crew. However, some of the more difficult labor was left to non-Anglo immigrants. The open ditch work was done by "Greeks, Bulgarians, Serbians, some Montenegrans, and some Mexicans" as "American men just wouldn't work out in the open in the temperatures that existed in the summertime."[43] Tensions existed among different ethnic groups who worked on the aqueduct, as well as with Mexicans who were working on the Southern Pacific Railroad in Owens Valley at the same time. Abraham Hoffman described a racially motivated dispute that occurred at a Little Lake bar in Owens Valley: "When largely Anglo aqueduct workers ousted Mexican Southern Pacific employees from a Little Lake saloon, the Mexicans soon returned with reinforcements. The aqueduct partisans barricaded the doors and windows of the saloon while the Southern Pacific [railroad] workers besieged the building for three days and nights."[44] Eventually reinforcements arrived from the aqueduct, and the aqueduct employees were able to leave, although the saloon was a shambles. After this incident, the owner began to close the saloon at sundown.

The Los Angeles Aqueduct was described as a military venture, but it was more often than not a mutinous project. Fights broke out among the aqueduct crews. Strikes were common along the aqueduct line. In 1911, the workers went on strike after meal prices were raised five cents a piece. They demanded a corresponding wage increase, noting that the food consisted of spoiled meat and weevil-infested bread. Earlier, in 1909, men had been ordered to pay 70 cents per day for aqueduct food, whether they ate it or not; many employees had been seeking their own sources of provisions because of the terrible quality of the food at aqueduct camps. After several weeks, the unions sent a letter to the mayor, warning that "as there seems no possible way to secure justice the aqueduct employees will have to try by all means in their power to make the taxpayers aware of the facts in the present situation."[45] Socialist leader Job Harriman charged "that construction was faulty, that working conditions were intolerable, and that it had been launched to serve a few landowners in Los Angeles."[46]

Nonetheless, the workers' strike was lost as many men were replaced by the plentiful transient labor force. Like the residents of Owens Valley, the workers of the aqueduct did not have many options, moving from place to place in search of another ten-day work shift. Sam Lewis, who left Los Angeles in search of the "wide open spaces" that he had heard about along the aqueduct, was later disappointed to find that his work was primarily underground. He explained that, "gas was so bad in the Soda Hill tunnel it made everyone sick one day. I had enough underground. High places suited me better, so I stayed with my horses and wide open spaces."[47] Stories like Sam Lewis's were common; men drifted in and out of the Owens Valley in search of work or adventure with the aqueduct construction team. Men like Casey Jones and Tom Spratt ("Indian Tom") became notorious for their bootlegging operations and wild parties at Brown. Revelers claim that Tom Spratt often ended the parties with gunfire. (Later, Spratt was asked for his help in the bombing of the aqueduct, but he declined.) Oftentimes, these men would regularly switch jobs, working as packers, then bootleggers, then miners, then aqueduct employees. They were called the "Hobo Crew" locally, and they later installed the power lines that followed the aqueduct path. Mojave, the main aqueduct city, became known as the "wickedest town in the West." Crime rose along the aqueduct, including raids on cookhouses and the too-common theft of payday salaries.[48]

After the completion of the aqueduct, many of these transient workers tried to stay in the cities that sprang up overnight along the aqueduct. The towns of Inyokern, Leliter, and Brown had grown to serve these workers with schools, hospitals, stables, offices, and bars. Brown, in the Sand Canyon, had as many as three thousand transient residents during aqueduct construction. Many employees hoped to tap into the plentiful source of water and start their own irrigation projects along the aqueduct. Henry F. Schuette, a resident of one of these camps, explained: "The aqueduct brought people in, and all the people saw the valley and figured that the water was being piped down the hill so we'd have water here. The whole valley was homesteaded."[49] In Indian Wells Valley, aqueduct workers formed their own water company, the Inyo-Kern Land and Water Company, and planned to start their own subdivision scheme. Robert Thompson explained, "They envisioned a city the size of Los Angeles, covering the whole Indian Wells Valley."[50] The dreams of the aqueduct workers to realize their vision, however, would fail. None of the settlements were given permits for water by the Department of Water and Power.

In fact, the few homesteads that were given aqueduct water outside of Los Angeles were the Department of Water and Power guard stations. In Owens Valley, the aqueduct guards were even *required* to keep their lawns green to showcase the wealth of the Department of Water and Power. Litha Crowell Mattis remembers: "It was part of my father's job to keep the yard looking nice. The Department of Water and Power made a showplace of these stations. Of course, we had all the water we needed. The Department of Water and Power had a gardener that would come up and help my father with telling him how to prune the roses and how to take care of the yard."[51] Meanwhile, others homesteaders were not allotted any water. In 1919, the Inyo-Kern Company starting making its own plans to tap into Owens River water, receiving $8 million in pledges to bring water down from Mono Lake by building their own aqueduct. They asked the federal government for another $23 million, but the government refused. Robert Thompson explained, "Unfortunately, the Los Angeles Metropolitan Water District had greater clout in Washington, and the government refused to give either the water rights or the money grant."[52] The collapse of homesteader efforts such as Inyo-Kern, combined with poor working conditions at the aqueduct, often led to worker unrest. The workers on the aqueduct, with their unstable employment, dangerous work environment, and overpriced or inadequate living conditions, often became openly rebellious. In July 1927, when the aqueduct was blown up, a participant in the dynamiting reported that "the party mainly consisted of employees of the aqueduct construction."[53]

The conflict over water has generally been portrayed in books such as Remi Nadeau's *The Water Seekers* and W. A. Chalfant's *The Story of Inyo* as polarized between Los Angeles and Owens Valley. But the sides in this battle were never so clearly defined. Owens Valley residents themselves were dramatically divided between those who favored selling out to Los Angeles and those who hoped to stay. Businessmen, for instance, pitted themselves against farmers; farmers were more likely to have the opportunity to sell out because they owned water rights. Instead, businesses simply went bankrupt due to the loss of clientele. Owens Valley Paiutes also suffered dramatically; off-reservation employment disappeared as whites left the area. But many farmers who sold out early did not protest the aqueduct construction. On the Department of Water and Power side, many of the aqueduct workers sided with anti-aqueduct factions of Owens Valley. Because of this confusion over loyalties, the Department of Water and Power began looking for plots against and enemies of the aqueduct. In 1915, the Board of Water Commissioners wrote, "From the beginning all sorts of selfish interests have antagonized the development of this magnificent project. These interests have for the most part waged a battle from the ambush. They have used the knife in the dark. They have not permitted their identity to be disclosed."[54] In 1917, warnings of a dynamiting plot at Haiwee reservoir led the City to place extra guards along the aqueduct. When the aqueduct failed in two places, dynamiting was suspected and Mayor Woodman declared that he would order guards to "shoot to kill."[55] The main suspect, however, turned out to be an employee of the Los Angeles Gas and Electric Corporation, a private electric company struggling for control of Los Angeles's electricity market.

In the 1920s, several hundred guards were hired to protect the aqueduct along a two-hundred-mile front. Routinely searching vehicles for bombs and other weapons, the City turned Owens Valley into a virtual police state.[56] Ellen Snodgrass Cooper told of her brother-in-law's experience of living in Owens Valley after the construction of the aqueduct: "Bill told of Owens Valley when it was lush with farms and orchards. Then the City of Los Angeles started buying up the land. Some of the farmers didn't want to sell and these farms were mysteriously burned down. Shotgun guards were placed along the Owens River. He said it was not possible to get a drink of water from the river. There was a lot of resentment against the city as people watched their orchards and fields dry up for lack of water. Many times the aqueduct was dynamited, until a guardhouse was built in every canyon where it came above ground."[57] In 1927, Casey Jones was advanced "the fabulous sum of $1,000.00 by reliable Inyo County citizens" to blow up the aqueduct siphon in NoName Canyon. The following day, a blast carried away 350 feet of steel siphon from the Los Angeles aqueduct, and a large reward was offered for the arrest of the "culprits." Casey Jones, however, was never linked to the bombing by the Department of Water and Power. Later he accepted the offer of a "well-paid job as one of several hundred guards hired by the City of Los Angeles." The money that Jones earned as an aqueduct guard then enabled him to hire protection for a successful moonshine business in the area.[58] After a 1927 bombing, a City newsreel announced, "The police are after the fiends that did this rotten job. Let's hope they get 'em. There is no punishment too strong." Eventually three women and fifteen men were named as the "ringleaders" and arrested, but when they went to trial, there was not one conviction.

Don Powers, a Sand Canyon resident, described the response of the City after another successful bombing in 1927. He said, "They set up a machine gun emplacement and a huge spotlight at each end of the siphon with 2 men on duty 24 hours a day, and two men with submachine guns at the gate where the road crossed the aqueduct."[59] Six hundred police were sent up to Owens Valley to protect the aqueduct. William Mulholland's granddaughter, Catherine Mulholland, remembers that at the time, her family had to use false names when traveling in Owens Valley. But, she recalls, "They sent machine guns up there and it stopped." Powers described coming home at the age of ten from a cattle drive: "When we reached that area about midnight," he wrote, "Stanley and I were dozing in the saddle when those searchlights found us. It was a rude awakening. They kept those lights on our faces until we got to the gate where the two guards checked us over. Each had a Thompson machine gun on us. It was a nerve wracking experience."[60] Meanwhile bulldozers sent up from Los Angeles were knocking down old farmhouses, hoping to erase signs of development in Owens Valley. Tom Spratt's home, tucked up in Grapevine Canyon, became a kind of refuge for those working on the aqueduct line. Spratt supported himself by working brief stints on the aqueduct, bootlegging for aqueduct workers, and leading pack expeditions. He also provided shelter for those who had bombed the aqueduct. The Department of Water and Power was constantly looking for "hideouts" like Spratt's, places where people might be conspiring, drinking, and hatching into "terrorists."

Before World War II, aqueduct sabotage was generally blamed on Owens Valley residents, regardless of the actual culprits. But during World War II, fear of aqueduct sabotage shifted to foreigners—mainly the Japanese. Michael Sayer's book *Sabotage! The Secret War Against America* describes a 1934 letter from the Japanese consulate to Mr. Norman at the Department of Water and Power. The letter read, "If you have any books or pamphlets covering the entire water system of this city, we shall appreciate it very much if you will kindly forward us copies of same."[61] Sayer explained that Norman instantly contacted the U.S. Department of Justice and military authorities and did not give any information to the consulate. The title of this chapter is "Tokyo Terrorists." Sayer explained the reasons for the constant fear of aqueduct sabotage during World War II: "The city of Los Angeles, together with its war industries, is dependent on a water supply reaching it by means of an aqueduct system. Sabotage of this system would effectively cripple the chief city of the West Coast."[62] Paranoia thus shifted from fear of Owens Valley farmers to fear of the Japanese, or Germans. Whoever posed a threat to the continued supply of Owens River water to Los Angeles was seen as a potential traitor or enemy to the country. This fear of sabotage to the city's water supply was depicted in several films and advertisements, including Alfred Hitchcock's *Saboteur* (1942). In *Saboteur*, an international ring of Nazi terrorists threatens Los Angeles's water supply in a plot to blow up Boulder Dam. The antagonist of *Saboteur* claims that the dam is "a great monument to man's unceasing industry and to his stubborn faith in the future." The protagonist, in turn, must reveal the identity of the saboteurs and thus save Los Angeles and its war industries. Because so many defense contractors had located in Los Angeles before and during World War II, following a westward wave of settlers, protecting Los Angeles in wartime was seen as a patriotic duty.

During World War II, even more trained guards were hired to live along the aqueduct. In Sand Canyon, three dormitories were built to house some of these guards; the foundations still remain. Litha Crowell Mattis explained: "The guards were hired to guard the aqueduct against sabotage. . . . They were all issued guns, including my father."[63] Rather than being attacked by Nazis, however, Los Angeles's water supply was still more likely to be the target of disgruntled Los Angeles employees. Department of Water and Power workers repeatedly went on strike during World War II. In 1942, the year that *Saboteur* was released, the Department of Water and Power had another strike on its hands, a job action that was well publicized due to close associations between the Department of Water and Power and the *Los Angeles Times.* Department of Water and Power employees requested a $40-a-month across-the-board raise. The Department of Water and Power Board flatly turned down the demand, stating that "this Board has not been, and will not be moved to inconsiderate action by any so-called pressure group." On August 28, 1942, a full-page advertisement reaffirmed the position that any threat to the water supply was an act against the country: "Whatever impedes, or threatens to impede, the flow of water or electricity to homes, shops and factories, to hospitals and other institutions, directly affects the activities, the lives and well-being of every citizen of the community. Indispensable in times of peace, avoidable interruptions to such services when the nation is fighting for existence are unthinkable and in good conscience cannot be tolerated."[64] Department of Water and Power employees returned to their jobs only after another full-page ad was printed in the *Los Angeles Times,* this one stating that the Department of Water and Power would "discharge any employee absenting himself from duty."[65]

By February 1944, however, another strike was in effect, this time resulting in an Executive Order from the president to take over the plant for the "successful promotion of the War." This time employees had asked for a $15-per-month raise and again were accused of un-American activities. Mayor Bowron urged an investigation in order to determine the "underlying causes of and conduct of the strike, to ascertain what part was played by a sinister local political clique, and if organized labor was not used as an unconscious tool to further their purpose to discredit the administration of the city department."[66] The president called in the army to stop the strike because 150 war industries had lost power during the strike due to a large storm. Also, reports of sabotage to electric lines reached the department from various parts of the city. Workers returned to their jobs after the army was called in, again deferring negotiations until a later date.

In the 1990s, the Department of Water and Power had the longest strike in history on its hands. This time the employees demanded that their benefits remain intact and that they receive a cost-of-living increase. Ninety percent of the Department of Water and Power's eleven thousand employees walked off the job. Arguing that the walkout posed a threat to "public health and safety," the Department of Water and Power went to court to have the strike ended. Arguing that power loss and water quality issues might endanger the public, the Department of Water and Power won its case. DWP strikes would now be illegal, though this strike ended in a 3 percent pay increase for the following year. During the strike, the department hired camera crews to "discourage illegal activities by either strikers or employees," and after it was over, it hired a psychologist to help employees "cope."[67]

Interestingly, the Department of Water and Power attempted to "normalize" relations between management and labor by claiming that they were a "family." Although this "family" may experience dysfunctional moments, the Department of Water and Power argued, the "family" is ultimately a place of "healing." The Department printed a list of "coping strategies" to help deal with the transition back to work entitled, "Healing Relationships: The Strike Revisited." The article stated, "Because the Department is so much like a family, any breaks in the usual bonds of trust and mutual respect take longer to heal."[68] Dr. Ann Rubin, a Department of Water and Power counselor, commented, "People have friends, raise children, and spend their whole careers here. The pain to a family breaking up is much greater than that experienced by a group of unrelated people. When family bonds are broken, they are much more difficult to repair than when relationships with work associates are fractured."[69] The Department of Water and Power's corporate counselor helped traumatized family units deal with the effects of the strike, minimizing employee disgruntlement. Families, it was suggested, had to stay together and needed to handle conflict in a less "painful" way. Strikers had broken the "bonds of trust."

Only five months later, however, the Department of Water and Power changed its trope from harmonious family to "terminal patient," as a June-July article announced Department of Water and Power layoffs: "It was startling but not unexpected. An auditor's recommendation that the Department of Water and Power cut its work force by up to 25 percent over the next five years or eventually go out of business seemed like the grim diagnosis a doctor would give a terminal patient." It continued, "In fact, an audit is much like a medical exam, where a doctor studies a patient, makes a diagnosis, then offers a prescription. . . . It's up to the patient—or company—to decide whether to listen to the doctor's advice and be healthy or sick, live or die."[70] The cause of this sickness was supposedly the upcoming deregulation; the prescription was firing employees, as many as 40 percent. The Department of Water and Power employees had been called a "sinister political clique," a "family," and finally, a "terminal patient."

In 1998, I visited the Department of Water and Power archives and was troubled by the construction sounds all around me. The Department of Water and Power librarian told me, "They're downsizing and changing everything here, including the building." An architectural firm that specializes in "space utilization" designed the Department of Water and Power building in downtown Los Angeles.[71] The walls of the building are made entirely of movable panels that may make rooms larger or smaller depending upon the number of people employed at any given time. Adjustable to meet the needs of the economy, the building can be quickly adapted to cover the absences of employees who have been proven "expendable." With more than seven miles of movable partitions in the building, the office space is "entirely flexible"—in response to the economy. Deregulation was on the horizon and the librarian explained this change: "Everybody's becoming a marketer, never mind being an engineer. They're just going to sell the stuff, they're not going to make it anymore." She then remarked that she planned to leave the state.

I asked about the heavy security I encountered upon entering the building, including a sign that demanded that all packages be searched. She explained, "Oh, they think somebody will bomb them, with all the downsizing and reorganization going on around here." I then understood her to mean that the Department of Water and Power's own employees might bomb the building. The plans for reduction in the workforce were far from clear. The Department of Water and Power is a government agency with a mandate that no layoffs will be allowed. *The Intake,* however, explained a way around this problem: "To achieve the reduction in staffing in

accordance with the city's current policy of 'no lay-offs' . . . we have to look
at the numbers to determine which positions should be decreased."[72] *The
Intake* warned that early retirement incentives would not be a part of the
plan. "There will not be any golden handshakes," General Manager Ken
Miyoshi said. The plan, it claimed, was simply to reduce "staffing requirements" in line with the "no layoff" policy. This is what the employees called
"downsizing" and what led the Department of Water and Power to think
that it would be bombed.

In 2003, the situation at the Department of Water and Power had only
worsened, probably due to fears of a terrorist attack on the water supply.
There were security guards everywhere. When I tried to leave the building,
one guard stopped me. I had been taking a picture of a public exhibit in the
lobby called "Diversity in Los Angeles." "You can't take pictures in here,"
she said. "What are you doing?" I explained the premise of my book and
said I was working on security issues at the Department of Water and
Power. She looked suspicious but let me go, explaining again that I could-
n't take pictures. But as I was getting on the elevator, I heard someone yell,
"Hey you, wait," while running toward me. I came back and another guard
questioned me for several minutes, wondering why I was taking pictures.
"You know, we have to be careful, given the situation," he said. "There are
no pictures allowed in here."

"Even of a sign about ethnic diversity?" I asked.

"No pictures," he said. Before he took my camera, I quickly left, hoping
they would not run after me again. It was clear that they thought I was
some sort of terrorist—though why a terrorist would want to take a photo
of an exhibit about cultural diversity was not clear to me. But because I said
I was writing on security issues and taking pictures of guards as well, they
were confused. I am sure they were simply obeying orders to look for anyone suspicious. Los Angeles must have the most heavily defended water
supply system in the country.

Richard Knox, who was conservation manager for the Department of
Water and Power for thirty years, described life at the Department of Water
and Power: "I think it is important [to] understand how one comes to a position of power at DWP: (1) Slavish loyalty to management. (2) Never raise
ethical questions. (3) Ruthlessly pursue your superior's objectives. If you are
successful at achieving your management's goals by these means, promo-

tions will be yours."[73] Knox now lives in Owens Valley, where he works as an activist against the Department of Water and Power. Knox believes that what little money he does have—his pension from the Department of Water and Power—has been threatened because of his activities. At a protest against the Department of Water and Power, Mayor Richard Riordan shook Richard Knox's hand and said, "I've got bad news for you. Your pension program is being looked into." Although Riordan later claimed that this was "a joke," Knox said he "did not take his comment as being lighthearted . . . it serves as an indication of his tacit approval for the DWP to continue to deny the fundamental rights of Owens Valley residents to express their views without fear of retaliation."[74] Ironically, the placard that Knox had been holding read, "This placard is for those who can't be here because they fear retaliation because . . . they work for the DWP. . . ." Knox said he should have added: "because they are retired from the DWP."[75]

The Department of Water and Power has long portrayed itself as a benevolent ruler overseeing the very life of the city. Jerry Gewe said that the DWP's feelings about the aqueduct are "very parochial" because the organization is so focused on protecting the city. In reality, the city itself seems to be perpetually rebelling—in the form of strikes and disasters and deregulation and rioting. On September 16, 1976, the aqueduct was attacked again, when the Alabama Gates were bombed. The next day, a dynamite stick attached to an arrow was found on the Mulholland Statue in Los Angeles—it had failed to explode. Earlier that year, the aqueduct gates had been opened with a blow torch. In the Owens Valley, there is also an ongoing battle over DWP signs, which are constantly being vandalized. For instance, at the DWP's Haiwee Dam, to the north, the sign is full of bullet holes (see figure 1.3). In the 1990s, you could still find anti-aqueduct paraphernalia at the Jawbone Canyon Store, including postcards that show the aqueduct springing a leak or being bombed. One postcard reads, "L.A., there is your water." The aqueduct had been blown up several times at Jawbone Canyon, and the store owners took pride in this fact. But in 1998, the owners were arrested for allegedly operating a methamphetamine lab, which they claimed was a setup. The following month, the store mysteriously burned down.[76]

Today, Owens Valley residents work largely in the tourist industry, supplying services to Angelenos on their way to the Sierras. They generally

1.3. Haiwee Reservoir Sign, CLUI photo by Steve Rowell. Used with permission.

have no front lawns, only square patches of dirt in front of their houses. Los Angeles, in turn, became known for its lawns and green spaces while Owens Valley lots dried up. One Owens Valley resident recently complained, "People don't even flush their toilets anymore except when it gets really bad—and all the time they keep pumping water right out of here to people hundreds of miles away."[77] Owens Valley often complains of being treated like a colony of Los Angeles by the Department of Water and Power, which owns 99 percent of the land in Owens Valley. The Department of Water and Power leases its land to tenants and is responsible for much of the infrastructure (including the Paiute reservations) in Owens Valley. According to one Owens Valley resident, "The entire valley is a colony. We are colonials. Whenever we want something, we have to go to the DWP and ask them for it."[78] Another resident remarked, "We haven't had the resources to fight Los Angeles. . . . We're not unlike a Third World country in that respect."[79] Interestingly, even Los Angeles accepts its role as colonial "protector" in the valley. Jerry Gewe complained about Owens Valley: "They're unhappy with us. We're taking their water. We control them. They're treated as a colony. . . . But when they have a problem, who do they turn to to solve the problem? We pay all the taxes up there that enable them to maintain their infrastructure. When they have a natural disaster, it's always our equipment that bails them out. It's definitely a love/hate relationship."[80] This inequitable relationship has made it difficult even today for Owens Valley residents to define themselves as having needs that are different from those of Los Angeles.

Once, a man on a horse in the rugged Sierras was seen as an appropriate "guardian" for the city, glorifying the myth of the cowboy-engineer. But today, the city requires more protection than that. Since September 11, urban water supplies have been linked to national security issues and, therefore, treated less as local problems. David Isenberg of the Center for Defense Information, Terrorism Project, announced, "As drinking water is essential to human life, denying it for any period could cause panic and disrupt society."[81] In 2002, the FBI warned the nation's water suppliers to prepare to defend themselves against possible attacks on supply systems to urban areas. The Department of Water and Power, for instance, is currently trying to conceal the aqueduct path. Where the aqueduct crosses the road, near the Haiwee Dam, the name of the aqueduct has been covered in duct tape, purportedly to protect the aqueduct from terrorism or vandalism. The name of the Owens River has similarly been covered in duct tape (see figure 1.4). After September 11, the Department of Water and Power also started making daily helicopter flights over the aqueduct. The Department of Water and Power announced to the public that it would double its security forces. Los Angeles's Mayor James Hahn explained, "The FBI, CIA and other state and federal authorities have requested increased security for water and power facilities and we are here today to ensure the citizens of Los Angeles that we are working hard to ensure the safety and reliability of our water and power services. These actions are vital to protecting the residents of Los Angeles from the impact of possible terrorists' attacks."[82] Besides doubling their security forces, the DWP has proposed to increase water testing by 50 percent, add two new helicopters for increased aerial patrols, add twenty-four-hour security presence at water facilities, hire an outside security consultant, and work more closely with federal agencies to coordinate response to terrorist threats.

1.4. Owens River, CLUI photo by Kazys Varnelis. Used with permission.

While threats to water supplies are generally described as external—for example, threats from Al Qaeda operatives—internal pressures are often more debilitating to public utilities. "Terrorism" has constantly haunted the Mulholland-hero, the mountain man, and the aqueduct army. But in fact, the "terrorist" is the very public that the aqueduct was once constructed to serve. The terrorist is the worker, the non-Anglo, the local from Owens Valley. It is the teenager who bombed the aqueduct in 1976. It is all that could and does go wrong with the aqueduct. Today it is the dust. The Department of Water and Power is still trying to boost its image as savior while threatened with deregulation, employee unrest, and continuing water struggles in Owens Valley. Dust is the new financial drain and saboteur. Because it is not a *human* threat, this dust is particularly challenging to the Department of Water and Power. Owens Lake dust is challenging precisely because it cannot be demonized as Al Qaeda, or Nazis, or any kind of illegal activity. It is a creation of the Department of Water and Power.

Scholars have long portrayed the historical Owens Valley–Los Angeles conflict as a polarized regional microdrama that is isolated in the past, without looking at the colonial context or the continuation of the conflict today. These books present a cast of characters who are seemingly on trial:

William Mulholland, J. B. Lippincott, and others. Historians have tried to decipher whether these men were guilty or innocent, trying to delve into their personal lives—and even consciences—to decide if their motivations were above board. The pro–Los Angeles narratives, like Catherine Mulholland's *William Mulholland,* tend to focus on the "genius" of William Mulholland. These books build histories based on the promotional materials of the Department of Water and Power, which still immortalize Mulholland as a hero. One recent DWP brochure claimed, "Every time a faucet is turned the water it releases is a reminder of the man whose life was devoted to public service."[83] Along these lines, pro–Los Angeles narratives focus on the inevitability of Los Angeles's growth, the sacrifices of the men who worked to build the city, and the beauty or value of Los Angeles today. Other books focus on the powerful City of Los Angeles destroying (an often overly beatific) Owens Valley—for example, Marc Reisner's *Cadillac Desert,* William Kahrl's *Water and Power,* and John Walton's *Western Times and Water Wars.* These books tend to place Owens Valley in a passive or defeated role while depicting Los Angles as a pollution-filled mistake. Owens Valley as victim appears to be already pronounced dead, without any reference to the current struggles that are occurring.

But I do not have on rose-colored glasses about pre–Los Angeles Owens Valley. If the United States government *had* approved a big dam in Owens Valley rather than an aqueduct for Los Angeles, the state of California would look much different. Owens Lake, however, would probably still be dry, drained by the federal government rather than by Los Angeles. Due to small-scale irrigation projects, Owens Lake was already shrinking before Los Angeles diverted the Owens River. This shrinkage in turn caused a debate among Owens Valley farmers about the value of the lake long before it was drained. In the early 1900s, for instance, thousands of migrating ducks were found dead in the lake, due to the lake's shrinking size. R. G. Taylor reported that the concentrated salts of the lake had crystallized on the ducks' feathers, making it impossible for them to fly away.[84] They were trapped on the lake and starved to death. Owens Valley residents were divided over whether to try to rescue the lake. Farmers were also confronted with increasingly alkali conditions in the soil, making farming itself more difficult. In some ways, the valley was already in decline before the city appeared.

Also, it is important to remember than neither Owens Valley nor the Department of Water and Power presents a unified voice. Owens Valley has had a history of intense racial conflict—both before and after the aqueduct was built. There have been battles and tension between Paiutes and settlers, Mexican miners and white farmers, and, later, between locals and Japanese internees. Historically, Owens Valley residents are not a homogenous group. In short, Owens Valley was fraught with racial strife and environmental problems even before the aqueduct issue emerged. These difficulties would not have been solved by the Owens Valley Project. Nor does the Department of Water and Power present a unified voice. It is full of internal problems and class issues. Ultimately, this is not a city versus country argument but a history of development that tends to benefit the white and wealthy wherever they are. The flows of water are directed to those with the most money.

The difference now is that the environment itself is fighting back. Owens Lake is rewriting a long history of manifest destiny about the City of Los Angeles. It is speaking for the residents of Owens Valley who were long ago silenced. But beyond that, it is deconstructing a long narrative of *faith*—in progress, in people's abilities, in the public good. Owens Lake speaks of failure, disease, and catastrophe. In *Empire*, Antonio Negri and Michael Hardt have suggested that disease is the main symptom of colonization in reverse—the undoing of the American notion of "progress." They write, "Disease is a sign of physical and moral corruption, a sign of a lack of civilization. Colonialism's civilizing project, then, is justified by the hygiene it brings. On the other side of the coin, however . . . there is possible not only a civilizing process from disease to health, but also ineluctably the reverse process, from health to disease. Contagion is the constant and present danger, the dark underside of the civilizing mission."[85] In the case of Owens Lake, the construction of the aqueduct was a "civilizing mission" that promised to solve the problem of polluted water in Los Angeles. In this sense, it brought cleanliness and hygiene to the city. But now this mission is being overtaken by disease in Owens Valley. In part, the hesitation of Los Angeles to clean up the dust may be due to its intransigent belief in the "public good"—or in protecting Los Angeles against all outsiders. But today, the sheer scope of these "outsiders" seeking water is growing. In turn, the City of Los Angeles may be forced to rethink its belief in unhindered growth and "free" water. The cost of its water, in the end, may be much greater than the City of Los Angeles ever realized.

The Department of Water and Power once saw itself as an army fighting for the dream of William Mulholland: to build a Great City in the desert. The Department of Water and Power has long been invested in protecting the city's water supply and defining any threats to its "vision" as betrayals. In reality, its "army" was always mutinous. But in the hills of Owens Valley, men still live with guns ready for anyone who attempts to challenge this vision—even though the challenges now come mostly from within. Today you can still meet one of these aqueduct guards along the banks of the Owens River, a Rottweiler hanging out of his truck window. He will be waiting there with a 12-gauge shotgun. Be careful when you approach, as this is a man who can feel "their eyes on the back of [his] head" when he walks. Although he was talking about mountain lions, the gun was obviously not only for lions.

T W O

MANUFACTURING WHITENESS

Mike Odom pointed to a block of indeterminate industrial equipment—stacks with steam pouring from them, large metal boxes, instrument panels—and said that this was where the ravens fell. "They don't die from suffocation, but from the fall," he explained, "We're always finding them there and having to throw them out." I was touring the Los Angeles Filtration Plant, the first stop of Owens River water in Los Angeles. Cascading over the San Gabriel Mountains, the water ends up at the largest ozone filtration plant in the world, operated by the Department of Water and Power. Odom explained, "They get a good dose of that nitrous oxide and just black out." Mike Odom was in charge of ozone generation at the filtration plant—a job that he likened to generating those "blue streaks of electricity in the Boris Karloff movie." Indeed, there was an eerie *Frankenstein* feel to the filtration plant. Besides potentially running into a dead raven, I noticed the lab seemed to be entirely mechanized and guarded. I could picture Dr. Frankenstein there, madly working away in total secrecy and privacy. Mike Odom, however, was no Victor Frankenstein. He was a big lumbering sort of man who was shy but delighted to have someone to talk to about the facility. He walked with the slow confidence of someone who had "made it" in the field of ozone filtration. "You wouldn't believe the competition in this field," he explained. He was proud to show me the best facility in the world, and he seemed to feel he had the best job in the world as well.

The tour started at a small fish tank, which Odom said came "straight from the Owens River"—fish and all. "This is the water before it's treated," he explained. No one was around, and the fish stared blankly through the glass, waiting for food. Then we walked out onto a platform over a series of pools, which resembled a fish hatchery. This was where the water settled before it was sent through the carbon filters. Here, ozone was injected into the water, which is the most advanced—and expensive—way of purifying water. The water was "flocked" (short for *flocculation*) by the ozone, then sent through carbon filters, which Odom put through a backwash demonstration to show me the amount of dirt that was filtered out. The control rooms for the filters sat like lonely fire stations over the pools of water and were all empty, but after a mysterious phone call, the process seemed to begin by itself. We watched the muddy water pour over concrete walls, and I saw the extent of Owens River mud that actually collected in this place. Behind the facility, hills of this mud are being sculpted to look like natural hills.

The problem with Owens Valley water is not that it is polluted, in fact, but that it is muddy. Moving quickly over hundreds of miles through concrete aqueduct channels, Owens River water is churned up and filled with silt particles. Water suppliers used to believe that dumping enough chlorine into the water would kill anything that was dangerous. But it has been recently discovered that chlorine actually bonds with any organic material in the water to form a carcinogenic material called TCB. The solution is ozonation. Ozone causes organic material to "flock" together into large enough clumps that can easily be filtered out through carbon filters.

There were oxygen machines with attached breathing masks mounted on the walls throughout the facility. Odom informed me that they were "in case of emergency"—specifically, an ozone leak—which, it turned out, was the biggest fear around the facility. "It's always a possibility," he explained and showed me the instrument that monitored levels of ozone in the area. "If this needle goes above this line," he said, pointing to a red bar on a meter, "the whole system will automatically shut down, and emergency evacuation procedures will begin." The machine was in the basement, where the walls were lined with spouts of dripping water ("for tests") and instrument panels. Strangely, there was still no one in sight, and the only sounds in the room were from the ominously beeping ozone lights. "This is where people like to film movies," Odom explained. "Chase scenes, industrial footage, that sort of thing."

The facility seemed immense and deserted, and as we walked through cold, clammy basements with shooting steam and dripping water, I began to wonder if humans ran this operation. Aside from the secretary at the front desk, I had still seen no one else. I was wondering precisely who would need to be evacuated and who performed the "tests," when we turned the corner and encountered a glassed-in room with three or four people in it. "This is the control room," he explained. "We can monitor everything from here." Indeed, the control room looked like the helm of the starship *Enterprise* to me. I began to think of the filtration plant as a great big ship, delivering water straight from space to a thirsty nation. The instrument panels were blinking, and I was told that we could watch the flow of Owens River water on its journey through the entire facility on these panels as managers monitored its quality and checked the levels of its flow.

Not all of Los Angeles gets the treated, billion-dollar Owens River water, and not all of that water is actually of the same quality. Those who live closest to the filtration plant, in the San Fernando Valley or on the Westside, receive the most and highest quality water. This is because in some areas the Department of Water and Power mixes polluted groundwater with aqueduct water until the polluted water is diluted to the point at which it is drinkable by EPA standards. The Department of Water and Power, in its yearly water quality reports, breaks the city up into four districts: Central and Eastern L.A., San Fernando Valley, Western Los Angeles, and the Harbor Area. Central and Eastern L.A. receive the highest number of pollutants, including areas such as Watts, Koreatown, Little Tokyo, Chinatown, Boyle Heights, and Los Feliz. The Water Quality Report for 1999 showed that the water for this region contained aluminum, arsenic, barium, fluoride, nitrate, tetrachloroethene, trichloroethene, dichloroethene, and uranium. This pollution was caused by "discharge or oil drilling waste and from metal refineries, runoff and leaching from fertilizer use, leaching from septic tanks and sewage, discharge from factories, dry cleaners, and auto shops (metal degreaser), and discharge from industrial chemical factories." The water in Western Los Angeles, in contrast, contained only fluoride, arsenic, and radium. The source of this pollution was "erosion of natural deposits."[1] This region contains the towns of Pacific Palisades, Bel Air Estates, Venice, Century City, Westwood, and Beverly Glen. As Owens River water is distributed throughout the city, more chlorine is also added to counteract organic materials that are picked up along the distribution route—and with this chlorine the carcinogens, TCBs, travel. I asked Jerry Gewe what determines who gets what type of water. He said simply, "Hydraulics." Today, only those who live in the wealthier parts of Los Angeles tend to have ample access to Owens River water. D. J. Waldie suggested, "If you live high [in Los Angeles] you share history and hydrology with Los Angeles's Anglo ascendancy."[2]

In 1911, William Howard Taft suggested that the aqueduct should terminate in the San Fernando Valley "because it is the logical geological spot."[3] At the same time, the San Fernando Valley's underground aquifer could act as a storage basin for Owens River water. Because the San Fernando Valley is north of Los Angeles, it is closer to Owens Valley. Owens River water would have to pass through it or some other northern valley on its way to Los Angeles. Taft and others believed that the aqueduct water should first be stored in the San Fernando Valley and then distributed throughout Los Angeles. Not coincidentally, the place where Taft proposed that the Los Angeles Aqueduct should end was also the place where the Los Angeles River began. Water used for irrigation in the San Fernando Valley, it was believed, would seep into the ground and could be used again. Underneath the San Fernando Valley was a huge underground aquifer that ultimately bubbled up as the headwaters to the Los Angeles River. The underground reservoir that fed the Los Angeles River was therefore considered the perfect storage place for Owens River water. The water board described this aquifer: "It would appear as a great natural reservoir, created by Nature for the express purpose of holding the water of Owens River, until needed by the City of Los Angeles. . . . Some of the water used for irrigation is sure to sink deep into the ground, and we estimate that at least one-fourth of all the water used in the San Fernando Valley will eventually return to the Los Angeles River as underflow, and can be utilized a second time. This water is just as valuable as water direct from the Aqueduct. On account of the return water, and for other reasons, it is highly desirable that the San Fernando Valley should have an adequate allowance of water for irrigation."[4] Other areas vying for excess aqueduct water, such as the San Gabriel Valley, were eliminated because they would "yield but little return water by seepage."[5] The water board claimed that using Owens River water twice—first for farming and then for drinking—would yield more water.

The water used for irrigation in the San Fernando Valley did, in fact, dramatically increase the flow of the Los Angeles River. The problem, of course, was that post-irrigation water was not suitable for domestic use. It was waste water, contaminated with pesticides and other farm pollutants as well as street runoff and industrial discharge.[6] The construction of the Los Angeles Aqueduct directly led to the degradation of the Los Angeles River and this groundwater source. Owens River water would bring increased pollution to the Los Angeles River, although at the time of the aqueduct construction, this additional water—albeit polluted—was a major selling point behind the choice of the San Fernando Valley. The men who had bought up dust bowl land in the San Fernando Valley could now subdivide and sell richly irrigated farmland. Those who could afford to moved closer to the aqueduct terminus, in the San Fernando Valley, after water became available. The people downriver, however, began to receive polluted water as pollution in the Los Angeles River increased. The volume of water in the Los Angeles River also increased, contributing to disastrous flooding problems. In time, as these problems became evident, water officials attempted to keep the Los Angeles River from flowing on the surface by pumping the cleaner groundwater. Parts of the Los Angeles River, to a large extent, would cease to flow altogether—except when they flooded. The Los Angeles River would ultimately be encased in concrete in an attempt to control this flooding.

The Los Angeles River would come to signify pollution, homelessness, and unsanitary conditions. Owens Valley, in turn, became a site for recreation—as well as clean air and water—for those classes that could afford to leave Los Angeles. Inasmuch as the Los Angeles River was mocked or degraded, the Owens River was praised (see figure 2.1). But they were both to become increasingly artificial, severed from their natural watersheds. Class interests would largely determine the difference between how and where these rivers flowed. Because both of these rivers were considered detachable from their surroundings, their representations could be easily manipulated. Marc Reisner writes, "By effectively detaching the West's water

One can be seen with the naked eye; the other hard to find with a spyglass.

2.1. Owens River–Los Angeles River, *The Los Angeles Times,* August 18, 1905.

from the land, the prior appropriation doctrine fundamentally favors movement of water from one river basin to another."[7] This doctrine, which favored whoever first "used" a river by diverting it, also favored those with the money to implement such diversions. Access to clean water, in this sense, always came with a price tag.

The aqueduct plan emerged, in part, because of pollution problems in the Los Angeles River. In 1850, the Common Council prohibited the throwing of garbage and washing of clothes in the Los Angeles River. But Benjamin Hayes reported that "this latter regulation was disobeyed by the native women, who continued to gather there."[8] In the late 1800s, one resident wrote that "the course of the Los Angeles River is the . . . proper outlet for the sewage of Los Angeles. To such disposition of the sewer water, no one would have a right to complain, for it would be precisely the drainage provided by Nature."[9] Another resident wrote that the water was "so offensive to the taste and smell, as to be not only undrinkable, but positively nauseating."[10] Around the same time, stories began to circulate of corpses—usually those of people of color—polluting the river. Catherine Muholland wrote, "Then variations of the story appeared: it was a cow, a horse, a sheep; two drowned 'Chinamen,' then a Chinaman and a horse, then two Chinamen and an Indian; finally, an Indian and a mule."[11] A town doctor even declared that "the offensive effluvia was nothing less than that emanating from decomposed human remains."[12] At this time, when the river was being constantly defined as "foul" and undrinkable, it also began to be confined, through channelization, to a designated route through what was then called "Nigger Alley"—the last street before the river. The term was used for people of various ethnicities, including Native Americans, Italians, Basques, Jews, and Slavs. North of Nigger Alley, the Mexican barrio of Sonoratown, as well as Chinatown, emerged in the 1860s.

The Los Angeles River increasingly became described as a home for transients, who camped there when the river was dry, rather than a source of water. In January 1902, the *Los Angeles Times* complained of an "ever shifting class that inhabits the bed."[13] In an article appropriately called, "Vagrant Rivers," Bernice Eastman Johnston associated the Los Angeles River not only with "shiftiness" (in the sense of constantly leaving its banks) but also with the hazards of wilderness. The land surrounding the river, she claimed, was a "vast forest, undergrown with impenetrable thickets and laced with hidden pools and swamps . . . half-wild cattle and horses found hiding places in the jungle of sycamores, willows, alders, wild grape vines and bramble bushes."[14] In contrast to the "well kept lawns" of the already growing suburbs, the Los Angeles River became associated with an unpredictable lawlessness, "penetrated" by a few trails and "made hazardous by prowling grizzly bears." The riverbed was also seen as a place where Indians and transients could hide out, "prowling" and ambushing unwary citizens from the cover of willows.

The pollution and unseemliness of the Los Angeles River started a general trend of white, westward movement away from the river in the 1880s, when local Anglos started subdividing housing lots on Bunker Hill. Margaret Collier Graham wrote of the growing contrast between downtown and the suburbs as early as 1876. She described her discomfort walking downtown: "We have been walking around nearly all day through the narrow streets full of strange Spanish and Chinese faces, passing long rows of low adobe houses swarming with dusky children and reeking of foreign odors." Collier Graham suggested that her only appreciation came from looking past the "squalor and nastiness" of downtown to the "groves of green trees, orange, fig, walnut, and acres of grape vines" that dotted the hills surrounding Los Angeles.[15] In 1882, the newer parts of town were described by a visiting journalist: "the beautiful, new and refined Anglo-Saxon part of the town with its fine architecture, its well kept lawns, its evergreen trees."[16]

Los Angeles's older water system inevitably became polluted as the city grew; then it became associated with people of color. It was seen as a Mexican or indigenous system—not a "forward-looking" or progressive system. The Gabrielino Indians who had first settled along the Los Angeles River were described by the Department of Water and Power as mere animals. In January 1926, Water and Power employee Charles Houser wrote for *The Intake*, "Alta California was populated with a race barely above the animal nature. They were later called 'Indians'. . . . The Indians of California had seventeen absolutely distinct languages. The vocabulary of each language consisted of only a few hundred words, and their talk seemed to one who did not understand it to be made up of slobberings and gruntings."[17] Mexicans were often described as lazy or lacking the initiative necessary for a monumental project like the Los Angeles Aqueduct. A 1924 *Intake* described California in the 1850s: "The Time. Almost seventy-five long years ago, in the dim and misty past, in the Year of Grace, Eighteen Hundred and Fifty-One. THE PLACE. The straggling, unkempt adobe village of Los Angeles, part Mexican and part American, basking lazily beneath a summer sky, without intuition to foresee or incentive to day-dream of the great future lying across its path in the coming years."[18] The narrative of "dreaming" or "imagining" Los Angeles out of nothing is constantly juxtaposed with the lack of imagination of non-Anglos. It served as a colonial justification for taking Los Angeles from the Indians and Mexicans who did not have the "initiative" to make anything of it. The City's rhetoric was one of "vision" or being "envisioned" ex nihilo. Those who envisioned the city were seen as both its prophets and leaders. Kevin Starr wrote, "Prophesying the bringing of water to the desert and to the cities on the plain, they saw themselves embarked upon a work of social redemption Biblical in metaphor and suggestion."[19]

Ironically but perhaps not surprisingly, Spain and later Mexico actually led the European world in modern dam-building methods and irrigation systems. From Mexico, dam-building and irrigation schemes then moved north to New Mexico, Arizona, Colorado, and California. In Owens Valley, Paiute irrigation systems predominated before the diversion of the Owens River. In Los Angeles, the early Spanish inhabitants built elaborate canals or *acequia* systems for managing the flow of the Los Angeles River. According to historian Norman Smith, "Spanish dams were without equal or rival, in Europe or anywhere else."[20] The Spanish had adopted many Middle Eastern irrigation techniques before expelling Muslims from Spain in the seventeenth century. Smith writes, "Spain, in short, was the birthplace of modern dam-building."[21] Spanish dam-building techniques were exported throughout the world, particularly to America. But just as Spanish technology co-opted and then erased indigenous and Muslim systems, so Anglo-America wanted to erase the influence of Mexican irrigation on water development schemes.

The new suburban developments attempted to recreate the atmosphere of the Anglo-European "gentleman's" estate with lawns, gardens, fountains, and pools. This preoccupation was linked to "white flight," the desire to escape from the pollution of the Los Angeles River. In contrast to the uncontrollable and dirty Los Angeles River, Owens River would offer precisely controlled water flow, neatly ordered lawns, and pure drinking water. William Mulholland had a dream, he said, of Los Angeles becoming a model of green beauty in the West. He objected to the suggestion that Angelenos use *less* water during times of drought, encouraging them instead not to fall beneath the per capita water usage in the East. The "beauty" of the city had been carved out by men like Henry E. Huntington, owner of the Southern Pacific Railroad, at his 500-acre botanical gardens and estate. The city's beauty been established in the country estate, the suburban lawn, and the fantasy-machine of Hollywood, where African jungles and the English Lake District could be found side by side on the back lots of movie studios in the San Fernando Valley. All these dreams required water, which represented status and the ability to make more dreams. Kevin Starr has called Los Angeles the "most exquisite invented garden in history." He also said it is a "vampire."

The model for Los Angeles's future would be the "beautiful" city, whose beauty was based on water consumption for agriculture and landscaping. In

1902, the Board of Water Commissioners reported, "we must not expect that this City can hope to reach a low per capita consumption, as measured by that of Eastern cities (and it is not desirable that she should, a bountiful supply of water being necessary to the maintenance of the beauty for which she is famous)."[22] At this time, water consumption in Los Angeles was 50 percent higher than that of most eastern cities, with 300 gallons being used per capita every day. The Board of Water Commissioners stated that this figure was 50 percent greater than the average consumption of forty-seven cities in the United States ranging in population from forty thousand to four hundred thousand.[23] But in 1911, William Howard Taft justified this overuse, pointing out that that because of its beautification programs, 300 gallons per person was not exorbitant.

Los Angeles, of course, is known for its tidy suburban lawns and back-yard swimming pools. It became a model of suburban development throughout the nation. The Los Angeles Aqueduct enabled a further po-larization between black and white areas of the city. If the bed of the Los Angeles River was increasingly associated with blackness, the Owens River would promise to bring whiteness, purity, and beauty to the Los Angeles suburbs. Roosevelt openly promoted the racial division that followed and repeatedly expressed fear about the mingling of different races in cities. He stated, "It is highly inadvisable that peoples in wholly different stages of civilization . . . shall be thrown into intimate contact. This is especially un-desirable when there is a difference of race."[24] In 1914, a year after the aqueduct opened, the first "whites only" bus system was established in Los Angeles.[25] Resistance to people of color moving into white neighborhoods began to emerge around the same time. After 1918, white property owners began to place race-restrictive covenants on properties, enforced by the courts, which prevented the "use or occupancy of property by Blacks." African Americans who attempted to move away from downtown areas to the nicer beachfront developments and suburban housing projects of East Los Angeles were often met with hostility or even violence. In the 1920s, these satellite suburbs were described as the "happy hunting grounds of the Klan," with Klan activism reaching an all-time high.[26]

Los Angeles's "elite" also began to move to Owensmouth, now Canoga Park, where the water was delivered from the Owens Valley. "White flight" from downtown Los Angeles toward the aqueduct terminus in the San Fernando Valley was promoted in advertisements by real estate speculators, who courted white tourists to the suburbs of Los Angeles. Some suburban developers openly excluded nonwhites; developer Frank P. Cross advertised in 1924: "Purchasers of these Lots are restricted to the Caucasian or White Race."[27] In 1928, former Klan member John Porter was elected mayor of Los Angeles. The Westside, including Hollywood and Bel Air, was entirely blocked to black immigration, while the movement of blacks south and southeast was highly contested. White homeowners were known to riot against sales to African Americans, while the KKK burned homes and crosses downtown. By 1930, 70 percent of African Americans lived in one assembly district in the Central Avenue area—the remainder lived in ad-joining districts such as Watts, Eastern Los Angeles, and the West Adams district.[28] Raphael Sonenshein explained, "In dynamic Los Angeles, growth was moving quickly out of the central city into suburban areas. It was here that the new opportunities for wealth were being created, but successful at-tempts were made to exclude Blacks."[29] Blacks had been restricted to ap-proximately 5 percent of the residential area of Los Angeles. During World War II an area called "Little Tokyo" was also opened to blacks—because most of its Japanese residents had been relocated to internment camps. This area was renamed "Bronzeville," and quickly became over-congested, with makeshift residences and unsanitary conditions.[30]

In 1943, the City housing authority stated that "in addition to the pos-sibility of race riots nurtured by subversive elements within the commu-nity," there was the problem of "mal-content that exists because of this intolerable housing condition." A DWP employee recalled entering houses during World War II that "had no make-shift or no inside plumb-ing facilities at all."[31] Following World War II, conditions only worsened when Japanese residents returned from relocation camps to "Little Tokyo." Those who attempted to evict black residents often had their businesses or properties looted in retaliation.[32] Police Chief Daryl Gates described the Central L.A. area in 1951 as "stretching east to Chinatown and the Los Angeles River." It was, he said, "a mixture of blacks, Hispanics, Asians, and whites, many of them newly arrived immigrants."[33] Gates complained that in 1951, the area contained "a bunch of beaten-down, dilapidated old ten-ements, rife with crime, narcotics, gambling, drunks, prostitutes, and wholesale scumbags."[34] Zoning laws were not enforced, and unapproved warehouses and junkyards sprang up overnight. Garbage went uncollected, and rat and roach infestations were uncontrolled.

Around this time, the LAPD began to practice a strategy of "containment" for criminals and the homeless. The area to which they were "contained" stretched from Broadway to the riverfront, Los Angeles's Skid Row. In the 1960s, Chief Gates claimed that the LAPD looked to Vietnam for lessons in containing crime in downtown Los Angeles. After the Watts riots in 1965, Gates explained, "[We] began reading everything we could get our hands on concerning guerilla warfare. We watched with interest what was happening in Vietnam, and in particular studied what a group of marines, based at the Naval Armory in Chavez Ravine, were doing. They shared with us their knowledge of counter-insurgency and guerilla warfare."[35] In 1969, Gates first used the "SWAT" method, which he said stood for "Special Weapons Attack Teams," against the Black Panthers in South Central Los Angeles. SWAT trained "deep in the San Fernando Valley" and received permission from the Pentagon to use a grenade launcher against a group of Panthers, whom Gates called "modern-day mountebanks, a rabble-rousing street gang."[36] The Panthers surrendered, however, before the grenade that would have blown up their building was launched. In 1970, the LAPD started a "Public Disorder Intelligence Division" in its Wilshire office to spy on subversive groups downtown.[37] Downtown was increasingly seen, by the police and the general public, as harboring terrorists, subversives, and "scumbags." If Owens River water was instrumental in creating wealth for Los Angeles's suburbs, the Los Angeles River was seen as watering the ghettos of Los Angeles after the aqueduct was completed. Los Angeles was a forward-thinking city, and the Los Angeles River represented the past (see figure 2.2).

In the 1960s, Anheuser Busch celebrated the wealth provided by the Owens River by building Busch Gardens, an amusement park built in its Budweiser brewery in the San Fernando Valley. You could take a boat ride through the brewery on Owens River water, surrounded by tropical birds while drinking beer also made from the Owens River. Some say the feral parakeets that can be found around Los Angeles today are descendents of escapees from Busch Gardens, which is now shut down. This fantasy land of Midwestern beer garden and tropical landscape is the perfect symbol of Los Angeles. Owens River provided the promise of an

2.2. "Here's How!" *The Los Angeles Times*, March 22, 1915.

escape from the increasingly crowded and polluted urban conditions of inner city Los Angeles.

Today, the San Fernando Valley, which once clamored to join Los Angeles, is now trying to secede from downtown Los Angeles. Claiming that it "subsidizes" the rest of Los Angeles, the San Fernando Valley could vote on secession in the near future. Opponents claim that the movement represents a racist hostility toward the inner city. Mayor Richard Riordan complained, "I think it is just downright immoral to abandon the poor people of this city."[38] The segregation of the San Fernando Valley from a "contained" downtown parallels anxieties over "sharing the wealth" through taxation. If the San Fernando Valley could more thoroughly insulate itself, it would also be removed from the flooding and pollution problems of the Los Angeles River. Buying Owens River water directly from the Department of Water and Power, the San Fernando Valley would no longer have to subsidize the costly treatment plants for polluted groundwater in other parts of Los Angeles.

The Los Angeles Aqueduct enabled the development of the independent farmer and suburban family on the edges of the city, creating a satellization effect. Beyond this, the Los Angeles Aqueduct enabled the City to promote its new "recreational" properties along the Owens River. Owens Valley served the dual purpose of providing nature for tourism and water for Los Angeles. Nancy Walter commented, "Sierra water going south only passes the tourists coming north."[39] One of the reasons for the promotion of tourism in Owens Valley was simply that the Department of Water and Power did not want their watershed lands to be developed and potentially pollute the Owens River. In fact, every effort was made to keep this from happening in the early 1900s. In order to help the DWP achieve this goal, Theodore Roosevelt set aside the Inyo National Forest in Owens Valley in 1907, which included over a million acres and prevented further settlement in Owens Valley. The mayor of Bishop explained, "The Department of Water and Power originally tried to buy up the towns so they could shut them down. They used to talk about grass growing on the streets here one day. But then the area became a tourist draw, and that became impossible. It is still Department of Water and Power policy to limit growth, however. The more growth they have, the more hassles."[40]

The Department of Water and Power initially promoted its undeveloped land as a selling feature of the Los Angeles Aqueduct. Los Angeles once hoped "to annex this vast country to the city of Los Angeles by a shoestring strip following the aqueduct."[41] Commissioner Whitsett of the water board proposed that Los Angeles annex Owens Valley within its city limits, but the City ultimately rejected this plan. Still, at the northern end of Owens Valley, a sign stood for a long time that read, "Los Angeles City Limits."[42] Instead of annexing the Owens Valley, the Department of Water and Power next claimed that it wanted "the land purchased to be used by the people of Los Angeles as a recreational center."[43] Department of Water and Power employee P. B. Hardesty traveled to Switzerland in 1927 to get ideas about promoting Owens Valley. In his article entitled "Unveiling the American Alps," he wrote, "We hope to learn much from Switzerland that will aid our Board of Water and Power Commissioners in developing the Owens River Valley region into one of the great outing and vacation lands of America."[44] In what was perhaps a confusing metaphor, the Owens River Gorge north of Bishop was described as the "Grand Canyon of California."[45] In 1928, The Intake editor wrote an article entitled, "High Sierras Offer Fine Playground." He suggested that one of the ways in which Los Angeles was the "most fortunate of the great cities in the world" was that "it has in its possession the most magnificent playground to be found anywhere in the world." The article goes on to describe the necessity of a city having a playground: "Perhaps a great city can manage to get along without a playground, although I don't see how. The people of a thickly populated community must have a place where they can find relaxation from the stifling life that goes inevitably with stone streets and skyscrapers. . . . Indeed, to be frank about it, they must have somewhere to go when they can get away from an overdeveloped and supercomplex civilization. It is a safety valve, deprived of which the people come to be without vision, and so perish; they collapse because they have divorced themselves from nature."[46] This notion of "nature" as a place from which people have been divorced and to which they must return paralleled an Edenic myth of racial purity in the West. This notion of "nature," however, was based not upon preservation but upon recreation.

Los Angeles explorers began venturing up the mountains to alpine streams and fisheries after the construction of the road to Owens Valley.

Though the local pupfish population (now endangered) refused to bite a line, largemouth bass, as well as trout, carp, and catfish, were introduced to solve this problem, making the Owens Valley one of the best fishing spots in Southern California. The first fish were brought over the Sierra Mountains on pack animals, but later fish were brought in cans on the railroad. The bass tended to clean out the carp and trout, however, as well as Owens pupfish and Owens tui chub. The pupfish, which had been a staple food source for the Paiutes, slowly disappeared. Other fish—the Owens specked dace and Owens River sucker—disappeared from the Owens River Fish Slough altogether. In 1915, the *Inyo Register* reported that the "world's largest fish hatchery" would be built in Owens Valley, the Mt. Whitney fish hatchery. Within five years, over 3 million trout were planted annually in the Eastern Sierra.[47] Today, fishing is still a major industry in the area, though fish are now dropped by airplane into the alpine lakes. The fish have been studied to determine the damage to them from the impact of this fall—now they are only released when they are large enough to survive the fall.

Big game hunting was also promoted in Owens Valley. In 1933 and 1934, tule elk were transported to Department of Water and Power property in Owens Valley from Yosemite and the Bakersfield area. Due to overhunting and irrigation, tule elk were on the verge of becoming extinct in the San Joaquin Valley. In 1904, the last tule elk herd was handed over to the Department of the Interior, which then undertook to transplant the animals to several areas in California. Currently, the Department of Water and Power maintains a herd of tule elk on irrigated pasturage in Owens Valley.[48] Like trout, however, the tule elk herd displaced native bighorn sheep and antelope. Owens Valley became a hunting and fishing preserve for tourists from Los Angeles, who were predominantly white. The marketing of the Owens Valley for tourism paralleled a growing concern with maintaining and establishing a sense of "whiteness" in Los Angeles.

Theodore Roosevelt, who was ultimately responsible for the creation of Los Angeles, was also a leading preservationist and a friend of John Muir. Roosevelt's desire to preserve wilderness, however, intersected with his belief that overcivilization led to a "flabby" or effeminate type of man. Roosevelt romanticized the cowboy, big game hunter, and frontiersman, and he advocated the preservation of wilderness in order to maintain spaces where these manly specimens could pursue their interests. Roosevelt described the life of a cowboy: "The whole existence is patriarchal in character: it is the life of men who live in the open, who tend their herds on horseback, who go armed and ready to guard their lives by their own prowess, whose wants are very simple, and who call no man master. Ranching is an occupation like those of vigorous, primitive pastoral peoples, having little in common with the humdrum, workaday business world of the nineteenth century; and the free ranchman in his manner of life shows more kinship to an Arab sheik than to a sleek city merchant or tradesman."[49] Theodore Roosevelt was the most famous advocate of the "strenuous life" of hunting, camping, and other wilderness sports as an antidote to the overcivilization of American men. In *Wilderness and the American Mind*, Roderick Nash places Theodore Roosevelt squarely in the camp of other "wilderness cult" members such as John Muir and Henry David Thoreau.

In 1903, Theodore Roosevelt went camping with John Muir in Yosemite and discussed wilderness preservation. For neither Muir nor Roosevelt did the "wilderness cult" include Indians. Roosevelt believed that Indians would naturally "die out" as the West was settled. Muir seemed to regard Indians as dirty beggars, complaining often of their uncleanliness. Writing of the Northern Paiutes, Muir covets their environment: "Two things they have that civilized toilers might well envy them—pure air and pure water." But demonstrating the prevalent prejudices of the time, he continues, "These go far to cover and cure the grossness of their lives. . . . Most Indians I have seen are not a whit more natural in their lives than we civilized whites. Perhaps if I knew them better I should like them better. The worst thing about them is their uncleanliness. Nothing truly wild is unclean."[50] This valorization of the natural world at the expense of the Paiutes is particularly telling in terms of the rise of environmental consciousness in American history. By fashioning himself as "wild," Muir had to explain natives as not-wild. The Owens Valley became "wild" only by removing people—including Indians.

Ironically, when the National Park Service was created in 1916, Yosemite introduced "Indian field days," a yearly festival in which Paiutes were paid to supply entertainment to visitors to the park. Since the tourists preferred the more glamorous Plains Indians attire, however, Paiutes were required to wear those costumes rather than their own and act out prescribed roles. Owens Valley Paiute Viola Martinez described her disturbing experience of Indian field days: "The first time I saw it, there was a live play where there were horses and houses were burning, Indians coming around and setting fire to them. I thought the Indians were terrible. . . . I was little. . . . I didn't even know what it was all about. All I knew was that the Indians were horrible. They were coming in and killing the whites."[51] The stereotypical movie-Indian dominated the Yosemite landscape for a short time, before Indian days were disbanded altogether. During Indian days, white tourists could experience the thrill of what they imagined it was like for white settlers to move into the wilderness. Tourism was detrimental to the local Paiutes in other ways, as Viola Martinez noted painfully, recounting the white tourists' fascination with Indian babies. Martinez explained what happened to her sister: "Whenever Alice was around, the white people just loved her. One couple, particularly, took a real shine to her. When they would go up to the Mammoth Lake area, June Lake and all those places, they'd ask my mother if they could take [Alice] with them. The result was that they stole her. . . . Of course, anything that happened to the Indians, the whites didn't care. . . . Nobody did anything about it."[52] Indians became another tourist commodity during the establishment of the High Sierras as a wilderness retreat. Those who frequented these parks were almost exclusively white—as is still the case today. In contrast, Los Angeles now has the highest concentration of city-living Indians in the United States. (The 2000 Census count shows 138,696 American Indians in Los Angeles County—and this number is considered a gross underestimate.) Indians fleeing difficult conditions in these new wilderness areas ended up scattered throughout the City of Los Angeles.[53]

Theodore Roosevelt did more than any other president to set aside wilderness areas in the United States, and more national parks, monuments, and wilderness areas surround Owens Valley than anywhere else in the nation—besides Alaska. These include Yosemite, Devils Postpile, Death Valley, Kings Canyon, and Sequoia National Park. The parks near Owens Valley, in the Sierra Nevada Mountains, receive more recreational visitors than the Grand Canyon, Yellowstone, and Glacier National Parks put together. Park attendance, however, is predominantly made up of Caucasians. Recent studies of National Park use show that at Yosemite National Park in California, 3.6 percent of the visitors are Hispanic, 3.3 percent Asian, 1.4 percent American Indian, and .4 percent black. In "Whiteness of National Parks," Michelle Boorsten explains the current discrepancy in national park use: "The people who created these places were primarily affluent white people. This hasn't been a major part of the culture of people of color in the U.S. up to this point."[54] The "whiteness" of national parks today thus reflects statistically the history of marketing these parks to Anglos.

The Los Angeles River is a river that has become devoid of "nature," so much so that one politician suggested that the riverbed be painted blue so it would look natural from the air. The Los Angeles River, which once supported the entire city, is now deserted and forgotten (see figure 2.3). It is generally a river that is *missed;* freeways crisscross this abandoned space as if it were a railroad depot or industrial wasteland. The Los Angeles River is either not seen or seen by most as a sign of urban decay. The Art Deco bridges that cross the river are now falling down and forgotten, in the midst of old railway tracks and an industrial mélange of apparently uninhabitable territory. By the 1930s, the parks commissioner of Los Angeles would say,

2.3. Los Angeles River. Photo by Karen Piper. Used with permission.

"It would be expensive and difficult, if not impossible, ever to make the river bed a thing of beauty . . . but it is not necessary to have it so ugly and unsanitary."[55] In *Close-Up: How to Read the American City*, Grady Clay talks about parts of cities called "breaks," where the grid of the city is interrupted by some kind of barrier. He writes, "Breaks form psychological, as well as geographic, barriers; they set up relationships that confuse, so that territory on the other side seems strange and unreliable. Land beyond the break has an uneasy look about it; development is spotty and irregular."[56] The Los Angeles River appears to be such a "break" within the city, a place that causes unease, malaise, or confusion.

In the 1980s, sweatshops began to locate around the Los Angeles River, particularly near Vernon, taking advantage of the cheap land and labor there. Today, the Los Angeles River is the most polluted urban river in the nation. The Los Angeles River serves as a playground, drinking fountain, laundromat, and community center for the homeless of East and South Central Los Angeles. Central American refugees in the MacArthur Park area have been known to sleep in the Department of Water and Power's storm drains and drink the river's polluted water. While most of this water is treated and released from the Department of Water and Power's Tillman Reclamation Plant and is therefore "clean" if not "drinkable," the rest is from the city's streets, lawns, and industrial plants. The homeless are drinking this treated sewage because there is no other water available. One of the control measures against Los Angeles's homeless is to eliminate public facilities, including bathrooms, parks, and drinking fountains in the downtown neighborhoods. Downtown Los Angeles, therefore, has fewer public facilities than any other North American city.[57]

In the spring of 1992, as I was driving through Skid Row on the way to the Los Angeles River, I saw a man urinating against a Department of Water and Power office. The office was windowless, and a steel guard door had been pulled over the main doors, as the Department of Water and Power had recently abandoned this office. The Los Angeles River is an oily brownish color, and it runs in a neatly confined trickle. Today, it is hard to imagine much life in the graffiti-ridden sections of the Los Angeles River channel. There are a few plants clinging to life where underground water has broken through the concrete floor, but the river is dry for most of the year, except for the lower portion that is kept flowing with wastewater from the Tillman sewage treatment plant. There are a few green shoots of grass or trees that have broken through parts of the concrete that had given in to the pressure of the water. From the bed of the river, the city is hidden behind its concrete walls. Instead, in the storm drains waiting to feed into the river, homeless men crouch in dirty clothes, with all their goods piled around them. The concrete river has now become a good canvas for graffiti artists. Its walls are peppered with tags, throw ups, and intricate murals.

Painting the Los Angeles River blue may not be so strange for a city like Los Angeles. The blue paint would mask the graffiti, the garbage, and the history of segregation and racism that the river represents. It would simulate nature, a kind of cleaned-up spectacle for those flying into or out of the city. Los Angeles has long been called the quintessential "postmodern" city because of its artificiality. Kevin Starr writes: "Los Angelenos were always struggling against a sense of emptiness, of void even, in their psychological encounter with the city . . . aggravated by an underlying uneasiness as to whether or not Los Angeles was truly there in the first place. The City of Los Angeles had made itself happen through will and water; but even when it happened, Los Angeles remained in some eerie way an emptiness, a void, the Nowhere City."[58] Or, as Sam Weber once said, "Living in L.A. is like living in an hallucination." The Los Angeles River, painted blue, would also feel like a kind of hallucination, a simulated river to cover up the visions of popular local artists.

The Los Angeles River is also portrayed in Hollywood as anything but a river. In the 1950s movie *Them*, it was most notoriously portrayed as a place infested with giant irradiated ants who had crawled out of its storm drains. In *Grease*, it was the site of the famous drag race between John Travolta and his rival gang. In *The Italian Job*, it became an escape route for gold thieves in souped-up BMW Minis. In *Terminator 2* and *Repo Man*, the Los Angeles River was also featured as a part of a futuristic nowhereland. But one of the most novel portrayals is in Mick Jackson's *Volcano* (1997), in which the Los Angeles River, rather than carrying water, becomes a channel for lava flows.

Volcano fits into a whole history of apocalyptic literature about the city— beginning with Louis Adamic's infamous essay of 1926, "There She Blows." *Volcano* also feeds into public fears following the 1992 Rodney King riots. The 1992 riot was most commonly described by CNN and other news affiliates as an "eruption," associating rioting with natural disaster. It was also called a "barbaric frenzy," a "potlatch of violence," and an "adolescent carnival."[59] *Volcano* makes these associations between race rioting and natural disaster. A volcano erupts in the storm drains of the Los Angeles River during drilling for a subway link between downtown and the San Fernando Valley. The volcano first erupts downtown in MacArthur Park and starts heading west toward Santa Monica. Interestingly, men in DWP hats suddenly appear, as the Department of Water and Power comes to the rescue in this film, building a series of dams to stop the lava flow. The Department of Water and Power has to stop the flow of lava in thirty minutes, before it hits West Hollywood and Santa Monica. Their response is "build a dam in thirty minutes—you've got to be crazy." Luckily, the storm drains for the Los Angeles River can be used to control the flow of lava. *Volcano* recounts much of the history of the Los Angeles River in less than two hours, including the attitudes about race that have historically surrounded the river. Like *Them,* it creates the vision of a bizarre, mutant, or out-of-place substance emerging from the Los Angeles River that must be explained and controlled. It demonstrates anxieties about the river as an unknown or even alien entity; the people who live around it and the "nature" that it contains are both seen as dangerous, out of control, and potentially able to escape their designated space and attack the "better" parts of Los Angeles.

The City of Los Angeles hoped to turn its back on the Los Angeles River after the acquisition the Owens River. However, anxieties about this forgotten space, like the unconscious of Los Angeles itself, would continue to erupt. The Los Angeles River has now become a place of urban legend, a no-man's land of alternative identities. The local Mexican American community claims that *la Llorona,* or the Crying Woman, lives there. *La Llorona* once drowned her own children—and then herself—in a desert arroyo. According to the tale, she lured them into the suddenly rising waters and watched as her children were swept away. She now continues to haunt the Los Angeles River, luring unsuspecting people to their death. Children are regularly caught up in Los Angeles River floodwaters; the riverbed is now a kind of playground for inner city children. The waters that rush down the Los Angeles channel can rise over one's head in a matter of minutes, not unlike the flash floods of the open desert. In 1934, the death toll reached an all-time high of 180 as the river overtopped its banks and spilled into surrounding neighborhoods.

The problem of flooding would continue to draw the public's attention back to the Los Angeles River. The building of the Los Angeles Aqueduct actually contributed to the flooding problems of the Los Angeles River. First, post-irrigation wastewater increased the flow of the Los Angeles River. By 1914, Bernice Eastman Johnston wrote, "it became obvious that [the Los Angeles River] must yield to a civilizing restraint."[60] In an attempt to control the river's flow, the entire river was lined with concrete between 1938 and 1940. The Sepulveda Basin and dam were also designed to control the flooding in the foothills. Still, the river flooded five times between 1941 and 1944.[61] Suburbanization in the San Fernando Valley only exacerbated the problem of flooding by keeping rainwater from seeping into the ground altogether. Water instead quickly ran off the pavement surfaces into storm drains that directly fed the Los Angeles River. This lack of seepage into the aquifer caused an overabundance of surface waters during rainfall, leading to severe flash flooding. It also caused water to flow straight out to sea rather than recharging the groundwater supply. In 1983, the Los Angeles River killed six people. In 1992, seven people, including a fifteen-year-old boy, were killed. The lack of connection between surface water and groundwater has also led to the lowering of the water table, leading to aquifer cave-ins, aboveground subsidence, and property damage. To stop some of these problems with intrusion and subsidence, Los Angeles has been artificially recharging groundwater by pumping in waste water. Los Angeles has been left with a "feast or famine" water supply problem. Water defined as "waste" (sewage water, flash flood waters, and other polluted waters) is overabundant in some areas while clean water becomes impossible, for some, to acquire.

Today, the Army Corps of Engineers believes that the flood control system could fail at any time and would like to build eight-foot concrete walls around the lower portion of the river, which is already encased in concrete. Some have critiqued this idea for its very ugliness, which would add to the "urban blight" of the inner city areas that surround the lower river.[62] Today, according to the corps, a breach in the Los Angeles River levee would flood between 75 and 82 square miles of residential and commercial development in Southeast Los Angeles. There are 500,000 people living in the eleven areas under threat, most of them Latinos and African Americans. One city official estimated that a flood would "pour down on these houses in a wave that will have the momentum of a freight train."[63] Raising the concrete walls along the Los Angeles River, however, would visibly cut off East Los Angeles from downtown Los Angeles. But for those who see the Los Angeles River as a threatening and unfamiliar place, these walls may represent insulation from that very threat.

Interestingly, both the Owens River and Los Angeles River have been ignored or neglected. In the case of the Owens River, what matters is the product, which is water for the Department of Water and Power. In the case of the Los Angeles River, what has mattered is sewage disposal, a place to flush the unwanted refuse of Los Angeles. Both these rivers are now encased in concrete, markers of urban control. Owens River water enters Los Angeles as billion-dollar treated water. The treatment plant where the Owens River is "made," however, is not simply a sign of success for Los Angeles. It is also a place that is ignored or taken for granted by the people of Los Angeles—much like the Los Angeles River. The replacement of the Los Angeles River with the Owens River and the movement of white communities toward the latter also served to establish racial difference in Los Angeles. In selling the aqueduct, the Department of Water and Power would also sell the idea of "whiteness" or white sanctuaries to incoming Midwesterners. The Los Angeles River, for decades, would only exist as a kind of hallucination or problem area to be crossed. It would assert its identity only by refusing to stop flowing altogether—by continuing to flood.

Owens River seems also unwilling to perform its role these days—it has a new pollution problem. The same arsenic that is found on Owens Lake bed is now being found in the Los Angeles Aqueduct. This arsenic is said to originate from water flowing into the aqueduct from Hot Creek Gorge, a volcanic hot springs north of Owens Lake. This arsenic-laden water, which once fed Owens Lake and is now contributing to its airborne arsenic problem, is also starting to scare the people of Los Angeles. Between 1968 and 1991, Los Angeles aqueduct water contained an average of 20 ppb of arsenic.[64] Under the Clinton administration, the EPA lowered the allowable limits of arsenic to 10 ppb. In 2003, George Bush reversed the EPA's decision and set the limit at 50 ppb. The Department of Water and Power is currently searching for the best way to filter arsenic from its water. It has not yet been determined how much Owens Valley's airborne arsenic, which settles into the open aqueduct channels, contributes to this problem. But once again, an elaborate system of racial and class divisions based on the supposed "purity" of Owens Valley water may be undone by problems at the water's source.

Mike Odom knows this and recognizes that his prized filtration plant may soon become outmoded. For now, he is proud to be generating ozone for the Department of Water and Power. Ironically, most people do not even know about the filtration plant or the efforts that are being made to keep their water clean. The area around the filtration plant, including the Van Norman Dam, is now used by the Los Angeles Police Department for SWAT training. The lower part of the reservoir was drained in 1971, after the dam cracked during an earthquake. Now the DWP land is used by the LAPD as a racetrack and mock town for training purposes. Its remote location and DWP security help to keep the training strategies top secret. Crowds once gathered to watch the Owens River tumble into the San Fernando Valley. You can still see the same sight today but it is difficult to stop to watch; it is at the intersection of Interstates 5, 210, and 405. The local interchange of these freeways is called the "bucket of worms" and has collapsed twice—once when it was being built in the 1970s and once in the Northridge quake of 1994. Interestingly, the sound walls around the freeways extending into San Fernando Valley are constructed from cinder from Owens Valley. Twin Mountain Rock Company is taking down a cinder mountain and relocating it to Los Angeles. Usually, the traffic is traveling so quickly on the freeways in this area, and so many lane changes must be made, that the Owens River may appear, if one is lucky, only as a blur in one's peripheral vision on the way out of town. Most people probably do not even know what it is. The water comes out of the mountain and heads down a series of steps in a long artificial waterfall, illuminated at night by alternate colors of blue, red, and green. It then heads into the Los Angeles Filtration Plant: the land of dead ravens, the movie backlot, the aquarium of Owens River Fish.

As the last stop on our tour, Mike Odom took me to a drinking fountain with a sign over it that read, "The Finished Product." Water bubbled up in this room into a ceramic-lined pool that fed directly into a 36-inch intake pipe, all enclosed behind a wire fence in the basement. This pipe took the water to smaller and smaller pipes and, finally, to the customers through Los Angeles. I was anxious to taste the "purest" form of water from the Owens River, straight from treatment plant. But when I went for a drink, Odom stopped me. "You don't want to drink that water," he said. "That's not really safe. We don't use that fountain anymore." I noticed that rust had built up on the faucet, and a pool of stagnant water was lying at its base. I wasn't really sure what was "pure" and what, after all, was not.

THREE

THE DEPARTMENT OF WATER AND POWER VERSUS THE PAIUTES

Owens Lake is where the Paiutes were drowned when they refused to leave the Owens Valley. On July 11, 1863, the Paiutes were told that they were to be moved from Owens Valley to Fort Tejon and would be shot if they refused to comply. Many Paiutes resisted the caravan, dropping out along the way and hiding in the hills; when the caravan crossed the marshes of Owens Lake, "dozens and dozens of Indians hid themselves among the tules [a kind of reed surrounding the lake]."[1] One of the soldiers described the battle that ensued: "We then chased them toward the lake. Some of the Indians got within forty yards of it, a place of safety, so they thought, but it proved death to them. Of those who went into the lake, but few came out."[2] The Indians attempted to outswim the soldiers, but because of a heavy wind they made little headway; they became easy targets. Dorothy Clora Cragen described that night: "Darkness came on but there was a bright moon, and the soldiers and citizens formed a line along the west shore, and remained there until the bodies began to wash ashore. One citizen, taking a shot at an Indian in the water, raised his fist after he had shot, and said to the struggling form, 'Die, damn you, in the lake,' and the Indian did."[3]

Thirty to forty Paiute and Shoshone men, women, and children were shot or driven into Owens Lake to drown that night on their way to Fort Tejon.[4] For the Paiutes, Owens Lake, though it had once sustained them, became a place of death and loss. It was also a place of hiding, a murky in-between space of camouflage and life that was not circumscribed by the rhetoric of the settlers. In 1909, *Sierra Club Bulletin* reported, "it is said that some of the bodies still lie in the bottom, perfectly preserved by soda which has crystallized about them."[5]

Many people know of the conflict between Owens Valley and Los Angeles, but few have heard the impact of this violence on the Paiutes. *Cadillac Desert, Water and Power, The Water Seekers*—all of these histories recount the struggle between Mulholland, Roosevelt, and the farmers of Owens Valley. This narrative of quasi-mythological white men, however, leaves out the people who, to this day, are victimized from both sides in this battle. In *Rhetoric of Empire,* David Spurr claims that in settler cultures, the territory and native people are often debased or ignored in order to provide a justification for colonial development. Spurr calls negation the process by which "a space for the expansion of the colonial imagination and for the pursuit of desire" is cleared.[6] This negation occurs by simply not acknowledging the pre-colonial presence or significance of the environment and people. Debasement is the condemning of that territory in order to justify colonial development projects as a sign of "civilization."

In the case of Owens Lake, negation and debasement were surprisingly prevalent in explorer journals and settler narratives. Even the earliest known record of exploration in Owens Valley (from around 500 B.C.) is not entirely positive. Found on a rock north of Bishop, a note written in Gaelic by a Celt from what is now Spain has been translated: "The desolate Valley by the river is less cold."[7] Owens Lake, which was named after Richard Owens, is particularly lacking in praise from explorers. In 1834, Richard Owens headed toward Owens Valley, and though he never made it there, his fellow-explorer John Fremont named the lake in his honor.[8] This expedition, as well as others that followed it, did not report favorably on the condition of the lake. It was called a realm of "mystery and malaria," around which Indians might be hiding (in the reeds) and disease might lurk. In *The Land of Little Rain*, Mary Austin described the marshes surrounding Owens Lake as "black and evil-smelling like old blood." She continued: "Last and inevitable resort of overflow waters is the tulares, great wastes of reed (*Juncus*) in sickly, slow streams. The reeds, called tules, are ghostly pale in winter, in summer deep poisonous-looking green, the waters thick and brown; the reed beds breaking into dingy pools, clumps of rotting willows, narrow winding water lanes and sinking paths."[9] Those places that could not be "penetrated" by explorers were considered somehow dangerous, "sickly," or out of control. But for the Paiutes, the Owens Lake supplied a food source; materials for housing, canoes, fish traps, and baskets; and a place to hide. The very thing that made the tules despicable to settlers—their lack of order and control— made them valuable to Paiutes. Owens Lake became the "last resort" of the Paiutes, who lost their lives in its waters.

In 1859, Captain J. W. Davidson surveyed the "fitness" of Owens Valley for an Indian reservation. Davidson described Owens Valley in his report: "It may be said literally to be a vast meadow, watered every few miles with clear, cold mountain streams, and the grass (although in August) as green as in the first of spring." The meadows, he said, "extended for miles," with "fingers of forest" following the streams down to the lake.[10] Davidson recommended that the valley be turned into an Indian reservation, but his glowing reports of the valley also attracted stockmen and farmers to Owens Valley. "To the Grazier, this is one of the finest parts of the state," Davidson had written. "To the Farmer, it offers every advantage but a market."[11] He described contact with the Paiutes: "The signs and trails of Indians today show them to be in great numbers, and to be running from us."[12] He continued: "These Indians subsist on the flesh of such game as they can kill, the Deer, Antelope, & Rabbit, Upon the seeds of various grasses, the Acorn, Pinon-nut, & the Tuber of a species of nutritious grass. . . . Whole fields of this grass, miles in extent, are irrigated with great care, yielding an abundant harvest of what is one of their principal articles of food."[13] These are only a few of the food sources on which the Paiutes were known to subsist. Yearly deer drives and mountain sheep hunts were an important part of the culture, as were pine nut harvests and the collection of brine fly larvae from the shores of Owens Lake. The larvae were dried and ground with flour, and Davidson noted "hundred of bushels" of the larvae drying in the sun.[14] The grasses that were cultivated, mainly yellow nut grass and wild hyacinth, were all native to the area, though other grasses, such as wheat grass, were also raised. Paiute irrigation covered over fifty-seven miles and ten creeks, with one of the major tracts existing at Bishop Creek. There was also evidence that the Paiutes rotated their fields, allowing one to go fallow while the other was cultivated.

Captain Davidson reported that the Paiutes were "an interesting, peaceful, industrious people, deserving the protection and watchful care of the Government."[15] Davidson also reported that the Paiutes requested military protection, as they had already been subject to the raids of cattlemen and miners passing through the area. Davidson wrote: "They expressed a desire to have a military post among them, as well as they could understand its nature, to live under the protection of the Government, and to have seeds and some simple instruments of Agriculture furnished them."[16] But Davidson's recommendation for a vast Indian reservation, complete with military protection against cattlemen, was overlooked as the area was becoming an important thoroughfare for cattle drives to Los Angeles.

In 1861, Samuel Bishop settled at the site of the present-day town that now bears his name, in order to let his five hundred to six hundred head of cattle take advantage of the luxuriant grasses there.[17] The grasses on which Bishop let his cattle graze were most likely the irrigated fields of the Paiutes, who were later blamed for killing his cattle. Robert A. Sauder concluded that Bishop's stock ranch was placed "close to, if not on, the Paiute's irrigated fields."[18] By fall of that year, close to a dozen ranches were established in the valley, and Paiute fields had been seriously damaged. In 1862, Col. James H. Carleton looked into the situation and reported: "I have heard that the white men went into Owen's Lake Valley and took their stock onto the fields of grass which is cultivated by those Indians, the root of the grass which is used by them as an article of food, and that, on the Indians remonstrating with them, they persisted in keeping their stock in these fields. . . . The poor Indians are doubtless at a loss to know how to live, having their fields turned into pastures whether they are willing or not willing."[19] Besides grazing their cattle in Paiute fields, settlers diverted water already used by the Paiutes for irrigation. One Paiute described the emerging tension between cattlemen and Paiutes: "When they [Paiutes] go out to irrigate the seed beds, the white man says not to take any of the water. If you do my horses and cattle will not have anything to eat."[20] With one of their staple food sources taken away, the living condition of the Paiutes began to quickly deteriorate. A second winter staple, the pinon pine nut, was also being destroyed by the cutting of pinon pines to make charcoal for the mining industry. By the winter of 1861, Paiutes were forced to kill cattle in the valley in order to survive.

The worsening relations between the settlers and Paiutes led the settlers to request military aid in dealing with the Paiutes. In 1862, Colonel Evans was sent to the Owens Valley to investigate the situation. He reported that after arriving in the area where the Indians were supposed to be, he "found no Indians, they having scattered at our approach . . . like partridges." Ultimately, he claimed, he was "compelled to go back into the valley to camp for the night without catching an Indian."[21] Still, Evans concluded that a military post should be established in the valley for the protection of the settlers. He wrote in his report, "From all the information I could get . . . I am of the opinion that the Owen's River Indians, together with detachments from the Tejon, Tulare, and Mono Indians, and some of the Piutes, have banded together, numbering not far from 800 to 1,000 warriors; that they have 100 or more good guns, and are determined to carry out their threat that no white man should live in the valley."[22] On July 4, 1862, the U.S. Army came in and established Fort Independence, claiming it was Independence Day for the settlers. The army began a more methodical process of starving the Indians by destroying their winter stores, burning their camps, and forcing them up into the hills.[23] Capt. Moses McLaughlin, who had been sent to run the camp, explained his strategy: "It is now a well-established fact that no treaty can be entered into with these Indians. They care nothing for pledges given, and have imagined that they live better by war than peace. They will soon learn that they have been mistaken, as with the forces here they will soon either be killed off, or pushed so far in the surrounding deserts that they will perish by famine."[24] In the fall of 1862, with winter setting in and food supplies dwindling, the Paiutes were invited to a "feast" at the fort in order to discuss a treaty. They were given food to bring home to their families, offered work, and urged to return the next day. Ben Tibbitts recalls, "In the next few days we went down to Fort Independence where we were captured and kept."[25] The Paiutes were "kept" at Fort Independence over the winter, but dwindling food supplies and lack of adequate shelter made their upkeep impossible.

By the summer, talk began of removing the last of the Paiutes from Owens Valley. Captain McLaughlin recommended the establishment of a military commission "to try and punish those found guilty, which would, I think result in the putting to death every male Indian over twelve years of age."[26] Instead, it was decided, they would simply be moved. On July 10, 1863, McLaughlin assembled all the Indians at the parade grounds, counted 998, and then told them of the plans for their removal. Historian Dorothy Clora Cragen reports, "For fear that they would become excited and cause a general stampede, he had the soldiers placed in such a manner as to completely surround the Indians with a wall of firearms."[27]

During their journey to Fort Tejon, many Paiutes died of thirst. Once they reached the camp, living conditions did not improve. The Paiutes were placed in an area called the "bog" and forced to forage for their own food. By 1864, Captain Schmidt described the condition of the Indians: "I found 380 Indians located about 300 yards below the Fort, as follows: 120 bucks, 170 squaws, and 90 children almost in a state of starvation; as they are under no one's charge, no one to care for them, they must look out for themselves. They are the remnants of nearly 1,100 Indians that were brought in from the Owens River."[28] Many had died from starvation and disease; others had been shot while trying to escape and return to Owens Valley. Captain Schmidt recommended that Fort Tejon be closed in 1864.[29]

By the time most Paiutes returned to Owens Valley, the situation had changed entirely. Fort Independence had been closed after the Indian removal. Mining was booming in the Coso range, on the eastern side of Owens Lake, and Owens Valley had an influx of Mexican miners. This mining, in fact, was primarily responsible for the establishment of Los Angeles as a major city. The constant supply of silver bullion from the Cerro Gordo mine, which had to be transported to the city for processing, started Los Angeles's boom. By 1870, two-thirds of Owens Valley's miners were listed in the census report as foreign-born—about half of those were from Mexico.[30] Chalfant wrote, "The locality bore the unusual designation of the 'Spanish mines.' A record book of Coso District . . . is written in Spanish and signed by eighteen Mexican names, with no other nationality represented."[31] The mining town of Cerro Gordo also had an established Chinatown as well as Keeler. Locally, these workers were known as the "China Gang" and were treated very poorly by Anglos. Many of their social activities were held in caves or tunnels for protection from harassment. The houses in Owens Valley were primarily of adobe construction, until an 8.3

or higher earthquake struck and leveled these buildings in 1872. African Americans also moved into the area for mining work, though they experienced the same prejudicial attitudes that had been directed toward the Paiutes. In 1865, a letter to the editor of the *Visalia Delta* noted, "The soldiers . . . were used the other day to quell a Negro insurrection. The darkies that came from New York to work the Coso mines are not well pleased with their new home, whose deserts can offer no amusements to the unthinking mind . . . and they are threatening to secede, which is no approval of life in a sagebrush region."[32] White settlers brought other African Americans into Owens Valley from the South as agricultural labor, though most fled the area due to racial tensions. In 1866, a race riot broke out in Independence. And in 1873, troopers were called in to protect the jail from a lynch mob.

Paiutes were commonly hired as agricultural laborers after their return from Fort Tejon in 1864. Owens Valley had quickly become covered with orchards and small farms, driving the cattle barons north. The Paiutes, when they returned, lived either on public lands (*campodees*) or on white homesteads (*rancherias*). Indians living on or near homesteads would be allowed to settle there in exchange for their labor, working for as little as 50 cents a day. (In the San Joaquin Valley, Indians were hired for $1 a day.[33]) Alternatively, Paiutes would squat on public lands. Dorothy Clora Cragen writes, "Their lands were gone, and they had no way of making a living except to work for the Whites, and the Whites often cheated them, underpaid them, and sometimes did not pay them at all except perhaps with old clothes, food of no value, and other articles that the White people did not care to keep."[34] Prejudice against the Paiutes remained strong, though there grew to be an increasing interdependency between Paiutes and whites. Still, marriage between Paiutes and whites was considered scandalous; Anglo-Mexican marriages were more common. If a white man married a Paiute woman, he would be cast off from white society. Instead, white men commonly raped Paiute women or kept them as mistresses. Dorothy Clora Cragen described: "It was common practice when riding over the country to lasso an Indian woman, particularly a young one, kill any Indian man who attempted to protect her, and take her by force."[35] This violence against Paiute women reflected a general ambivalence toward the Paiute laborers. Though Indians were in high demand as farm laborers, they were also considered a "problem" throughout this time, due to their homelessness and poverty. Paiutes were used as cheap labor and despised for their living conditions, which came to be seen as an inherent indictment of their race.

Some Paiutes hid out in the hills, refusing to settle on white homesteads and working only intermittently while supporting themselves as much as possible with a subsistence lifestyle. "Joaquin Jim" was the most notorious of these Paiutes, known for the guerilla-style raids he led on the settlers. By 1866, the raids had become so successful that a petition for Joaquin Jim's removal from Owens Valley circulated. It read: "It is a well-known fact that Joaquin Jim is now and ever has been an enemy of the whites . . . that the many murders and outrages committed in this valley since the withdrawal of Government troops from this locality is traceable to the implacable animosity of this captain or chief to our people."[36] Joaquin Jim's near-mythological status as "bandit Indian" led to several false rumors of his death, spread by men who hoped to gain notoriety by killing him. In 1866, a scalp that was purported to belong to Joaquin Jim was exhibited on Main Street in Los Angeles with the following advertisement: "Scalp of the famous chief, Joaquin Jim, can be seen at Dick Wilson's new saloon on Main Street. The sunning of his moccasins has been of benefit to the Owens River travelers."[37] The scalp, it was later discovered, was not Joaquin Jim's. In reality, Joaquin Jim would continue on as a hero of the Indian resistance in the Owens Valley. To the Paiutes, he symbolized great cunning and strength; to the settlers, he represented lawlessness. Indeed, lawlessness among the agricultural laborers had been the greatest fear since the "Negro insurrection" of 1865. The settlers depended upon Paiute labor, but resented their presence as the unsettled, uncontainable "other."

In 1873, another plan for Indian removal was recommended by the federal government, which announced a plan to move all Indians from the southern Sierras to the Tule River Indian reservation in the southern San Joaquin Valley. This time the people of Owens Valley were strongly opposed to the removal. On May 3, 1873, the *Inyo Independent* reported, "No catastrophe could befall our general farming interest that could equal the removal of our Indians to a reservation." The *Inyo* defended the Paiutes' work, claiming, "Their labor is of essential importance in public economy and supplies a want in that direction that no other can do as well. . . . The value of, and demand for their labor, both field and household, insures them good treatment at the hands of the whites, and a support free of cost to the government."[38] This campaign against the reservation plan continued in local papers for months until the plan was ultimately dropped. The policy in dealing with the Paiutes would then shift from removal to assimilation.

U.S. Indian policy at the turn of the century stated that Indians could claim U.S. citizenship as long as they renounced tribal practices and affiliations. In Owens Valley, census bureaus began to ask in their surveys if Indians saw themselves as "Fixed or Moveable?" The question was meant to ascertain whether the Indians were living in permanent houses or in traditional tule reed "winter" houses, which would be abandoned for summerhouses in the Sierras (see figure 3.1). If the Paiutes were considerecd "moveable," meaning they still moved from house to house, they could not apply for U.S. citizenship; the question was designed to ascertain the success of assimilation policies. The correct answer, in terms of advantages to the Paiutes, would be "fixed," whether or not Paiutes at the time felt they

3.1. Paiute Tule House. Courtesy County of Inyo, Eastern California Museum. Reproduced with permission.

were fixed in Owens Valley; ironically, Paiutes had been constantly treated as "moveable" since the settlers first entered Owens Valley. But at this point in time, Paiutes were asked to assume a fixity as a solution to the problem of "homelessness" in Owens Valley. The largest population, however, was still "scattered all over the valley and lived or squatted along streams, old ranches, close to the towns, or at isolated points."[39]

In 1912, President Taft attempted to remedy this problem by setting aside 67,120 acres of Owens Valley, ten miles north of Bishop, for "allotment purposes to homeless Paiute or other Indians living on or adjacent thereto."[40] This land, commonly called the "volcanic tableland," contained the largest petroglyph collection in Owens Valley. The idea behind this allotment was for Paiutes to start their own small farms and so better subsist in Owens Valley. However, the Department of Water and Power was purchasing water rights at the same time that President Taft set aside land for the Indians. In 1917, the Superintendent of Bishop, Dale H. Reed, wrote to the Commissioner of Indian Affairs, "I have to say that we are endeavoring through every means to induce the Indians to plant every available foot of land belonging to them . . . but the Indians have but little or no water for irrigating purposes."[41] In fact, some have suggested that, like President Roosevelt's establishment of a National Forest in Owens Valley, the withdrawal of lands for "Indian settlement" was really a cover to prevent settlement in Owens Valley. Whatever the case, this land would eventually be transferred into the hands of the Department of Water and Power by the federal government, and lost to the Paiutes.

When the Department of Water and Power began purchasing lands in the Owens Valley, they assumed that the Paiutes would move out when the white settlers were forced to leave. Most Paiutes depended upon white landowners for their employment, and those who did not were still not able to acquire water for their own irrigation projects. The Paiutes, however, proved to be more "fixed" than the Department of Water and Power had hoped. Those who owned land and who had become U.S. citizens were generally offered less than half of what white settlers received for their property; many refused to sell. Others remained on the land set aside by President Taft, even with water supplies dwindling as Los Angeles purchased water rights to the surrounding creeks. The Paiutes' worsening living conditions, combined with the Department of Water and Power's increasing encroachment into the Owens Valley, again prompted the search for a solution to the "Indian problem." In 1930, the Department of Water and Power wrote a "field report" with recommendations for dealing with the Paiutes. This report stated, "Because of the past continual abandonment of so many of the Owens Valley ranches, the market for the Indian's labor has gradually decreased until at the present time, it is almost exhausted, with the result that the major and usual means of self-support for the Indians is not available."[42]

The 1930 Department of Water and Power report proposed a land exchange with the Paiutes, claiming, "The proposed plan for the exchange of lands would assist materially in handling the Indian situation in Owens Valley. At the same time, it would increase the Department's land holdings by approximately 70,917 tax-exempt acres, and its water rights."[43] This figure included the 67,120 acres of reserved land, as well as 3,126 acres of scattered homesites then in use by Paiutes. The Department of Water and Power worded this proposed exchange in terms of humanitarian aid to the Indians; but there were land and water rights at stake that the City wanted. The report stated, "In very few instances are the Indians living under what could be termed favorable conditions. Nearly all of them use immense quantities of water from the streams for irrigation. None have the advantage of good sanitary sewerage disposal. Some are living in dugouts or crudely constructed shacks that are detrimental to their health and a disgrace to American Ideals."[44] This "philanthropic" attempt by the Department of Water and Power to bring Paiutes up to "American Ideals" by giving them houses and a sewage system could be read as a front for what was really desired: "immense quantities of water." The Department of Water and Power wanted "homeless" Indians who might use and degrade the water quality to disappear from Owens Valley.

In 1932, the City of Los Angeles followed up on this report with three recommendations for dealing with the Indian "situation" in Owens Valley: "(1) Indians be moved from the Owens Valley to new locations. If investigation shows this plan to be impractical, it is then suggested that (2) the same idea of improved homesites be carried out within the Owens Valley." The third option, a combination of the two, was to move all Indians who would "voluntarily" go. The report explained the rationale for this plan: "It is believed . . . that over a period of years the success made by the Indians moving to the new locations would gradually induce the ones remaining in the Valley to migrate, eventually solving this problem by complete removal of all Indians from Owens Valley."[45] Paiute opposition to this suggested move was strong, as many of the elders remembered the last forcible move and were suspicious of this one. Still the Department of Water and Power persisted, recommending coercive tactics in its final report, which read, "It would appear only logical for the Government, and others, to adopt some workable plan for removal of the Indians to a new location and compel them to accept the Government's edict under a plan of toleration, sympathy, and cooperation."[46] The wording of this statement contains an obvious contradiction; the Indians would be "compelled to accept" an "edict" of "cooperation."

But in 1933, President Roosevelt partially solved the problem by withdrawing the 67,000 acres from Indian status, setting the land aside instead as reserved federal land for the City of Los Angeles. The land, he claimed, would be reserved "in aid of legislation for the protection of the water supply of the city of Los Angeles." Paiute elder Allen Spoonhunter commented, "In the early 1900s there was a great deal of collusion between the Department of the Interior and the DWP. . . . The DWP was influential in having that 67,000 acres withdrawn." After this important reversal of President Taft's decision, only 3,000 acres of Indian lands remained. The Department of Water and Power still promoted the confiscation of these lands, hoping to move all Indians from Owens Valley. The issue was only resolved in 1937, when Congress determined that the relocation of all Owens Valley Indians would not be possible. Congress concluded, "The question of removal of the Indians from the valley to some other point has been given careful consideration, but due to their strenuous objections and the difficulty in locating lands that will meet their needs in localities offering opportunities for employment and other advantages, that plan has been abandoned."[47] The Department of Water and Power, in turn, prepared a report for dealing with the continued presence of the Paiutes in Owens Valley. It read, "Since . . . many or all of them will no doubt be a permanent fixture or problem in the Owens Valley for many years to come, this report has been prepared with the view that the Indian problem be now attacked in a serious manner."[48] In 1937, the Department of Water and Power undertook to exchange 3,126 acres of Paiute land with water rights for 1,511 acres of Department of Water and Power land without water rights. The City listed the advantages to the people of Los Angeles:

1. Increase the City's water supply . . .
2. Secure title to a large plot of Government land in Owens Valley which will be tax exempt.
3. Relieved of the future burden of paying taxes on 1511.48 acres of land in Owens Valley.
4. Have the now badly scattered Owens Valley Indians moved on to four (4) compact and segregated areas where the utilization of water will be handled under an efficient system and waste of water reduced to a minimum.
5. Protection of the City's water supply from contamination by concentration of the present scattered Indians into compact and efficiently operated modern home units.
6. Moving the present badly scattered Indians to compact and regulated units near the towns where moral, school, health, labor, market, etc. conditions can be better met when compared to present conditions.[49]

Note the emphasis in these "advantages" to Los Angeles on words such as *compact, regulated, concentration,* and *segregated;* this regulated environment is the proposed solution to the "badly scattered" state of the Paiutes. The solution is control, concentration, and confinement. By locating the Paiutes on regulated and segregated plots of land, the City reduces the threat of subversion. Note that the word *compact* is used three times, suggesting that the natives can be controlled precisely by being "compacted" onto small plots of land. The houses are described as "units" of control: "efficiently operated modern home units" or "regulated units" or "segregated areas where the utilization of water will be handled under an efficient system and waste of water reduced to a minimum." In *The Order of Things,* Michel Foucault described organizing space as the main method of modernist control: "One must eliminate the effects of imprecise distributions, the uncontrolled disappearance of individuals, their diffuse circulation."[50] In the case of the Paiutes of Owens Valley, a long history of other agencies controlling their "diffuse circulation" had been in effect already.

This proposal ultimately gained more water for the City of Los Angeles by taking it from the Owens Valley Paiutes. The Department of Water and Power objected to the "immense" quantities of water being used by Paiutes in the Sunland irrigation tract outside of Bishop; this tract was a traditional irrigation plot that diverted water on a seasonal basis before allowing it to flow back to the Owens River. The Paiute tribes were moved to four small reservations, some of the best agricultural land in the valley, but without water. P. J. Wilke states: "Seasonal hunting and gathering were impossible given the limited number of ecological zones which could be exploited on most of the small reservations. The government would have liked to make farmers of all the Indians, but the reservations were often unsuited even for that. The reservations were, in fact, concentration camps."[51] Paiutes had long held a complex and paradoxical relationship with white settlers in their practice of agriculture. Initially, their practice of agriculture was denied—primarily because it was not recognizable as such by Anglo-American standards. Indians were considered "savage," pre-agricultural communities in need of civilization and development. Summing up a common attitude toward the Paiutes, Roy Harvey Pearce wrote, "All explanations of the essential weakness of savage society had as a basic tenet the assumption that Indians were not farmers, and all plans for civilizing Indians assumed they needed to be farmers."[52] Although Euro-Americans may have assumed that Paiutes needed to farm, they also dismissed the fact that Paiutes already were farming. The reason for this dismissal may have been the desire to keep the Paiutes in a "savage" state and thus explain and excuse their "extinction." Captain Davidson wrote, "They were once a numerous tribe, but they are now exemplifying the fact that the Indian race is giving way before a higher and better power than ever ran wild in woods."[53] "Running wild in the woods" was equated with the inevitability of disappearance in the face of settlement and civilization. Theodore Roosevelt, who granted Owens River water to Los Angeles, made the same argument about the Indians: "The Indians should be treated in just the same way that we treat the white settlers. Give each his little claim; if, as would generally happen, he declined this, why, then let him share the fate of the thousands of white hunters and trappers who have lived on the game that the settlement of the country has exterminated, and let him, like these whites, who will not work, perish from the face of the earth which he cumbers."[54]

By the time Paiutes were actively encouraged to farm by the U.S. Government, the Department of Water and Power had acquired nearly all the water rights in Owens Valley. Instead, the Paiutes were offered "compact" houses, sometimes only one room on a "homesite" where property was divided into 2-½-acre plots. Ed Connerly of the Toiyabe Indian Health Project noted, "Close housing situations are as alien to the Indian cultural lifestyle as the governmental enforcement of reservation boundaries and the private ownership of land."[55] While 2-½–acre plots may not seem small now, white homesteaders at this time were given 160 acres, which was considered the minimum for a working farm. In the desert lands of the West, even 160 acres was considered far too small and the allotment went up to 640 acres. Meanwhile, the 2-½–acre plots were later scaled down in many instances to one acre. The DWP plan was presented to the Paiutes, offering them:

1. A one, five or ten-acre tract of good, fertile land with a first class water right
2. A suitable new and modern house, etc. for each family unit
3. An efficient and modern domestic irrigation water supply system . . . and efficient and modern sewage disposal system.[56]

In reality, however, water rights would be taken away from Indians in exchange for the right to purchase water from the DWP. The plan had to receive a majority vote from the Paiutes before it could pass. An election was supposedly held in Owens Valley, and Congress later maintained that the Indians "appear to have voted," but the ballots do not exist in the Department of Water and Power archives or anywhere else.[57] Also, the Fort Independence Indians, who violently opposed the land exchange, were not allowed to vote "because of the specific terms of the Executive Order relating to that group."[58] The military post at Fort Independence had already been transformed into the only reservation in the valley before the land exchange, giving the Paiutes there a unique status.[59] However, the Executive Order pertaining to the Fort Independence Indians merely stated that their lands were "permanently withdrawn from settlement." It did not reflect their ability to vote on the transfer of Paiute lands. Nancy Walter commented, "The issue is whether or not the presentation was given in such a way that the Indian was not aware of the disadvantage or full implications of the land exchange, only the advantages—a new house, a domestic water supply, out buildings, land for a garden or pasture, or living closer to town."[60]

The Paiutes who remember the "vote" present conflicting versions of its significance. Walter commented, "Those who lived in the Bishop area tend not to remember a general vote taking place. Instead they remember a petition for signatures or a small group of leaders making the decisions. . . . There are very definite statements when the vote at Fort Independence is brought up for they all remember that the Fort did not want to exchange lands."[61] What the petition may have said is not now known, as it has also been lost from the archives. What many Paiutes remember today is that they did not want to move to the new lands and were not aware that they were giving up rights to their old properties.

The Land Exchange Act reached Congress on March 3, 1937. A "number of" Paiutes from the Owens Valley traveled to Washington, D.C., in order to comment on the process. They were never heard, and Representative Burdick attempted to derail the whole process because of the refusal of Congress to hear the Indians. Burdick brought the Paiutes to the attention of the Speaker of the House, commenting, "I want to inform the gentleman that there are a number of Indians here from California who desire to be heard on the bill." The Speaker, Mr. Rogers, responded, "In that connection I would say they have never communicated that information to me, and I did not know of it until a few minutes ago. . . . It is too late now, of course." Burdick again tried to stop the measure from going through, stating: "It occurs to me that the Indians themselves have no voice in this matter. We are conferring authority upon the Secretary of the Interior to transfer this tract of land if in his judgment he thinks it is for the benefit of the Indians. I am convinced, Mr. Speaker, that there are Indians here now who desire to be heard on this bill, and as long as they are here I am going to use what influence I have to prevent the passage of the measure." And again the Speaker responded, "The Indians should have been heard, but they did not make their wishes known. We did not even know that they were here." Three times Burdick brought up the issue of hearing the Indian's perspective on the matter, and three times he met the same response.[62]

The bill was introduced in the House of Representatives on March 3 and pushed through for passage by March 10. Burdick commented, "It seems to me, Mr. Speaker, that we are going mighty fast to bring up for passage on the tenth of March a bill introduced on the third of March. This is the speediest action I have seen on legislation in this House." The House wanted the bill to go through without ever hearing the Indians. The fact that a vote was never mentioned and that the Indians had "never been heard on the matter" was never contradicted. Burdick stood by his statement: "I am not in favor of Indian legislation that is favored by a city without taking the Indians into consideration. As long as they are here and desire to be heard on the bill, I think we are making a mistake to pass it without hearing them."[63] Burdick also claimed that he had not been given enough information to make a decision about the bill. He stated, "I am not entirely satisfied that this bill should be passed, nor have I sufficient information to make up my mind that it should not be. One fact, however, that stands out plainly is that we are transferring 3,840 acres of Indian lands and receiving back for the Indians 1,470 acres."[64] Nonetheless, the bill passed.

Owens Valley Paiutes found themselves living in a Department of Water and Power planned community without their consent and without water rights. The DWP acquired 10,733 acre-feet of water on Indian lands in Owens Valley. In return, the Indians were to receive 6,064 acre-feet per year of water, purchased by the United States Indian Service, from the City of Los Angeles. The Paiutes lost their communal irrigation plots and were subjected to the planned housing project of the Department of Water and Power, paid for by the federal government. On February 3, 1939, President Roosevelt authorized a relief bill in the amount of $305,000 for the Inyo County Indian projects. The Paiutes were allotted 2-1/2 acres per person if they registered for it.[65] Those Indians who did not sign up for land allotments ended up losing their land, thus reducing the overall size of the reservations. But one Paiute commented on the community's fear of the forced move: "They didn't want to get in and have their government or town or the county corral them in and can't get out. Walled in like prisoners. . . . That's the way they have been treated all these years."[66] Those Paiutes who were more educated or who spoke better English tried to explain the necessity of Indians getting on the list for land. Viola Martinez explained that because her uncle spoke English well, he made sure her family's names were written down. Others resisted the whole allotment process, as Martinez commented: "Tom Gustie was very eager to have Indians from Bishop be aware that they had the opportunity to request land to live on there. . . . Many of them just didn't understand that it was necessary for them to make a request. They just assumed it was their land. Why did they have to ask permission to come back to something that was already theirs?"[67] Those who had been sent away to boarding schools also often lost their land allotments.

Viola Martinez, who was sent to the Sherman Boarding Institute in the Los Angeles area, ultimately came back to claim her allotment. But her sister Winona did not want to return for her allotment, claiming that she had been taken off the reservation as a young child and felt that "no one had ever cared about her" in Bishop.[68] Those who had been sent to boarding schools often chose to assimilate into Los Angeles culture, despite their hardships there. (One Indian described her heartbreaking experience at the Sherman Institute: "Land of oranges, land of perfume. Time of torture."[69]) By the time she returned to Bishop, Viola's language was lost. Paiutes returning to Owens Valley were often forced to live in cramped and uncomfortable quarters among people who no longer spoke the same language.

The Department of Water and Power influenced the design and development of reservation allotments, even demanding that the federal government give the DWP complete control of the Paiute lands. The Department of Water and Power report demanded "that as soon as possible, the Federal Government agree to withdraw from the Owens Basin and that it cooperate, in the future, by rendering financial assistance to the Department of Water and Power, which Department will execute the proposed program outlined herein."[70] The Department of Water and Power wanted sole control over the Owens Valley Paiutes without further interference from the federal government. It should have been the responsibility of the federal government to do the fieldwork and research and come up with the land exchange proposal, as well as implement it. The fact that it was not demonstrates the amount of power that the Department of Water and Power held over every aspect of development in Owens Valley. In 1940, museum curator Frank Parcher was named project manager of the DWP's Owens Valley Rehabilitation Project, with the task of "get[ting] the Indians to keep their places respectable and orderly in appearance."[71] The DWP took on an almost parental role in its relations with the Paiutes.

Paiutes today do not like to talk about the land exchange. Nancy Walter commented, "Among both the Indian and the non-Indian there has been a reluctance on the part of some people to discuss anything concerning water and/or the Department of Water and Power. . . . In a few cases these people felt anything they had to say would cause them trouble or grief." Those who moved to the new "reservations" often did so under compulsion and later regretted the move. Walter explained, "There are people living on the reservation today, who did not want to move to the new reservation and who had said they never would. To remember that time is, for them, troubling. . . . The memories . . . are painful."[72] In the 1950s and early 1960s, a national movement to close Indian reservations affected the security of those who had moved to the reservations. In 1953, Congress passed the Termination Act, which encouraged Indians to accept a per capita settlement for their reservation lands. The Northern Paiute group, which included Owens Valley Paiutes, was asked to draw up termination plans but refused to do so. Many Paiutes had refused even to move to the reservation lands and still squat on Department of Water and Power lands. Since the 1930s, several who called themselves the "Free and Independent American Indians" have squatted on land owned by the Department of Water and Power. One Owens Valley resident discussed their presence: "They were squatters, but nobody paid too much attention to them. Most of the Indians were fairly well employed by the cattlemen and sheepmen around the country."[73]

But on November 7, 1985, the Department of Water and Power demolished the home of Mary Turner, a member of the Bishop Paiute tribe who had refused to move from Department of Water and Power lands to a HUD house on the new reservation. Mary Turner had been visiting friends in Bishop and came back to a pile of rubble. The Department of Water and Power said that the structure on its land was "believed to be vacated" although there were some "clothes and furniture in it." A Department of Water and Power representative explained the department's perspective on the matter: "After the DWP and Federal government traded these parcels many of the Native American Indians refused to leave what once was their land. . . . We have waited for these people to vacate the houses and then we would go in and clean them up." Mary Turner noted sardonically, "They did a real thorough clean up. I only wish they would have given me a little notice first."[74]

The Department of Water and Power has a long history of bulldozing vacant properties in Owens Valley in order to conceal its involvement in the devastation of the valley. Robert A. Sauder wrote of the landscape in the 1930s: "Dying orchards, empty schoolhouses, and abandoned farmhouses and farm buildings became common landscape features. Los Angeles, the new landlord of Owens Valley, removed most traces of abandoned rural life as quickly as possible; houses and barns were bulldozed or burned and trees and orchards were either cut down or uprooted in order to hide from passing motorists the despoilation that it had wrought."[75] Similarly, the army bulldozed Manzanar to erase the history of internment camps. But in the case of the Paiutes, bulldozing has been used to force Indians off disputed lands and onto small reservations.

Scattered in small pockets throughout the Owens Valley, Paiute reservations are not even big enough to allow the Paiutes to bury their dead on that property.[76] Allen Spoonhunter of the Bishop Paiute tribe lamented that the tribe had just talked to the Department of Water and Power "about acquiring additional lands for a cemetery—just for burying our people." He shook his head and explained, "They said it's not possible. Not without a land trade." And the Paiutes have nothing left to trade. "They told us that they felt we got adequate land for present and future use in the land exchange," Spoonhunter said, "but we used to have over 1.5 million acres here, and then, through collusion, deception, and everything else, we're stuck with 1,500 acres."[77] Today, the Department of Water and Power is also involved in constant disputes over the acre-feet of water used every year by the Paiutes. The reservations, today, are both overcrowded and inadequately watered.

Signs of neglect and poverty abound on the reservations. The Lone Pine Paiute reservation sign is not welcoming; years of sun damage and a lack of paint have erased the name of the tribe. Behind it, Paiute children play on an old swing set in an overgrown playground outside the health clinic. The prospects for these children are not hopeful. The Department of Water and Power had not planned for growth in its land exchange or housing project, and so land assignments do not meet the needs of the Paiute children. If an elder dies on a reservation, the housing committee has to decide to which grandchild will inherit the land, as there is no longer room for all. Recently, a Paiute expressed fear over leaving the reservation for job training; he thought that in his absence his house might be given away.[78]

When Los Angeles city officials worked out the land exchange, they did not take into account that Indians might have children. Basing their studies upon a fixed population, however, was in direct contrast to the city's own growth-oriented attitude. The most plausible explanation, therefore, is that the Department of Water and Power maintained a discriminatory or xenophobic attitude toward non-white development. Nancy Walter writes, "The fact that the Indian population might increase and this in turn would increase the need for more water than allowed under the land exchange agreement was not taken into consideration by either the federal government or the city of Los Angeles."[79] Inexplicably ignoring—or willfully attempting to inhibit—the fact of population growth among Indians, the City also did not consider that the Paiutes might want to grow economically. Paiutes had suffered under the daily strain of poverty since their land base had first been lost, but the Department of Water and Power determined that this was their "natural" condition and so attempted to make it permanent. Mistaking poverty for "tradition," the City of Los Angeles allotted the Indians enough water for what it termed "subsistence" purposes, including domestic and agricultural use. The farms allotted, however, were not large enough for even subsistence agriculture, and because basic housing needs were not being met, farmlands were later divided to provide housing for relatives or other Paiutes.

Today, many Paiutes live in rental trailers on someone else's property or in identical concrete-block HUD houses with one or two bedrooms. These houses have high heating bills and maintenance costs and come with monthly housing payments, expenses that pose a severe financial burden on Paiutes who are either unemployed or underemployed. Instead of the idyllic agriculture community the Department of Water and Power had envisioned for the tribe, many jobs are in construction and mining off the reservation.[80] Paiutes often cannot afford the monthly payments for HUD housing, so they opt for cheaper trailer rentals. Indians returning to Owens

Valley from Los Angeles or elsewhere often missed out on allotments altogether and so camp out in trailers. Clyde and Winona Roach started the first trailer park at the Bishop Paiute Reservation. Winona's sister, Viola, recalled: "[Clyde] had friends that would come up [to Owens Valley] with trailers and would need places to stay and camp. He suggested [to Winona] that they have some kind of setup so they could have trailers. . . . The government was concerned about seeing that eligible Indians in that valley did have a piece of land [so] it was all according to law."[81] But in this fashion, many reservations have been subdivided into more and more crowded living conditions—those Paiutes who still own larger allotments of land are under pressure to subdivide for the sake of growth as well as the economic benefits of becoming a landlord.

Owens Valley reservations also have water quality problems, as well as inadequate sewage disposal facilities due to the lack of an adequate land base. The land exchange was initially implemented—and houses started being built—before the water rights had been negotiated. As a result, Paiutes went for over a year without a safe water supply. In 1939, a government employee discussed the problems created by not having the water system up and running: "At Lone Pine it was considered necessary to chlorinate the water as a precaution against a possible epidemic. You have probably heard that the Indians at Lone Pine are complaining constantly about the disagreeable taste of the water."[82] In 1986, Walter commented, "I have wondered if the system at Lone Pine has ever functioned properly for I have heard complaints about the taste and the color of the water for several years."[83] As well as having no place to bury their dead, the tribes have nowhere to put their sewage and no water with which to landscape. Spoonhunter explained, "We asked for water so we could do some landscaping, and they said no." The lack of greenery is obvious on Paiute lands, as in other parts of Owens Valley. Though the reservations are often close to the Owens River and so contain remnants of riverside vegetation, river water is not permitted to reach reservation lands. Instead, every drop is channeled off into the Los Angeles Aqueduct, and the reservation is supplied by underground wells. Riparian vegetation, as well as old lawns and attempts at agriculture, are now nothing more than dried-up brush in a drought-afflicted community. Paiutes work for the local businesses or the casino, as well as offering services for tourists . . . as indicated by an abandoned "Indian Taco" trailer (see figure 3.2). The fine print on the cardboard sign out-side says, "Welcome to Big Pine Indian Reservation."

If water could be said to bind a community together, a dearth of water would explain the lack of cohesion that is sometimes described among the Owens Valley Indians. Don Eargle wrote, "I had a strange sense of lack of overall community here, as if most families existed independently of each other."[84] Paiute identity is historically tied into the health of the Owens Valley, so it is no wonder that cultural values would begin to be lost along with the water. Also, the Department of Water and Power's control of the watershed has directly impacted traditional culture. For instance, the Department of Water and Power regularly cuts down willows and tule rushes along the creeks, both as a form of flood control and to protect their water supply. But willows and tules were of great significance to the Paiutes, who once made their homes—and still make baskets—from these materials. Paiutes no longer have access to the river that once sustained their tradition and culture. Indian attorney Dorothy Alther said, "It's a real problem here, the tribes are really landlocked. I think it's one of the primary reasons that so many of the tribes are having such a

3.2. Paiute "Indian Taco" Trailer. Photo by Karen Piper. Used with permission.

difficult time maintaining their identity and their culture. And it's really hard when you work with tribes that are unrecognized because they're so scattered . . . they have no land base to hold them together." Paiute children, having to move off the reservations and into cities, become separated from both their families and culture. This lack of cohesion and community among the Paiutes is one of the reasons historians have a hard time figuring out what happened as a result of the land exchange; many Paiutes acknowledge that even they had no idea what was going on. They had been moved before and after the land exchange and many were finally forced to move once more from Owens Valley.

Today the Paiute tribe is trying to negotiate with the Department of Water and Power for return of the water lost during the land exchange. Insisting that "they didn't trade water rights," one Paiute spokesman argued for the exchange's inherent unfairness. "It was a deal between the City and the Department of the Interior." In 1990, an Indian Water Commission was formed, with two representatives from each tribe to address the issue of water rights. Nancy Petersen Walter has argued that if irrigation ditches could be proven to predate European contact, then aboriginal water rights would apply.[85] In U.S. water law, whoever uses, or "appropriates," the water first gains rights to it in perpetuity. Currently the tribes only have "reserved" rights, which are rights reserved by the federal government for use on the reservation. If the tribes could win appropriative rights, demonstrating that they used the water first for irrigation, their struggles over water might be resolved. Paiute irrigation projects, however, were initially trampled by cattle, making identification difficult. Now they are threatened by the Department of Water and Power, which has proposed several hydropower plants for mountainside streams and creeks; these would flood indigenous agricultural projects, making dating impossible. Jerry Gewe of the Department of Water and Power is not optimistic about the possibility of Paiute water rights being reclaimed and suggests that he would oppose such a concession. "Basically they exchanged lands with us many years ago and they feel that they should have a much larger quantity of water, not that they could use it or want to use it," he said. "What they really want it for is money. What they want to do is get the water and then turn around and sell it to somebody else, either us or Ridgecrest or somebody else there. So it's really a dispute over money than over water. They aren't that much into agriculture, so they wouldn't want to use it anyway."[86] Gewe's comments reveal the complex attitude of settlers in relation to Paiute agriculture. Pauites had been placed in a Catch–22 situation in regard to agriculture since white people first arrived in Owens Valley. In *Key Words*, Raymond Williams points out that the word *culture* originally derives from *cultivate*.[87] Lacking cultivation, Paiutes were seen as lacking culture. Ironically, it was in the settlers' best interests to ignore the Paiute cultivation that existed. This provided a justification for killing Indians and supplied settlers with fresh fields where their cattle could graze. These cattle in turn trampled evidence of Paiute irrigation. Because it was not recognizable as a *European* form of cultivation, Paiute irrigation was not recognized at all. Seeing fields, Owens Valley settlers saw "grazing," "fields of corn," and "water." Similarly, the Department of Water and Power planned community was developed with agriculture in mind; the DWP then denied that Paiutes were an agricultural people. Mirroring claims in the 1800s that Indians would eventually "die out" and be replaced by a superior civilization, the Department of Water and Power was assuming that the Indians would not—or should not be allowed to—grow. According to Allen Spoonhunter, "There's no equity for us."

If the Paiutes do win their legal battle with the Department of Water and Power, they may ultimately donate the water to Owens Lake since they do not have enough land left for agriculture. Dorothy Alther claimed that the Paiutes have been concerned about the health impacts of the dry lake for some time, particularly those who live on Lone Pine reservation. When I asked Alther about local health problems, she responded, "Sandra Jefferson [Yonge] down at Lone Pine—she's got her inhaler with her. She said there's so many people on the rez that have inhalers that if you lose or misplace yours it's no problem because someone next to you has got one." A recent study by the Toyabie Indian Health Project in Lone Pine found that upper respiratory problems and infections among local Native Americans top the list of health problems in the past five years.[88]

But according to Spoonhunter, the Paiute tribes have not been that involved in the dust issue: "There's never been a real political effort to address that issue . . . primarily because the tribes never had the technical people or financial resources." At the office for legal counsel for the Paiute tribes, Dorothy Alther welcomed me into the small, one-room affair, without any sort of greenery surrounding the building. From the outside, it looked like an abandoned, historic building from the Old West, with a fake wooden facade. The office next door was for lease and the rest of the staff was off on an extended lunch when I arrived. Inside, Dorothy Alther addressed the problem of the dry lake, "I was real concerned about the dry lake because I saw it as a huge environmental problem that the tribes weren't really involved in . . . primarily because there was nothing to be involved in. I mean, they [Great Basin APCD] were just studying, studying, studying it." Scientific studies, it seemed, had been a sore point for the Paiutes for some time. When Paiutes did attempt to do their own "research," it was often dismissed as unscientific. For instance, Alther explained that the Toyaibe Indian Health Project was not recognized as "official" because the data collection was "non-scientific." Therefore, it could not be used to support the argument that there was a health problem among Indians in the Owens Valley, even though this was common knowledge on the reservation. The "scientists," unfortunately, had ignored the Indian health problem—yet when the Indians took the research into their own hands, they were ignored. Dorothy Alther complained that when the issue was put on *60 Minutes* and on the evening news with Tom Brokaw, the Paiutes were virtually ignored. She said, "None of them ever contacted us about the tribes' perspective, or whether the tribes were involved." Part of the problem may have been that the tribes weren't involved, initially. "Here's one of the biggest environmental problems in the country sitting right in the backdoor of one of my tribes, and we're not even a player. We're not even in the process," she said.

The tule marshes where the Paiutes once hid slowly disappeared when the water was drained from Owens Lake. But today these tules are returning to the Lower Owens River, thanks to a restoration project that the Department of Water and Power has been forced to implement. Ironically, the tules may not be allowed to remain in the river, since they interrupt the flow of the river. The Department of Water and Power, while required to rewater nearly sixty miles of the Lower Owens River, is constructing a pump to redivert that water back to the aqueduct before it reaches Owens Lake. Tule marshes, in limiting the flow of water, also keep it from returning quickly to the Los Angeles Aqueduct. In the Technical Memorandum on the Lower Owens River, the Department of

Water and Power suggested, "Channel dominance by tules, as well as the influence of beaver dams . . . influences stream flow and creates backwater effects. Excessive tule biomass can be a disadvantage in the development of a flowing and functioning river." For this reason, the Department of Water and Power devised a plan for the "control and management of excessive growth."[89] The tules may be controlled through herbicides, fire, or mechanical dredging. Already, the Department of Water and Power has sprayed seventy-five gallons of aquatic plant killer on the tules at Buckley Ponds.[90] Interestingly, only the Paiutes seem to object. Susan Hill explained that "tules seem to be regarded by most of the mainstream local stakeholders [in the Lower Owens River Project] as an intrusive and nuisance weed . . . that needs mechanical removal, but I learned that the Paiutes value the tules in many ways."[91] Basketweaver Charlotte Bococh complained, "Now the Department of Water and Power from Los Angeles seems to own most of the valley here. They keep track of the water levels, and they have roads right alongside the creek. And every year when the willows are just about ready to pick, they come and cut everything down. In some areas, they spray. The areas we used to always go to get willows are all cut down, and we really can't get anything there now."[92] The Indian Water Commission head described the impact of the Department of Water and Power on the life of the tribes: "To the tribes, water is life. Without it, they see only death here."

The Paiute and Shoshone Indians had survived comfortably in Owens Valley for at least ten thousand years before white contact, and the lake is considered by geologists to be 78 million years old.[93] Therefore, it is only in very recent history that the lake dried up and the Paiute homeland was destroyed. The word *Paiute* means "water people," I was told by the Paiute elder Michael Rogers outside a public hearing of the Great Basin APCD. In answer to my question about how long he'd been in the valley, he gave me his mother's name and his mother's mother's name. Somehow I had expected an answer in years rather than generations. He told me that the early settlers in Owens Valley once considered the Paiutes experts in locating water. He remembered Manzanar, the World War II Japanese internment camp, as a place where reduced visibility due to the dust led to the deaths of dozens of people in car crashes. "The cars just piled on top of each other there," he said. He remembered the birds that used to travel through the valley, mainly from stories his parents told him. His father had told him that the ducks were once "so thick you couldn't even see." When I asked about how the Owens Valley had changed, he said, "Now there's only the raven," he said, "because they eat whatever is dying. Now there's only the raven and nothing else."

FOUR

"WE ATE THE DUST": MANZANAR

Richard Stewart, a Paiute Indian, is the sole tour guide at Manzanar, a camp where over ten thousand Japanese Americans were interned in Owens Valley during World War II. He sits every day in one of the only remaining buildings, the old stone entry gate, which is unheated and has no running water. Stewart says of these conditions, "I'm used to it. I live here." Behind him, Manzanar is full of blowing tumbleweed and beer cans and grazing cattle. Bulldozed after the war by the Army Corps of Engineers, Manzanar reveals little of its history through its few remaining stone foundations. The army left one standing building, the old auditorium, which today has been finally turned into a visitor center. For years, Stewart faithfully took visitors to the old orchards, rock gardens, orphanage, guard towers, and hospital—which were merely signs on the dirt road or old concrete slabs or holes in the ground. The once-thriving orchards of Manzanar are hard to imagine today, as the camp itself is barely visible to visitors (see figure 4.1). Manzanar is primarily a wide patch of open dirt with little or no vegetation. Internees who revisit the camp often express doubts about their own memories of the place. Jeanne Wakatsuki Houston wrote of her fear of returning to Manzanar as an adult: "I half-suspected that the place did not exist. So few people I met in those years had even heard of it, sometimes I

4.1 One of the three remaining Structures at Manzanar. Photo by Karen Piper. Used with permission.

imagined I had made the whole thing up, dreamed it."[1] When she finally visited Manzanar, she claimed, her doubts were confirmed. "There was only tumbleweed and sagebrush," she said.

The reason that Manzanar is now open desert is that the Department of Water and Power made a deal with the U.S. Government that required that the land be returned to its original condition after the war ended. The government's lease of the land from the Department of Water and Power expired on June 30, 1946. The lease provided that the site be cleared and restored by September 30. Specifically, the lease required: (1) the complete dismantling of all structures, (2) the salvage and removal of all usable material, (3) a complete inventory of all recovered materials, and (4) the removal of all unusable material. In addition, the restoration of the land included the removal of "concrete slabs, foundation, curbs, piers, or structures that extended above normal ground surface." These materials were to be broken up and buried under "not less than 30 inches of earth cover leaving surface so as to conform with surrounding terrain" or hauled to the dump. Cellar excavations and other "unnatural depressions" were filled in. Fences were restored to their original condition. Scrap lumber was burned and the ashes were buried with "not less than one foot of earth cover leaving surface level with surrounding terrain."[2] The only things that could remain were ditches and irrigation structures in the agricultural areas, a few foundations, and the rock walls surrounding the roads. At the last minute, demolition of the auditorium was delayed and it was eventually sold to the Veterans of Foreign Wars of Inyo County, instead, for use as a clubhouse and meeting hall. Initially, it was sold with the condition that it be removed from the property—but later it was determined that the auditorium was too expensive to move. By the winter of 1946, Manzanar had practically disappeared. On December 2, 1946, the *Los Angeles Times* reported that except "for a few staff buildings left standing the war-born town of Manzanar which housed 10,000 Japanese internees today is flatter than Hiroshima."[3]

Manzanar once maintained the most modern infrastructure in Owens Valley. Today, all evidence of Manzanar is effectively erased, more so than at the nine other internment camps scattered across the Western United States. I grew up close to Manzanar and couldn't understand why busloads of Japanese Americans would travel each year to a dirt patch that looked no different to me than any other. The only difference seemed to be the gridlike dirt road, the white obelisk memorial that stood as a photogenic foreground to the Sierras, and a few dwarfed and gnarled fruit trees. There was nothing there, though sometimes I liked to run in circles around the roads and look for the bugs that were drawn to the rotten fruit. One of the reasons the property was neglected for so long was that the Department of Water and Power did not want it developed. When George Bush set aside the land at Manzanar in 1992 as a National Historic Site, the Department of Water and Power refused to give up its rights to the land, which was appraised at $530,000. Until 1997, the National Park Service could not even begin construction of the historical exhibit, due to resistance from the Department of Water and Power. District engineer Glenn Singley explained, "It was the rate payers of Los Angeles vs. the National Park Service. . . . This was about raising people's water bills."[4] Finally, the Department of Water and Power agreed to a land trade: 1,200 Bureau of Land Management acres for 800 acres at Manzanar. The National Park Service took possession of the land on April 26, 1997. But for almost fifty years, the history of the area had remained erased for the many pilgrims that came to visit their old home at Manzanar. The director of the Eastern California Museum, Bill Michael, was concerned about the time it was taking to start up the National Historic Site. "We as a country should be ashamed for what we did in World War Two at Manzanar," he said. "Now we should be ashamed again."[5]

Manzanar went through many transformations before becoming a Japanese American internment camp, though most people now equate the name with World War II. The fruit trees, for instance, are much older than the camp. In fact, the complex history of Manzanar in relation to the Department of Water and Power in many ways explains the DWP's recent reaction to turning the land over to the National Park Service. Manzanar was an orchard town long before—and even during—World War II. In 1905, the town of Manzanar was started as an irrigation colony, when George Chaffey purchased the two-thousand-acre Shepherd's Ranch in Owens Valley and named it Manzanar after the Spanish word *manzana*, meaning "apple." George Chaffey had earlier wanted to create an "American Nile Valley" called Imperial Valley in Southern California. After the British claimed to have "harnessed" the Nile in Egypt through the construction of the Aswan Dam (1899–1902), Americans seemed to want to prove that they could similarly conquer the desert. Lippincott wrote, "We have in the Colorado [River] an American Nile awaiting regulation, and it should be treated in as intelligent and vigorous manner as the British government has treated its great Egyptian prototype."[6] Chaffey's Imperial Valley settlement compared itself in advertising copy to the Egyptian Delta, with the Colorado River as its Nile. Imperial Valley would be the new Nile Valley with its wealth of irrigated corn and cotton.[7] Ultimately, however, Chaffey's project failed when the aqueduct channel broke in 1905. Water instead filled up a dry lakebed, creating the Salton Sea.

Chaffey started Manzanar after losing control over the irrigation project in the Imperial Valley and after failing—after eleven years—to start a successful irrigation colony in Australia. He became interested in Owens Valley while he was in Los Angeles setting up water delivery systems. Chaffey also gained the clout and cash he needed purchase Manzanar from his success in founding the irrigation town of Ontario, California. Chaffey subdivided Manzanar into small farms between ten and forty acres in size and began advertising the apple orchards to prospective homesteaders, selling Owens Valley as a lush agricultural region. More than five hundred acres were planted in apples, pears, grapes, peaches, and plums. But by 1912, with the aqueduct nearing completion, J. B. Lippincott hired the best legal counsel in Los Angeles to file for a right-of-way bill across lands owned by Chaffey. Embittered by another failed project, Chaffey left Manzanar.

Manzanar continued to thrive for a short time despite its precarious competition with the water supply of Los Angeles. By 1920, Manzanar had twenty-five homes, a store, community hall, fruit-packing plant, and twenty thousand fruit trees. Larry Van Horn called Manzanar at this time an "Anglo-Indian orchard community." He wrote: "I refer to the town as Anglo-Indian because of intermarriage. Paiutes and Shoshones married into the community. . . . The Indians I talked to, with family and other ties to Manzanar, are proud of their association with the orchard town and of Indian contributions to the irrigation on which the orchards depended."[9] The Paiutes had traditional ties to Manzanar, having established an irrigation community there long before the orchard companies moved in. In Paiute cosmology, Manzanar is close to the site where Owens Valley Paiutes originated. It is home. When the orchard colony was shut down by the Department of Water and Power, the Paiutes lamented the lost tradition and bounty of their irrigation community. Van Horn explains, "*How green was my valley!* is a sentiment expressed by several American Indian informants from their memories and from tribal oral tradition. It applied to Indian villages along streams in or near what is now the Manzanar site."[10] By 1929, the Los Angeles Department of Water and Power had purchased all the farms in Manzanar, and the community essentially died. In 1933, W. A. Chalfant wrote, "News comes that Manzanar, once a fruit growing and shipping point of importance, now owned by Los Angeles, is to be deprived of its water and lights. Its remaining orchards are doomed; its settlers must move."[11]

This briefly realized transformation of desert-to-irrigation-colony would occur, once again, when Manzanar became "Manzanar," the Japanese internment camp. On December 7, 1941, the Japanese bombed Pearl Harbor, and President Roosevelt signed Executive Order 9066, which called for all people in the United States of Japanese ancestry, most of whom were American citizens, to be placed in relocation camps. One hundred ten thousand people were imprisoned in ten internment camps throughout the country. In Southern California, the War Department requested that the Department of Water and Power donate the now-abandoned town of Manzanar for the first of these relocation centers. The Department of Water and Power refused, claiming that this would threaten their water supply. The City of Los Angeles was concerned not only about sanitation problems from runoff into the water supply but also about possible sabotage by the Japanese. Congressmen Thomas F. Ford of Los Angeles, who had consistently called for the evacuation and internment of persons of Japanese ancestry, worried about the site selection for Manzanar. He argued: "In my mind, I can see Tokio grinning with joy because of the opportunity this action will afford to sabotage the water supply of 1,500,000 people. . . . I most vigorously protest this action as in my judgment [an] inexcusable piece of stupidity. I sincerely hope that his military superiors in Washington will stop this move until a more thorough examination of the dangers inherent in the situation are investigated."[12] Nonetheless, Washington proceeded as planned to acquire Manzanar. The War Department threatened to confiscate the land, and the Department of Water and Power settled on a lease of $25,000 a year until six months after the war ended, with the condition that the property be returned to its original condition afterward.[13]

Manzanar held ten thousand people of Japanese descent for three and a half years between 1942 and 1945. Sixty-five hundred of the internees were American citizens. Eighty-eight percent of the internees originated from Los Angeles County.[14] By 1943, fifteen hundred acres had been cleared for farming by the internees, and the old town of Manzanar sprang back to life. Interestingly, the Paiute Indians again took part in the transformation of the land, helping to build, run, and eventually dismantle Manzanar. In fact, it has been claimed that 50 percent of the War Relocation Authority administrators came from the Bureau of Indian Affairs. Historian David Bertagnoli explained, "It was reasoned that, since they had been dealing with concentrated people on the reservation, they might have expertise in dealing with another concentrated minority group."[15] Viola Martinez, an Owens Valley Paiute who worked at Manzanar, described a certain camaraderie that developed between the Paiutes and the internees. Martinez said that one internee who asked her about Indians in the area explained her interest: "Well, in a way, the government has taken from you like they are doing to us."[16] Martinez agreed with the analogy, saying, "To a lesser degree and in a shorter period of time, what happened to them is what has been happening to the Native Americans."[17] Sometimes, however, this comparison worked against the Paiutes, such as when Manzanar employee and Paiute Tom Gustie was stopped by the guards because, he says, "They thought I was a Japanese trying to escape." He later joked, "I never should have told them. I could have lived there and not had to work. They brought the Japanese up here and fed them and everything. They never fed us."[18]

Employees and internees together worked to turn Manzanar into a self-sustaining desert community. The old ditch system was reconditioned, along with a preexisting dam on Shepherd Creek, and two new miles of canal were built for water siphoned off from the Los Angeles Aqueduct. The dam was raised eighteen inches and diverted water to the relocation center reservoir and settling basin. A few rows of pear and apple trees, which had been barely sustained by a shallow water table, were revived, yielding six hundred lug of apples and five thousand boxes of pears in the first year.[19] The excess was shipped off to other internment camps. Jeanne Wakatsuki Houston wrote, "People who lived in Owens Valley during the war still remember the flowers and lush greenery they could see from the highway as they drove past the main gate."[20] The farms provided the mess halls with lettuce, tomatoes, eggplant, string beans, horseradish, and cucumbers. In *Camp and Community: Manzanar and the Owens Valley,* numerous residents commented on the size of the vegetables and the success of the orchards. "My God, I never saw so many tomatoes in my life!" Robert Brown commented. "We had to ship them to Hunt's in Los Angeles."[21]

Besides the vegetable gardens and orchards, there were six elaborate parks at Manzanar. The hospital garden included "a large concrete-lined pond, a stream, dispersed boulders for seating, two winding concrete walkways, boulder stepping stones, wood-reinforced pathway steps, rock borders, and other landscape features." Pleasure Park, between Blocks 23 and 33, contained over one hundred species of flowers and included a rose garden, two small lakes, a waterfall, a bridge, a Japanese teahouse, a Dutch oven, and pine trees. Cherry Park, south of the Children's Village, contained a thousand cherry and wisteria trees. Another garden included a stream, rock alignments, and a buried pond. By the mess hall, there was a large concrete-lined pond, a stream with waterfalls, an island, a sidewalk, and rock alignments as well as a bridge.[22] The water came from the Department of Water and Power, diverted from the aqueduct. The buildings were constructed by employees of the Department of Water and Power, who worked alongside the Pauites. A. A. Brierly remembered that "the original plan was to take in the whole Owens Valley" as an internment camp. But H. A. Van Norman, the aqueduct chief, resisted, claiming, "If they put that land all back into cultivation, what is Los Angeles going to do for water?"[23] Instead, ten thousand people were confined to one square mile, just as the Paiutes had been earlier confined to compact sections of Owens Valley in order to preserve the water of Los Angeles.

The site of bountiful gardens and lush foliage appears to have had a significant impact on the residents of Owens Valley, who felt little control over whether the internment camp would be placed in Owens Valley. "There was a special sort of hostility in the Owens Valley that you didn't find in most of the other areas," Arthur Hansen commented.[24] This hostility, which was in part simple racism, appears to have been exacerbated by hostility toward the Department of Water and Power. Much of the criticism of Manzanar appears envious. Statements such as,

"They lived like kings" or "They had huge gardens" were common among those interviewed about their memories of Manzanar.[25] Ethelyne Joseph said, "They had a lot of freedom in their little realm of Manzanar. They had their basketball courts and their tennis courts and their swimming pools, so they really didn't live as though they were in an internment camp. . . . They didn't have it so bad."[26] Mary Gillespie said, "They were royally treated. . . . The Japanese had the best of everything. . . . There were all those beautiful trees down there."[27] Jack Hopkins concurred: "It was paradise out there. Really."[28] Those who worked at Manzanar, such as the guards, were known to pilfer from the camp. "It was just like any government project," Anna Kelley explained. "The Caucasians that worked there would come home with stuff."[29] This kind of *ressentiment* among the people of Owens Valley could be said to have been transferred from the Department of Water and Power to the Japanese. Owens Valley residents seemed to envy the Japanese for having stolen their water to "live like kings."

Interestingly, though many Owens Valley residents complained enviously about the idyllic conditions of the camp, most never went to Manzanar. Mary Gillespie, who repeatedly mentioned that the Japanese Americans were "royally treated" at Manzanar, later said, "I never went to the camp; I had no desire to."[30] Indeed, the hostility toward the Japanese was primarily directed against them when they entered the towns of Owens Valley. Jack Hopkins noted, "They would bring them in—maybe two busloads of Japanese—into town, and they'd scatter like quail up and down out main street buying this and buying that and buying something else."[31] Eventually, restrictions were placed upon the number of internees that could enter town at a time. A. A. Brierly described the xenophobia succinctly: "A Chinaman was content to be a Chinaman, and the Japanese wanted to be something more, and crowd in."[32] What can be inferred from this statement is that the "Chinamen" knew their *place;* the Japanese, in contrast, wanted equality, wanted to be white. There was also a prevalent fear of "the crowd" in rhetoric surrounding the Japanese Americans at Manzanar: "there were too many . . . they scattered like quail, they were always getting out." One man from Independence formed and trained his own militia to "save the women and children of Independence when the Japs broke loose!"[33]

But beneath this standard racist rhetoric is the discourse of envy. It was believed that the success of the Japanese Americans as farmers had displaced what should have been the success of the white farmers in Owens Valley. Mary Gillespie said, "They had all kinds of food and you know the Japs don't really live like that, they're used to fish and rice and their own food."[34] To the residents of Owens Valley, the revitalization of Manzanar signified only their own betrayal. The Japanese Americans of Manzanar realized what the locals had never been allowed to secure for themselves: a blooming desert. The hostility of the locals toward the Japanese was, in this sense, compounded. Manzanar came to represent, albeit in a microcosmic form, the lost history of Owens Valley. Residents of Owens Valley who felt victimized by Los Angeles often looked back to the days before diversion as almost an Edenic time. One Owens Valley resident remarked on the changes: "People who come to the Owens Valley don't have any idea what's happened to it. They come here and say, 'Gee, this a beautiful high desert valley.' But they weren't here when the trees were up and down the valley, and river was running and the brush was green."[35] Owens Valley residents watched the changes that occurred in their valley and felt helpless in the face of these changes. So to see this history resurrected for nonwhites stirred up both envy and racism in many people.

Interestingly, the idealized notion of a pastoral Eden in Owens Valley is mostly illusory. Owens Valley residents had just as little experience dealing with irrigation in an arid region as Los Angeles did. Because the land in Owens Valley was somewhat alkaline, it was paramount that farmers use proper drainage to avoid alkali buildups in the soil. They did not do this, however, and surface concentrations of alkali quickly ruined much of the good farmland. Also, water diverted for irrigation quickly lowered the lake levels. By 1895, the old Cartago wharf, which once stood in eight to ten feet of water, was two miles from the shore, and the lake had been reduced in size from 110 square miles to 75. In that year, concerns about the dropping lake levels led the *Register* to publish an article entitled, "Is Owens Lake Near Its End?"[36]

But the rose-colored glasses of old timers in Owens Valley led to bitter resentment against the Japanese. In 1943, Ansel Adams reinforced, through his photographs, the image of the "bountiful harvest" at Manzanar. Adams took portrait after portrait of smiling Japanese internees holding giant cabbages or standing in warehouses full of squash (see figure 4.2). Adams went to Manzanar to contribute to the war effort and demonstrate the "loyalty" of these Japanese American citizens. He explained, "The purpose of my work was to show how these people, suffering under a great injustice, and loss of property, businesses and professions, had overcome the sense of defeat and despair by building for themselves a vital community in an arid (but magnificent) environment."[37] He was forbidden to photograph the guard towers or barbed wire, and his images tended to depict the adaptability of the internees to a harsh desert environment. In his book, *Born Free and Equal,* Adams argued for the loyalty of the internees even under duress. Adams's images and text suggest that the internees took a certain pleasure in their internment, with all the contributing-to-the-war-effort rhetoric that was prevalent at the time. Adams was not opposed to relocation and called it simply "a detour on the road to American citizenship" for the Japanese.[38] As an apologist for the

4.2. Richard Kobayashi, Farmer with Cabbages by Ansel Adams, U.S. Library of Congress.

evacuation, Adams used his photos to demonstrate the success of the relocation program. He wanted to show Americans outside the camp that Manazanar internees were in fact industrious citizens who could make valuable contributions to any American community. Ironically, Adams's book was initially unpopular because it was seen as pro-Japanese. It created a picture of a productive, even utopian, relocation center that had been created—according to Adams—primarily by the internees.

In reality, conditions at Manzanar were far from ideal. Despite their elaborate gardens and farms, the internees complained of constant, severe dust storms. Cultural anthropologist Larry Van Horn wrote: "An everyday irritant to Japanese Americans interned at Manzanar was the constant wind that seemed to deposit dust and sand on everything. This was so despite the DWP making water available for crop irrigation. . . . Owens Lake dried up; its dust pollutes the air."[39] Indeed, the constant drive to build more gardens and bring more water in was in part an effort to fight the dust problem. One internee commented, "The main thing you remembered was the dust, always the dust."[40] In *And Justice for All*, Tom Watanabe remembers the dust storm as an almost nightly occurrence: "You had the dust storm come through. You get half an inch of dust. You either get in bed and cover yourself with a sheet or just stand out there and suffer. You couldn't even see three feet in front of you, and then by the time the dust was settled, you had at least a half inch of dust right on your sheet when you got under it. Used to come from underneath the floor."[41] The floorboards at Manzanar were built out of green wood, which shrank when it dried. Thus, residents would have their homes and beds constantly covered with dust. Helen Brill explained: "Every afternoon there was a terrible dust storm, and so then you had to hose out your barracks."[42] Kacy Lynn Guill, a ranger at Manzanar, said the internees used discarded tin can lids to try to seal out the wind. "They said they could tell where they had laid down at night because there would be an outline of their body in the dust when they woke up," she said.[43] Even after the floorboards were covered with tarp, the dust problem continued.

Probably the most prevalent theme in the internment memoirs that have been published—including the collected interviews in John Tateishi's *And Justice for All;* Monica Sone's autobiography, *Nisei Daughter;* and Rea Tahiri's film, *History and Memory*—is the inescapable presence of dust. In a famous photograph by Dorothea Lange, two people are shown ducking and running from the dust at Manzanar (see figure 4.3). In another photograph by Clem Albers, the fog-lake nature of Owens Lake dust is clearly seen as it immerses evacuees entering Manzanar (see figure 4.4). Many internees remember arriving at Manzanar during a dust storm and describe the place as "eerie." George Fukasawa recalls, "We got there right in the middle of one of those windstorms that were very common in Manzanar. The dust was blowing so hard you couldn't see more than fifteen feet ahead. Everybody that was out there had goggles on to protect their eyes from the dust, so they looked like a bunch of monsters from another world or something. It was a very eerie feeling to get into a place under conditions like that." Yoriyuki Kikuchi remembers, "Oh, everybody resented being put in such a place, especially when they were suffocated by sand!"[44]

Many internees, such as Joseph Yoshisuke Kurihara, described having to literally eat the dust: "Down in our hearts we cried and cursed this government

4.3. Dorothea Lange, "A Manzanar Dust Storm," July 3, 1942, Still Picture Branch of the National Archives and Records Administration.

4.4. Clem Albers, "Evacuees Arriving at Manzanar in California, 1942," Still Picture Branch of the National Archives and Records Administration.

every time when we were showered with sand. We slept in the dust; we breathed in the dust; and we ate the dust. Such abominable existence one could not forget, no matter how much we tried to be patient, understand the situation, and take it bravely."[45] Another internee described drinking the dust at Manzanar: "The most unpleasant thing about camp was the dust. We had a tin cup and a bowl with milk. A dust storm would blow sometimes for hours, and dust would seep into everything. I would see the dust forming on the milk and I'd try to scoop it away. It got to the point where I said 'Aah, just close your mind to it and say "Dust is good for you," and drink it.'"[46] This dust, which was clearly not "good" for anyone, was an unavoidable part of camp life and is often described as a part of the camp diet. According to Aly Colon in the *Seattle Times*, "It came through the floorboards, covered the blankets, even stuck to the bread. Sometimes it swirled so thick you couldn't see the barracks next door. You couldn't see the barbed wire that surrounded the camp. You couldn't see the towers filled with armed guards."[47] Jeanne Wakatsuki Houston described the dust as "a tide of sand pouring toward us," in which "the sky turned black as night."[48]

The "fine white dust" often described by internees is consistent with descriptions of dust from Owens Lake. Owens Lake dust is significantly different from regular dust due to its white color and fine consistency. It is often mistakenly referred to as a "mist" or "fog." Scientists have described this dust as a "pervasive, unusually fine-grained, alkaline dust that infiltrates the smallest cracks and contaminates residences."[49] Again and again, internees described their frustration at the effort to keep the dust out of their homes. Others tried to take a more lighthearted approach to having to live with the dust. In her memoir, Jeanne Wakatsuki Houston describes laughing at the sight of her clothes and her bed: "Now our cubicle looked as if a great laundry bag had exploded and then been sprayed with fine dust. A skin of sand covered the floor. I looked over Mama's shoulder at Kiyo. . . . His eyebrows were gray, and he was starting to giggle. He was looking at me, at my gray eyebrows and coated hair, and pretty soon we were both giggling. . . . Woody's voice just then come at us through the wall. He was rapping on the planks as if testing to see if they were hollow. 'Hey!' he yelled. 'You guys fall into the same flour barrel as us?'"[50] The sands at Manzanar became a part of the culture and understanding of the community itself. In the art of the internees, the dust came to represent the burial of the culture or the stripping away of identity. Paintings depict internees huddled together against the dust, or having clothes and umbrellas blown away by the dust.

Originally, the dust at Manzanar was not linked to Owens Lake. Instead, it was commonly believed by Manzanar residents and government officials alike that: (1) dust in the desert was normal, or (2) dust was caused by construction projects. At the time, Eleanor Roosevelt said, "The dust, caused by the massive disturbance of the soil from construction of hundreds of buildings at once, eventually settled, but the harshness of the climate stayed the same." But even though she claimed the dust had "settled," she nonetheless describes experiencing the dust during a high wind: "You are enveloped in dust. It chokes you and brings about irritations of the nose and throat and here in this climate where people go to recover from respiratory ailments, you will find quite a number of hospitals around the camps, both military and non-military, with patients suffering from the irritations that the swirling dust cannot fail to bring."[51] Basically, there were two types of dust at Manzanar: (1) loose sand from construction projects, and (2) fine-grained Owens Lake dust, which embeds heavy metals in the lungs. Though the first type of dust subsided with time, Owens Lake dust remained constant. Journalist Milton Silverman witnessed internees having to contend with both types of dust as the camp was being built. He wrote that "over, under, around and inside everything was the dust loosened by the tractors and scrapers, and blown by the interminable south wind. On mild days, the wind picked up only this dust, but [when] it really worked up to a blow, it carried . . . white soda dust scooped up from the deposits at Owens Lake more than twenty miles to the south."[52] Other local narratives speak specifically of dust storms occurring as early as the 1920s and early 1930s, although scientific studies of the dust did not begin until the 1970s. In 1934, Father John J. Crowley described Owens Lake dust storms: "Inyo's clerical callers learn rapidly that the customary black is no color for the desert traveler. When they find the dry bed of Owens Lake suspended, by a miracle of levitation, half-way up the slope of the Inyos in one of our south winds, thence settling on every man, woman, and beast in a fine dun coating, they long for the habit of St. Francis."[53]

Today, the Great Basin APCD has warned that areas north of Lone Pine, including Manzanar, are still "significantly impacted by Owens Lake dust."[54] The Great Basin APCD is particularly concerned about Manzanar because of "the health hazards posed to an estimated 250,000 to 350,000 visitors that are expected to annually visit the Manzanar National Historic Site, 15 miles north of Owens Lake."[55] Most of these visitors are older and particularly prone to respiratory illnesses. Dust levels in nearby Lone Pine have been shown to be over three times higher than the dust levels considered hazardous by the Clean Air Act. Today, the Manzanar National Historic Committee is seeking volunteers to do research on the deaths of over one hundred and thirty-five people at Manzanar in an attempt to confirm rumors of a disproportionate number of respiratory-related deaths. The total number of dust-related deaths may never be known, as the dust is known to be carcinogenic. Finally, there is the future impact on those relatives and survivors who continue to visit the camp. Unknowingly, these visitors may be receiving toxic doses of heavy metals during their stay.

Katharine Krater said that there was a "conspiracy of silence" around the subject of Manzanar in Owens Valley. "People just preferred not to talk about it," she said.[56] In *Voices Long Silent,* Arthur A. Hansen and Betty E. Mitson made the same claim about the Japanese Americans interned at Manzanar. The internees were reluctant to talk about their experiences there, though for different reasons; the memories were painful, or they felt embarrassed, or they wanted to put their lives as internees behind them. Many lived in disbelief that they could have been treated that way, or feared that it could happen again. Manzanar was closed in 1945. Today, you can see inscriptions in Japanese characters in the concrete of the empty reservoir and settling basin. Three inscriptions, which have been translated, read: "the army of the emperor occupied territory, 2/17/43, to Manzanar"; "banzai, the Great Japanese Empire, Manzanar Black Dragon Group headquarters"; and "beat Great Britain and the USA." During the majority of the war, these inscriptions were safely concealed by water from the Los Angeles Aqueduct. But after the war, Manzanar was bulldozed and the reservoirs drained; these hidden notes surfaced.

The buildings of Manzanar also still exist, but they have morphed into different histories and meanings. They can be found throughout the Owens Valley, Ridgecrest, and even Los Angeles. More than five hundred buildings were sold at the close of the war, many to returning veterans who were given a special price of $333.13 per barracks. Some barracks were sold whole and carted away to be turned into homes elsewhere and some were turned into scrap lumber and rebuilt. Architect Erwood P. Elden drew up four floor plans for houses that could be built entirely from materials salvaged from a barracks. The removal of the buildings, however, did not go uncontested. The project director of Manzanar, Ralph Merritt, wrote to the Department of Water and Power to request "a five-year lease on certain acreage and facilities within the present fenced area of the Manzanar Center."[57] Merritt claimed that he simply had grown attached to the place and after living there for twelve years did not want to leave.[58] But Merritt, who had previously been a rancher living near Big Pine, seemed to want land for more than personal property. Merritt, who had once been the successful owner of Sun Maid Raisins, had relatives in eastern California and was close friends with the descendant of John Shepherd, who had homesteaded the land at Manzanar since 1864. Merritt had also speculated in silver and mining ventures in Death Valley, so he was a well-established and wealthy member of the community by World War II. In his letter to the Department of Water and Power, he admitted that his motivations were not merely personal, claiming that Owens Valley was "in urgent need of housing facilities" for "schoolteachers in nearby towns" as well as "veterans and other residents." Merritt argued that "no housing now available should be destroyed or removed."[59] Instead, Merritt proposed allowing the leaseholder to operate twenty-six buildings, including apartments and single rooms, the administration building, the mess hall, and one warehouse. He also wanted "all present furnishings," along with water, sewage, and electrical lines. The water, he said, would be used for "lawns and dust control" and should be supplied without added charge. In addition, Merritt wanted twenty acres, to be "used for agriculture." Finally, he wanted the hospital buildings, children's village, or Blocks 29 and 34 together with water, sewage, and electrical lines. He claimed that he would use this property as "a tourist and recreational center." He wrote, "Because of the gardens now in this area and the adaptability of the buildings little new capital would be required for a tourist center of about 50 units."[60] It appeared, in fact, that he wanted to build a new agricultural community in Owens Valley, much like the old town of Manzanar.

Ignored by the Department of Water and Power, Merritt wrote again on May 9, though there were already negotiations between the FPHA and Inyo County Housing Commission for removal of the buildings. He reminded them of his request for a lease, arguing that his son, Peter, had worked at Yosemite National Park and could be employed at the new Manzanar tourist site, since he had "valuable experience in activities of that nature." He also desired to lease a small area in the vicinity of the hospital to establish "a semi-recreational and tourist facility, taking advantage of the approximately $5,000 worth of roses and other shrubs that the Japanese had left there."[61] Again, Merritt was ignored by the Department of Water and Power, and demolition of the area proceeded. Merritt, who had initially enticed the U.S. Government to place the internment camp at Manzanar before the war, did not appear to want to give up his re-created paradise. Interestingly, when Ansel Adams, who was a personal friend of Ralph Merritt, came to visit Manzanar, he agreed not to photograph the more prison-like aspects of Manzanar at Merritt's request. While most historians believe that this was a reflection of Merritt and Adams's support of the relocation policy, it could be that Merritt was trying to promote the idea of an ideal farming community in the desert—a historical Manzanar.

Today, photographer Andrew Freeman has tried to discover and photograph buildings that were once part of Manzanar. He has found that it is difficult to prove which buildings were from Manzanar. Many people, he said, do not want anyone to know that they own a Manzanar building. The National Park Service, in preparation for opening the Manzanar interpretive site, sent out flyers in 2002 asking people to call them if they owned a Manzanar building. They were frustrated with their lack of response. Andrew Freeman said, "They were afraid of losing their homes."[62] The Park Service did reclaim a double-wide building that had been abandoned at the Bishop airport. The service moved it back to Manzanar, where it sits on concrete blocks surrounded by orange pylons. The building is believed to be either the mess hall or the hospital, but since its removal from the airport, controversy has emerged as to whether it ever was at Manzanar, since the records for the building were lost. Since its arrival at Manzanar, a swarm of bees has set up habitation in the building and the park officials are trying to figure out how to exterminate them. Visitors are warned not to go near the building (see figure 4.5).

Denial and controversy surrounding the meaning and history of Manzanar have continued since its establishment. It is a perpetually indecipherable area. There has been a debate, for instance, about the existence and purpose of the guard towers. Were there eight guard towers or only one? Were the guard towers meant to guard internees from outsiders or monitor them as prisoners? Ross Hopkins, Manzanar superintendent, noted: "The Japanese were told they were put here for their own protection, but they all say that the guns were pointed inwards."[63] This debate about Manzanar culminated in a controversy surrounding the wording of a plaque that was placed at the site in 1973. The plaque reads: "In the early part of World War II, 110,000 persons of Japanese ancestry were interned in relocation centers by Executive Order No. 9066, issued on February 19, 1942. Manzanar, the first of ten such concentration camps, was bounded by barbed wire and guard towers, confining 10,000 persons, the majority being American citizens. May the injustices and humiliation suffered here as a result of hysteria, racism and economic exploitation never emerge again."

4.5. Mess Hall. Photo by Karen Piper. Used with permission.

The controversy surrounding this plaque largely centered on calling Manzanar a "concentration camp," a term that caused a controversy over the conditions of the camp itself. Some critics of the term claimed that it dishonored the victims of the Nazi camps, but others, who saw Manzanar more as a "summer camp," believed that it misrepresented the camp altogether. Anna Kelley said, "It shouldn't say 'concentration camp.' It wasn't one. . . . After the camp was built and the people had a chance to, like I say, make themselves comfortable, it was pretty good. It wasn't bad at all."[64] A. A. Brierly concurred: "I think it was a good thing they were locked up. I don't think that's what you would call a concentration camp. I don't know what you'd call it, but they were rounded up and kept there for their own protection."[65] Just as revisionists have recently tried to hide or downplay the atrocities of the concentration camps in Europe, so have some historians tried to paint a rosy picture of the Japanese American internment camps. Robert Ito remarked that among the odder claims was the idea that "the camps were so nice that East Coast Japanese Americans unaffected by the West Coast 'relocation' were clamoring to get in." Some of the more violent revisionists, according to Ito, have "threatened to burn down buildings at Manzanar, defaced and fired rounds at a plaque designating the site as a State Historical Landmark, scrawled swastikas and racials slurs around the area, and even accused Manzanar supporters of treason."[66]

In Bishop, a petition protesting the establishment of the park circulated. "We do not have any bitterness or animosity toward any Japanese who were loyal to the U.S.," the petition started. Then it went on to claim that camps such as Manzanar were necessary because the Japanese were "under suspicion" and "needed protection."[67] The petition was signed by more than a hundred people. "This has been a very contentious park," Ross Hopkins said. "People threatened to blow up the building. I had to unlist my phone number."[68] Many people in Owens Valley want to forget that Manzanar ever existed or to deny that it was a bad thing. The polarized images of utopian farming commune or concentration camp continue to swing back and forth like a historical pendulum.

As late as 2003, there was only one Paiute who took it upon himself to teach people about Japanese internment on lands that once belonged to his tribe. Interestingly, the Lone Pine Indian reservation tribal office was also housed in a Manzanar building. But many Paiutes did not want to see Manzanar developed as a historical monument, since they feared erasure of their own history of suffering at Manzanar. A letter from five Owens Valley tribal elders to the Inyo Country Board of Supervisors in 1979 claimed that "to develop an elaborate Japanese-American project means the desecration of the spiritual cultural heritage of the aborigines."[69] Richard Stewart, Manzanar's tour guide, became interested in Japanese history after studying Japanese pottery. Stewart led people on a tour that covered the history of the Paiute residents as well as that of the Department of Water and Power and the Japanese Americans. Stewart's tours were funded by a $3,500 grant from the Eastern California Museum, because the National Park service did not grant funding for this purpose. Sue Kunitomi Embrey, who lived in the camp, was thankful: "At least somebody will be there and do something so people won't come there and find nothing there except an empty lot and rusted cans."[70] At the time, Congress was planning to spend $310,000 to build a fence to keep out cattle and vandals. Ross Hopkins commented, "I think it's pretty pathetic . . . but the tours are a real tribute to the Eastern California Museum. Private citizens are taking their own time and energy to do something that really the federal government should be doing."[71] Stewart survived temperatures up to 110 in the summertime, with no air conditioning or even portable toilets. He gave tours five days a week during the summer and on weekends during the school year, when he taught elementary school. The guard booth where he spent his days when he was not taking people on tour was only 13 x 14 feet and had a dirt floor.

In September 2000, I visited Manzanar to see how developments were progressing. There was no one at the guard gate. Richard Stewart had apparently left for the winter, as the guardhouse was boarded up. The guardhouse was full of cobwebs and it looked as if it had been abandoned for years, except for the shiny new padlock on one window. There was a grid of dirt roads, however, and a manual for a self-guided driving tour. Sticking out of the ground were signs that said Auditorium or Barracks or Hospital. I drove to the orchards, where a few straggling trees still remained. There were apples hanging on one tree, and bear droppings full of fruit surrounded the tree. I tasted one apple, which was very bitter, like a cross between a crab apple and a pear. Two cars drove quickly through Manzanar, not stopping. A coyote loped through the abandoned gardens, which were only empty concrete-lined pools and dried sage and tamarisk (see figures 4.6 and 4.7). It was difficult to imagine the thriving gardens and the orchards and the amount of food that was produced at Manzanar. The Department of Water and Power did not want to return water to Manzanar for restoration purposes, so a few faded photographs were all that remained of the gardens. Pleasure Park still had the rocks that were carried to the gardens by the internees, but the grass was gone and the trees were struggling. The bridge over the pool crossed only dirt. For those internees who were still living there was only the dust to return their memories to them.

In April 2004, I returned for the opening of the Manzanar Visitors Center. More than a thousand people were there, including Japanese Americans who had been interned at the camp. It was fascinating to see the transformation, which, from the outside, consisted mainly of a large parking lot for buses. The inside of the auditorium, however, had been transformed, filled with memorabilia, multimedia presentations, and a wall covered by names of internees. It was, in fact, almost disconcerting to walk into the exhibit and feel the cool air and see the built-to-size guard tower and videos running on every wall. I must confess I felt more comfortable

4.6. Ansel Adams, "Pleasure Park," 1943, U.S. Library of Congress.

4.7. Pleasure Park today. Photo by Mary Piper. Used with permission.

outside, in a landscape that was familiar. Outside, besides the Disneyland-sized parking lot, the only thing that appeared different was that the number of portable toilets had increased from one to three. Also, there was that intriguing, neglected building on pylons that was full of bees. *This* is the desert I know, I thought. It is hard to say which version is more familiar to the residents of Manzanar or which is most appreciated.

At the entrance to Manzanar, there is a sign hanging that says Manzanar War Relocation Center. It *looks* like the original one, but I know it is not. The original sign was stolen and never recovered, even though it turned up on e-Bay in the early 1990s. To me, this stolen sign represents all that is unattainable about Manzanar. Once, Manzanar was forgotten, buried, covered over with dirt—as if this could make us forget the crime itself. Today, it is replicated and reconstructed in order to re-create at least the sensation that it once happened. Leaving the visitors center behind, I was relieved to see the same rotten fruit beneath the same old apple trees. At the cemetery, the same unmarked graves attest to the life that once thrived at Manzanar. This cemetery is marked by a white concrete obelisk built by the internees in 1943. It is still the place most remembered by those who return to visit Manzanar. The rope fence around the obelisk is covered in origami artwork, and the ground is covered in Japanese yen, broken plates, remnants of brick and concrete, stones wrapped in Japanese newspaper, dried flowers, and other memorabilia of a life that once was. The Japanese writing on the obelisk reads, "Monument to console the souls of the dead." Sadly, on the other side of the park, an Owens Valley resident bragged that he had driven to the park just to urinate on the new sign at Manzanar. When volunteers were sought from the Independence-based American Legion to post a color guard at the opening of the museum, no one volunteered. Legion post commander Carl King said, "So much has been said about [Manzanar]. You don't really know what the whole truth is."[72] Such is the embarrassing legacy of Manzanar, which to this day is covered in the unhealthy dust of Owens Lake. This is the element that unites all Owens Valley visitors, past and present.

FIVE

CONTROL MEASURES

During a field trip in 1996, I watched Bill Cox turn over a lump of dirt with a spade. He picked up the loose clod and rubbed it between his hands, watching the pieces fall away. "It's starting to crumble," his partner at the Great Basin Air Pollution Control District (APCD) warned. "I know," Bill admitted. Bill's idea was to turn the clay surface of the lakebed with a mechanical tiller, to make clods too large to be moved by the wind. The theory was that turning the wet dirt over and letting it dry in the sun would harden the clay subsurface into a cement-like block. Tilling is a dust control measure widely used in agriculture. "If you get big enough pieces of clay, the wind blows right off the surface and doesn't break them down. But they can't be too big. And they have to stay dry," he explained. This method of turning the dirt over to keep it from turning to dust, however, did not seem to be working as well as Bill had hoped. Bill dropped the clay clod and kicked it until it broke apart.

The Great Basin APCD had been working on finding a solution to the dust problem since 1987. In 1996, after almost ten years of looking for solutions, the Great Basin APCD decided to show the public what seemed to work best. The district had identified eight potential control measures: shallow flooding, vegetation, managed vegetation, tilling, salt flats, refilling the lake, and gravel and sand fences. They had decided against seven other potential control measures: compaction, salt composition modification, chemical stabilizers, sprinklers, lowering the groundwater table, tires and other waste materials, and riparian corridors. Twenty people drove around the lakebed that day in 1996, looking at experimental plots for the proposed solutions. The tour started off in a four-wheel drive bumping over the surface of the lakebed. I was in a car with Ted Schade, the engineer for the Great Basin APCD, and Brian Lamb, the district counsel. Brian and I were the only two that stayed until the end. Even then, the Great Basin APCD seemed to want to show us more, although it was getting late and we hadn't had lunch. We toured Carla Scheidlinger's saltgrass plots, Ted's flood irrigation projects, Bill's tilling. "We can take a bathroom break at the trailer," Bill suggested. He seemed to think that would be enough. It was a long day—four hours longer than we had been told it would be. Bill told us that the trailer in Keeler where he worked was sometimes so full of dust that he could not see from one end to the other. Across from Bill's trailer, near the lake shore, there was a surfboard sign that welcomed visitors to "Keeler Beach." It read: "Swim, Surf, Fish, Camps for Rent. This beautiful setting provided by L.A. Water Dept. Wear your haz. mat. suits at all times!" There were a few crumbling or dilapidated trailers on the property, and the "beach" crunched and sprayed white dust when I stepped on it (see figure 5.1). Keeler residents are retirees, artists, and a few oddballs who seem to have a sense of humor even in the face of declining options and poor health. But I had been told by one local that they were also likely to point a gun at anyone who stopped too long in front of their houses. James Wickser, a representative of the Department of Water and Power, once suggested that the DWP "give every person in Keeler a million dollars to relocate them."[1] The department did not follow through on this suggestion.

In 1975, the U.S. Navy was the first to notice and complain of the dust problem in Indian Wells Valley. Pilots had been having trouble with visibility on their test flights in the dusty weather. Then the Inyo County Board of Supervisors, after receiving a large number of complaints from the public, requested that the APCD look into the problem in 1979. The Owens Dry Lake Task Force was formed, consisting of the Department of Water and Power, the Great Basin APCD, China Lake Naval Air Weapons Station, Inyo County, and others. They met regularly and discussed vegetation, gravel, and flooding, among proposed solutions. In 1983, testing began on the lakebed, setting up sand fences to control the blowing sand. In 1987, the EPA designated particulate matter smaller than 10 micro-

5.1. Keeler Beach. Photo by Mary Piper. Used with permission.

grams (PM–10) to be a hazard to human health. The EPA, however, was not used to dealing with dust, so it did not designate Owens Lake a violator. Bill Cox and Ellen Hardebeck went to the EPA to argue their case that Owens Lake dust was as hazardous to the health as ozone (pollution), and the EPA agreed to declare the Owens Lake area a "non-attainment" area. The deadlines for fixing the problem, however, remained hazy.

In 1982, the Great Basin APCD had denied the DWP a permit to build a geothermal well because of a rule stating that the applicant must comply with air quality standards before a permit would be issued. The City was not compliant because of the Owens Lake dust problem. In response, the City had a bill introduced in the State Senate (SB270) that was authored by Senator Dills. The initial bill, which faced considerable opposition, exempted all water-gathering activities from the requirement to apply for a state permit. Eventually a negotiated and amended bill was passed. Senate Bill 270 states: "The Great Basin Unified Air Pollution Control District may require the City of Los Angeles to undertake reasonable measures, including studies, to mitigate the air quality impacts of its activities in the production, diversion, storage, or conveyance of water." The City of Los Angeles, from this date on, was required to pay the Great Basin APCD for studies that would ultimately determine the best way to mitigate and fix the dust problem. The district hired scientists and engineers to conduct research on the dust problem. These researchers were paid with money from the City of Los Angeles, which funded the APCD with approximately $4 million per year.

In exchange, the City would not have its water supply threatened. Los Angeles agreed only to fund the studies in exchange for a promise that it would not have to return water to Owens Lake. This promise was also included in Senate Bill 270: "The mitigation measures shall not affect the right of the city to produce, divert, store, or convey water." So the Great Basin APCD was put in the position of investigating measures such as planting saltgrass, spraying chemicals on the surface of the lake, layering it with tires, building fences to stop the sand, and tilling the surface of the lake. The task force had experimented with several of these possibilities, including layering the lakebed with a chemical stabilizer. This project failed and left residues on the surface. The task force had tried sand fences, which were partially successful although the wooden fences were eroded by the wind. The Great Basin APCD tried layering the lakebed with gravel. If the gravel pieces were large enough and uniform in size, this would be the most successful method to use without water. But it would be expensive for the Department of Water and Power to implement.

While it may seem strange that the Department of Water and Power would rather pay $4 million per year than give up any of its water, this solution is actually economically advantageous to the City. To the Department of Water and Power, the aqueduct is worth $170 million per year.[2] Los Angeles claimed that using 15 percent of aqueduct water to rewater Owens Lake was "exorbitant" and that this water would be better used by 100,000 families that it could supply in Los Angeles. Other alternatives, such as purchasing water from San Joaquin farmers, conserving water, or building desalination plants, had been called "too costly." Jerry Gewe said that purified seawater would cost $2,000 per acre-foot, whereas aqueduct water costs $400 per acre-foot.[3] So even though there were four desalination plants already in Southern California, in Santa Barbara, San Diego, and Catalina, the Department of Water and Power had rejected this option.

Gewe said that desalination prices were lowering and "eventually the price may get competitive," but that for now, "it is not an answer."[4]

In 1990, the Clean Air Act was amended to include stricter deadlines, depending on how serious the problem was. According to Ellen Hardebeck, Air Pollution Control Officer for the APCD, the new rules were based on the idea that "the worse you are, the more time you get."[5] As a "serious" offender, Owens Lake was given until 2001. It could also receive an extension until 2006, if necessary, meaning that sixteen years might be necessary to clean up the problem. By 1997, Hardebeck complained, "No controls have been installed on the lake in all this time. The city has never offered a solution of its own."[6] The most obvious way to stop the dust problem, of course, would be to bring water back to Owens Lake. This, however, was not seen as an option, for more than political reasons. Refilling Owens Lake would take 350,000 acre-feet of water a year. An acre-foot of water is the equivalent of an acre of land being filled one foot deep with water—one family consumes this amount in a year in Los Angeles. This is also the amount of water that evaporates from Owens Lake every year when it is full. It would mean essentially diverting all of Los Angeles's water back to the lake. The lake would take twenty years to fill, and because the dust-emitting areas of the lake are near the shore, the dust problem would not be solved until the end of the twenty-year period. The APCD spent ten years searching for a way to solve the dust problem that would work sooner, use less water, and meet environmental requirements. According to Ellen Hardebeck, "If no such methods had been found, we would have supported fill-the-lake as the only option, as we did at Mono Lake."[7]

The only water available for keeping the surface wet could be pumped from the water table beneath the lakebed itself; scientists estimated that between 33,000 and 56,000 acre-feet were available in the groundwater. It was brackish water, unsuitable for drinking, but it could be used to wet the surface of the lake. From 1993 to 1995, the Great Basin APCD successfully tested shallow flooding and vegetation using three wells it had drilled. The problem with implementing these methods permanently was that pumping water from beneath the lake could lower the water table and would further damage the lake's wetlands and spring mounds, potentially contributing to the dust problem. If the wetlands and spring mounds were destroyed, the saltgrasses that grew on them would disappear. California has already lost

90 percent of its wetlands, with only 400,000 acres of wetlands remaining out of an original 4 to 5 million acres. It tops the list of states with wetland losses.[8] The potential loss of wetlands in Owens Valley, therefore, is a legal and environmental concern. The Great Basin APCD installed a sprinkler system using this water but found that evaporation during a dust storm soon dried the surface.

On my lakebed tour in 1996, the Great Basin APCD employees showed me where shallow flooding had taken place, explaining that migrating snowy plovers had been found there. The project, which consisted of releasing water on the upper edge of Owens Lake and allowing it to spread down toward the center of the lake, attracted hundreds of birds that stopped to rest in the few thousand acre-feet of water that was experimentally pumped. Brine flies, once food for millions of birds, also came back to life at Owens Lake. The plan had been to turn the water off after June 15 of each year, since the dust problem mainly occurred in the winter when the strongest winds blew and lakebed crusts were weak. Ellen Hardebeck expressed concerns about turning the water off, however, given the effect on the snowy plovers. She said, "If you put out water, like in the shallow flooding, then snowy plovers will camp and have their babies near that water, and then if you turn it off at the end of the dust season, then you kill a lot of infants."[9] Snow geese, which now winter at the Ridgecrest Park and China Lake Golf Course, could also be drawn back to Owens Lake when the water is returned. Flocks of one to two thousand have been coming to Ridgecrest from September to March, and golfers have been complaining that the birds get in the way of their game. One year, a golfer confessed, "a poor goose suffered a fatal concussion from the blow of a golf ball."[10] If snow geese start nesting at Owens Lake, there could be die-off of birds too young to fly at the ending of the dust season.

Carla Scheidlinger of the Great Basin APCD showed me where she had planted the lakebed with forty acres of saltgrass, a native species that appeared to be taking well. Saltgrass promised not only to hold down the dust but also to provide a windbreak and minimize the dust in general. The saltgrass would be planted in a farmlike environment of four- to twenty-acre confined fields that were constantly irrigated. Saltgrass would be the only plant species introduced to the fields, because it spreads rapidly, tolerates high soil salinity, and provides good protective cover year-round. Biological, mechanical, and chemical control methods would have to be used to re-move pest plants and noxious grasses. The Great Basin APCD also won-dered if there would be enough water, even though saltgrass requires minimal irrigation in the spring. In response, Los Angeles offered to send its sewage water. "We'll have to ship it out from Los Angeles in trucks," Carla explained. "But it could be the solution to our nitrogen problems. We'll eventually have to fertilize somehow." In a note scrawled on a fax that Jerry Gewe gave me when I visited him, Ray Kearney of the Los Angeles Bureau of Sanitation wrote, "Biosolids may be a solution to controlling dust. If you get a chance to evaluate its use, let me know."[11] Biosolids in this case meant sewage.

The Great Basin APCD, I was told, had also tried growing salicornia, an exotic plant engineered especially for salty areas in Saudi Arabia. Its tips could be sold as a gourmet food product. The concern about salicornia, how-ever, was whether it was invasive. "We hope not," Carla commented during our trip. "That's why we're planting it way out here," she said, pointing to a distant field. The salt cedar had already invaded Owens Valley and was suck-ing up water from beneath the lake. Mary DeDecker, an eighty-eight-year-old resident of the Owens Valley, complained, "If you can find something that will survive in Owens Lake, you may well have found a monster that will eventually take over the whole Valley. . . . The solution is not to solve one problem by creating another."[12] In *The Risk Society and Beyond,* Barbara Adam and Joost Van Loon explained that this is a common phenomenon in dealing with risk: "Technological products enter the living world as 'foreign bodies' . . . Once inserted into the ecology of life, they begin to interact with their networked environments and from that point onwards scientists and engineers have inescapably lost control over the effects of their creation."[13] Recognizing this problem, the Great Basin APCD began gradually to con-centrate on methods that mimic existing natural processes—shallow flood-ing (seeps and springs), vegetation (wetlands), and gravel (desert pavement). But all of these methods required water. SB270, which at first was a com-promised solution, eventually became a huge roadblock to stopping the dust since it would not allow use of water.

The Great Basin APCD was also limited in its choices for dust mitiga-tion by the mandates of the Public Trust Doctrine. The Public Trust Doc-trine, which originated in early Roman law and was incorporated into

English Common law, held that certain resources should be held in common, including "the air, running water, the sea and consequently the shores of the sea."[14] As a trustee for the public, the State Lands Commission owns the beds of navigable rivers, streams, and lakes. The uses for which these resources are held are navigation, commerce, wildlife, and fishing. In 1983, the California Supreme Court ruled in *National Audubon Society v. Superior Court of Alpine County* that the Public Trust Doctrine also protects the "changing public needs of ecological preservation, open space maintenance and scenic and wildlife preservation."[15] In this historic case, the National Audubon Society won water rights for Mono Lake in order to preserve the public trust. The courts determined that "there seems little doubt that both the scenic beauty and the ecological values of Mono Lake are imperiled."[16] In the case of Owens Lake, the Great Basin APCD is not allowed to undertake any mitigation measures that will harm the public trust; for this reason, the idea of layering the lakebed with tires was dropped because it threatened the "scenic beauty" of the lake.

The California State Lands Commission had recently found three measures to be unacceptable and in violation of the public trust: gravel blankets, chemical stabilizers, and waste material coverings. Ted Schade stated, "If it weren't for the public trust, we would have layered the lakebed with old tires long ago. Our job is to stop the dust." Still, Ted explained, "We're going to have to use some gravel. We don't have enough water to do it all with shallow flooding and vegetation." The Great Basin APCD had recommended as one of three measures that a four-inch layer of coarse gravel be laid on the surface of Owens Lake. In theory, this gravel would prevent the formation of the salt crust because the saline water would not be able to rise to the surface, where it would evaporate and deposit salts. To prevent the gravel from sinking into the lakebed in areas with truck traffic or where groundwater was close to the surface, a plastic fabric would have to be spread over parts of the lakebed before the gravel was deposited. The gravel areas would have to be protected from water and windborne soil and dust with flood control berms, drainage channels, and desiltation and retention basins. The Great Basin APCD hoped that these strategies would make the gravel effective for many years, though no one could be sure. The APCD placed a small gravel blanket on the lakebed in 1990 and it still had not sunk, so the agency was hopeful about the results.

The problem with gravel, it seemed, was that no one really wanted it. The Great Basin APCD chose gravel, in addition to shallow flooding and managed vegetation, simply because there was not enough water to shallow flood or vegetate the entire dust area. But gravel would be very expensive, and the Department of Water and Power did not want to have to use it. Dorothy Alther explained: "I think the DWP is going to fight the gravel tooth and nail. I mean they're going to say this is going to cost us millions of dollars." Because there was no local gravel quarry, the use of gravel would require the development of a new quarry that would only further harm the environment.[17] The Paiutes were also against the use of gravel, instead supporting a combination of managed vegetation, shallow flooding, and salt flats. But when I asked Alther what sort of impact the tribes' comments would have in the whole process, she responded, "Very little. . . . In the greater scheme of things, we're pretty insignificant."

Meanwhile, the Department of Water and Power was invested in publicizing every failure of the Great Basin APCD. If there simply was no "reasonable" solution to the dust problem, the Department of Water and Power could not be held responsible for solving the problem. In the *Los Angeles Times*, a department spokesman described the failures of the APCD: "Over the years, a lot of things have sounded good, but they've all dropped out, because in the long run they just don't work. Nothing works the way it's supposed to in Owens Lake."[18] The City of Los Angeles once suggested that the lakebed be designated a national "sacrifice area" in order to overrule public trust law. In the 1960s, the Department of Water and Power already allowed part of the lakebed to be used by a tungsten mine for its waste, which contained flouride. "That was a fiasco of the 1960s," Ted Schade of the Great Basin APCD explained. "It's a ridiculous place for a waste dump. There are leaks all over from the groundwater. But they reasoned that, since there was a similar chemical compound on the lake's surface, that somehow it would blend back in. . . . It was a bad mistake."[19] Walking around on the lakebed, I found a sign that read, "Danger, flammable gas. Do not smoke. Do not enter." On the shores of the old lake, I had also once seen an unofficial dump full of abandoned cars, toilets, and refrigerators (see figure 5.2). Making the lake a national sacrifice area would legalize these uses and overrule the public trust law.

The public trust doctrine first came to national attention because of the court ruling over Mono Lake in 1983. Mono Lake, one hundred and twenty miles to the north, began to be drained by a second aqueduct built by the Department of Water and Power in 1941. The relation between Mono Lake and Owens Lake is particularly complex because they are vying for the same water source. "One region that seemed a candidate to be burdened, if the Mono Basin kept more of its water, was its neighbor down the Los Angeles Aqueduct, the Owens Valley," John Hart wrote. "Which place would you *rather* ruin?"[20] To its credit, the Mono Lake Committee worked hard to maintain a good relationship with the residents of Owens Valley. It recommended that Los Angeles reduce water use rather than pump more water from Owens Valley or take it from the San Joaquin Delta. John Hart wrote, "Los Angeles . . . would not have to raid any region whatsoever to replace Mono water—it could simply get by on less. The City could reduce water use by nearly one-quarter, without sacrifice, by installing more efficient pumping fixtures, irrigating lawns and gardens more carefully, encouraging the use of drought-tolerant plants, allowing higher residential densities, and reducing the water pressure in its mains."[21] The Mono Lake

5.2. Car Dump on Owens Lake. Photo by Karen Piper. Used with permission.

Committee has done more than any other group to demonstrate that Los Angeles can get by on less, though the City may not want to reduce water usage because of the cost involved in implementing conservation measures. Ironically, it is less expensive to use *more* water.

Still, the Mono Lake Committee saw itself as a competitor for water in Owens Valley. Also, it presented the idea of a landscape that was worth saving because it was still beautiful, unlike Owens Lake. David Gaines traveled the nation with a slide show of scenic images of Mono Lake, with work from professional photographers (see figure 5.3). Many years later, at a public hearing, a citizen of Los Angeles said, "I've never been to Mono Lake, but I know that it is beautiful." John Hart explained, "The camera did that."[22] What was being "saved" in Mono, aside from the California gull, was an image or idea of nature. Aldo Leopold once wrote, "Our ability to perceive quality in nature begins, as in art, with the pretty."[23] In describing Mono Lake, John Hart took this "quality" to the metaphysical level, writing, "This is the sort of place a new religion might come from. Who can stand on the lakeshore at twilight, with lightning glittering along

5.3. Mono Lake and Sierra Nevada. Photo © Larry Carver. Used with permission.

the hills, and not have the fantasy that some compelling Word is waiting to be spoken?"[24]

The Great Basin APCD was also involved in the Mono Lake solution. Representatives testified at a state hearing that the water level was set for Mono Lake at twenty feet below the natural lake level. Mono Lake, one hundred and twenty miles to the north of Owens Lake, will never be layered with gravel. Indeed, Owens Lake and Mono Lake, which are very similar types of alkaline lakes fed by Eastern Sierra streams, have been perceived in drastically different fashions. The difference may be clearly seen when talking to Melvin Bernasconi, the head of the Owens Lake Committee. Mel, who is over eighty years old and slightly deaf, says the motto of his committee is, "If you come up with something, we will support you." He talks constantly of the *Bessie Brady*, a steamship that in the 1870s transported ore from one side of Owens Lake to the other for mining operations across the lake. In 1874, the depth of the lake was measured at fifty-one feet. The *Bessie Brady* was the first boat to be used for business on an inland western lake, carrying seventy tons of silver bars across the lake every day.[25] Mel's dream is to build another steamship, as he explains: "It is a kind of a dream that some day we will build another *Bessie Brady* and we'll float it on the lake, and you can come along and take a ride with us. . . . Let our people rise together and fill the Owens Lake."[26] Mel's "visitor center" is his living room, and he writes poems about the lake and reads them at public hearings. Mel's recent poem is called "The Beautiful Owens Lake," which he proudly claims to have published in two newspapers. It reads, "Owens Lake, queen of the Inyo, murdered, murdered long ago. Spews poison dust out of her mouth in angry winds that rage and blow. Oh, Owens Lake . . . we pray for you to rise again and live forever more."[27] Mel Bernasconi shouts when he talks and laughs, seemingly always to himself. He recently read his poem at a public hearing, and when one person clapped, he laughed and said, "I thought that would impress someone." Then he limped away from the microphone with his cane.

In contrast, the Mono Lake Committee Visitor Center in Lee Vining is full of healthy-looking young people with shorts and smiles and tans, looking as if they have just come back from a hike in Yosemite. The visitors to the center are also generally REI-clad outdoorsy types and possibly a few foreign tourists milling through the bookshelves, listening to the natural "music" of rain and wind in the spacious front room. In the back room there is a slide show that demonstrates how spectacular the lake can look when captured by some of the best photographers in the nation. If you buy a book or T-shirt at the center, you'll be asked if you want to be a member of the Committee and handed a newsletter on the way out. This is the Mono Lake Committee at its best, celebrating its victories in the expanding, espresso-fueled town that was just a gas station and cheap motel a decade ago. Now the rooms rent for over $100 per night, as the cost for views of this lake has grown with its publicity.

The Mono Lake Committee, from its inception, had the support of the federal government, the National Audubon Society, Friends of the Earth, and the Sierra Club. Ornithologist David Gaines, a graduate student at the University of California, Davis, was galvanized by the declining bird population at Mono Lake and started a course called Bird Freaks Unite! The controversy started over Negit Island, in the center of Mono Lake, a nesting site for California gulls. As the lake levels began to drop, a land bridge emerged, connecting Negit Island to the mainland. The drama unfolded daily as, on national television, coyotes crossed a land bridge created by the receding waters to an island where they gorged themselves on helpless, nesting California gulls. *American Birds* magazine predicted "total destruction of the population."[28] David Gaines received a grant for $20,000 to study the lake, resulting in the formation of the Mono Lake Committee. Immediately, a dozen students were camped out by the lake, where they "sang, recited verse, lived largely on granola, beans, and rice, and were known to take in other nonstandard substances."[29] They also started counting dead birds. In *Water and Power*, William Kahrl called the Mono Lake Committee "a small band of bird-watchers and graduate students . . . activated by nothing more complex than their deep affection for a place few Californians will ever see."[30] David Gaines began traveling the country with a slide show of scenic views of the lake and mounds of dead birds. In 1979, two hundred and fifty people gathered at Mono Lake with buckets and pails full of fresh water to dump back into the lake. They carried signs that read, "California Gulls Need Love, Too!"

Finally, in 1986, Mono Lake was designated a Scenic Area by the Forest Service, which promised to monitor the lake area to protect "geologic, ecological, and cultural resources." In 1988, Congress allocated $4.3 million to build a striking visitor center on the shores of Mono Lake. And, in 1994, the California Water Resources Control Board required Los Angeles to return water to the lake to maintain its "scenic beauty and ecological diversity." The Department of Water and Power is now required to maintain a certain amount of water in Mono Lake.

Gravel will never be used at Mono Lake, which has dust problems similar to Owens Lake, though to a lesser degree. Because Mono Lake is designated a Scenic Area, its shores must be maintained in a "primitive, natural appearing condition."[31] In Owens Valley, the victories at Mono Lake were observed with surprise and suspicion. Charles Petit of the *San Francisco Chronicle* described the attitude of Owens Valley residents: "Such victories, largely by outside lawyers and recently arrived environmentalists, have surprised the region's old-timers. Few thought anybody could beat Los Angeles."[32] These victories were not for the people of Owens Valley, who watched the Mono Lake victories with continued resignation. Andrea Lawrence of the Mono County Board of Supervisors said to the State Air Resources Board, "In the ARB, your good people here joined with the District to help solve the Mono Lake dust problem. We in Mono, I need to tell you, are very, very grateful for that. It is a wonderful, wonderful decision. But then I must ask, why have you not offered this assistance when the pollution in Owens Lake is so much more severe?"[33] In 1992, the U.S. Bureau of Reclamation was authorized to pay one quarter of the costs of reclamation projects in southern California that would "offset diversions from the environmentally sensitive Mono Lake Basin."[34] In 1994, the Mono Lake Committee devised a water reclamation plan for the Central Valley that would effectively create 141,250 acre-feet per year of new water supplies for Los Angeles.[35] The "Big Ten" environmental groups all contributed enormous sums of time and money, the federal government offered $60 million to buy replacement waters for the Department of Water and Power, and the U.S. Bureau of Reclamation funded the solution for Mono Lake.

Ultimately, according to the Mono Lake Committee, the water made available to the Department of Water and Power through these measures far exceeded water lost to Mono Lake. Dorothy Alther explained, "Through the reclamation projects they were able to reclaim 100,000 acre feet of water per year. So if you deduct the 30,000 that Mono Lake is going to use, you've still got 70,000 acre feet of extra reclamation water per year.

And that is just one small example of where they've got water piled."[36] The Great Basin APCD needs only 50,000 acre-feet per year for shallow flooding on Owens Lake, but this request was met with strong resistance from the Department of Water and Power. Dorothy Alther complained, "I realized that that is a smoke screen—'Oh, we're water poor.'" For instance, about 80 percent of California's water goes to agriculture, which can be further broken down into types of usage. Around 60 percent of this water goes to cotton, rice, alfalfa, and pasture; but these crops generate only 15 percent of California's agricultural income. The top consumer of water, pastureland, also generates the least profit. But federal subsidies encourage beef production through low-cost water subsidies, which keeps this infrastructure in place. If the low-value crops of pasture, alfalfa, rice, and cotton were eliminated, there would be enough water for 70 million new Californians—or almost ten new cities the size of Los Angeles.[37] (Though, on the other hand, environmentalists are suggesting that rice provides marshland habitat for birds.) Recently, the Metropolitan Water District, which supplies water to Los Angeles's metropolitan area, announced that it was investigating the purchase of thousands of acres of farmland—and the water rights that go with it—from "economically pressed" San Joaquin growers. This move, district representatives announced, "would allow the district to channel millions of gallons of California aqueduct water to urban users."[38] But according to Jerry Gewe, "We can't make up that 50,000 acre feet of water [needed in Owens Valley] out of conservation in the short term alone. In the long term, we're committing to our growth."[39]

The Mono Lake trial ultimately proved that Los Angeles was not as water-poor as it appeared to be. But, as Jerry Gewe explained, buying any water essentially runs contrary to the policy of the Department of Water and Power: "Basically our operation is to take as much water as we can out of Owens River, because that water's free. That system is paid for, it flows by gravity . . . so we just take as much water as we can. Then we determine how much water we have available from surface runoff and make a decision how much [groundwater] we're going to pump. That's the second least expensive cost. . . . Once we made the decision on how much we're going to pump, we just buy the rest from the MWD, which has two sources, either the Colorado River or the State Water Project."[40] Tom Hayden also described the problem as a financial one: "The Department of Water and

Power has technical capacity and a budget, but it's in the business of selling water, so there's a conflict of interest there." The loyalties of the Department of Water and Power are first and foremost to its customers. Water, explained Hayden, "is the key to development, subdivisions, the expansion of power, the expansion of Southern California. . . . The developers and their friends lobby strenuously in favor of more studies or more flexible standards."[41] Ted Schade once remarked, "Around here water is more precious than gold. They [the DWP] won't give up water, just on principle."

Besides the financial costs, there are also political problems with taking Colorado River water, as California is already exceeding its apportionment of water, which must be shared with Arizona, Nevada, and Mexico. The residents of Arizona, in fact, resisted the Colorado River project in a manner that was even more organized than the opposition to the Los Angeles Aqueduct. In 1935, the governor deployed the state militia to keep Los Angeles from building a dam there. The militia installed machine gun nests to keep Californians away, which succeeded for eight months. But, as with Owens Valley, the Supreme Court ultimately settled the "California-Arizona War" by ruling that Arizona could not hold up California's work at gunpoint. Recently, Arizona and Nevada began to use the full amount of water due them from the Colorado River, leaving no surplus for California. The only other option for Los Angeles is getting water from the Feather River, six hundred miles to the north. But San Francisco and the San Joaquin Valley are in competition for this water. Farmers in the San Joaquin Valley are already protesting pressures from the Department of Water and Power, which now offers to buy water rights in exchange for farmers keeping their fields fallow. On Interstate 5, there is a sign posted that reads, "Owens Valley II?" Another problem in this part of California is the increasing dust storms that have resulted from blowing topsoil. At times, Interstate 5 has to be shut down because of poor visibility. Still, Owens Valley residents dream of often-inconceivable amounts of water being returned to them.

In 1996, one of the options presented as a "control measure" for the dust problem was the "fill the lake" option. After running through several other possible control measures, Duane Ono, at a meeting of the Owens Lake Advisory Board, held up a sketch of an Owens Lake filled with water. He announced with a note of satire in his voice: "And now 'the ever popular' fill the lake option. . . . There's not much we can say there. It's a pretty obvious solution."[42] Then he took the sketch down and went on to the next option. After the meeting, I asked Duane why this option was even being considered if no one was taking it seriously. He informed me that the California State Lands Commission required that it be studied as an option because of the public trust, but that everyone knew it was an impossibility. The studies performed on that option, therefore, were described as "cursory" and "not as in-depth" as, for instance, the salicornia or the irrigation. "We'd have to hire more lawyers than scientists if we were going to go down that road," he told me. "But it could happen," he continued, "if nothing else works." Duane admitted that then, "we may have to refill the lake." On the way back from my full-day lakebed tour in 1996, in a four-wheel drive with the attorney and the engineer, I asked about refilling the lake. They both said, "It won't happen. At least not in our lifetimes." Carla had simply commented on the possibility, "Well we'd all be out of work if that happened." What amazed me, then, was that the option could even be on the books, like some mythical paradise that no one believed in but nevertheless desired. When I later suggested to a Mono Lake Committee employee that I heard that returning the water to Owens Lake was impossible, she simply responded, "That's what they said about Mono Lake."

The refilling of Owens Lake seems to circulate as an illegitimate rumor in Owens Valley. It is a statement that is often disavowed, even as it is spoken. The subject is generally approached as if someone else—someone crazy—had said it. It is approached as a joke. And yet, it is always approached, even with all these mechanisms of disavowal around the approach. Postcolonial critic Gayatri Spivak once discussed rumor as a method of strategy against colonizing powers, a kind of unofficial discourse. She wrote, "Rumor evokes comradeship because it belongs to every 'reader' or 'transmitter.' No one is its origin or source. . . . This illegitimacy makes it accessible to insurgency."[43] In the case of Owens Lake, the subject seems to come up as a kind of absurd proposition. People know it would mean the end of L.A., but they seem to take a delightfully ironic pleasure in thinking of precisely this proposition. "I've heard that they'll have to refill the lake," they laugh, rolling their eyes as if to suggest how insane that would be while watching to see if you are in on the joke. All this is managed with eye contact rather than words, in rumor rather than writing, in innuendo rather than fact. It would be divine retribution for the colonized. It is impossible.

The process of "studying" Owens Lake, meanwhile, took twelve years to complete, until one Keeler resident complained in 1997 that all she could hope to do was "donate [her] body to science" when she died from the dust at Owens Lake.[44] Ironically, no matter how much disdain or mockery was directed at the proposition of refilling Owens Lake, no one seemed to discuss the absurdity of stopping dust from blowing without water. Because this was law rather than rumor, it seemed to be considered real. In the end, however, this would prove to be an impossible task. Many of the early solutions tried by the Great Basin APCD failed, and those that worked best required water. After twelve years of study, the Great Basin APCD was put in the position of having to ask for water. Water would have to be returned to Owens Lake, it seemed, but not first without a standoff between the APCD and the Department of Water and Power.

S I X

"THERE IT IS, FIX IT"

On July 2, 1997, at the Inyo County Courthouse, the Great Basin APCD Governing Board met to consider its staff's recommendations for mitigation of the dust problem, the State Implementation Plan (SIP) required by the Federal Clean Air Act. The courtroom was filled with seventy or eighty people who had shown up to voice their support for the plan. Representatives from the Big Pine, Bishop, Ft. Independence, and Lone Pine Paiute tribes, as well as the Shoshone–Death Valley tribes were sitting in the front rows. The commander of the Naval Air Weapons Station in Ridgecrest was also in front, along with a representative for the mayor of Ridgecrest. Five Department of Water and Power men were at the back, pushed outside the open doors because of the crowds.

To the chagrin of the Department of Water and Power, the SIP required Los Angeles to return 51,000 acre-feet of water to Owens Lake. Ellen Hardebeck, director of the Great Basin APCD, said it had no other choice. She explained, "We were completing the EIR [Environmental Impact Report] and realized that groundwater pumping wasn't an option environmentally, and the deadline was approaching . . . so that left us no option. We had to ask for DWP water."[1] Knowing that demanding aqueduct water might violate Senate Bill 270, the Great Basin APCD instead did not specify that water must come from the aqueduct. Dorothy Alther explained the APCD's strategy: "So what they're saying is, fix it, in this way, with this amount of water, but you don't have to take it from the aqueduct. You can take it from anywhere you want. You can buy it from Nevada and haul it in in trucks. You can bring it in from a hose from the ocean. We don't care. We're not ordering you to take it from the aqueduct."[2]

After hearing of this plan, the Department of Water and Power had cut off the salaries of the members of the Great Basin APCD. The DWP challenged the SIP and 80 percent of the entire budget of the Great Basin APCD even though the law required that it pay. It also sent a letter to the Inyo County Auditor, threatening him with legal action if he allowed the APCD to spend any of the previous year's remaining funds to cover lost salaries. The letter stated, "Please be advised that the City of Los Angeles, which is represented by this office, takes exception to said action of the District [their request for funds] and will take all appropriate legal action to protect its interests. We strongly recommend that you and your office obtain independent legal advise before complying with this order of the District Board."[3] This move was obviously a threat by the Department of Water and Power to try to coerce the APCD into not adopting the control measures that required water. Then negotiations between the Great Basin APCD and Department of Water and Power broke down completely. Infuriated, the Great Basin APCD compared the DWP publicly to Scrooge, Saddam Hussein, and an abusive spouse. Great Basin attorney Brian Lamb called negotiations between the Department of Water and Power and Great Basin APCD "a nightmare." Andrea Lawrence of the Great Basin APCD said, "I would be inclined to call it blackmail."[4]

The Department of Water and Power did not dispute this charge. In fact, it openly suggested that it had the power to shut down APCD operations by withholding money. Jerry Gewe explained: "Should the Great Basin approve that SIP on July 2, we will be in court. It's too important to our customers. . . . But they're going to have funding problems. And we'll find out whether the community is really that solidly behind the district to invest their own money in it if we shut off the flow of cash."[5] With a doctorate in astrophysics from Harvard University, Ellen Hardebeck had been with the Great Basin APCD since 1985. But in 1997, Hardebeck was very aware that she might soon be out of work. She complained, "They have appealed every penny of our funding and that includes our attorney, that includes my salary, many of the people who work here. . . ."[6] The Department of Water and Power had cut off funding to the Great Basin APCD even before the appeal was heard. Beginning on July 1, 1997, the Department of Water and Power withheld funds for the entire fiscal year of 1997–1998. The responsibility then fell upon the California Air Resources Board (ARB) to hear the appeal; the ARB did nothing. Dorothy Alther stated, "I think the fact that the Air Resource Board has not acted in a more expedited way on the funding appeal has signaled to me that Department of Water and Power has got some real leverage at that level. The Resource Board is saying to Great Basin, 'Why do we have to move so fast on this?' And Great Basin is saying, 'Because we're out of money in two weeks. We are shutting down.'"[7] One member of the Great Basin APCD, who asked to remain anonymous, said simply, "The DWP's plan is clearly to crush us." The Great Basin APCD, it seemed, was going to be put out of business by the Department of Water and Power and the State of California. Andrea Lawrence of the Great Basin APCD commented, "How the heck do we pay our staff's wages? This is medieval; these people are acting like they have the divine right of kings."[8]

Besides appealing the Great Basin's APCD's funding, the Department of Water and Power claimed that the solutions proposed by the APCD, which included shallow flooding, vegetation, and gravel, were not "reasonable." The Department of Water and Power submitted 121 pages criticizing the Great Basin APCD's Environmental Impact Report (EIR). Yet as one professor who reviewed the document noted, "Many [of the DWP's claims] do not include that much substance. Many are duplicative, as if numerous critics had each been asked to note what might be wrong and similar responses were tossed together in an unsorted pile. Perhaps most revolting, the Department of Water and Power calls the probable demand for the use of water for the clean up a 'regulatory taking' as if the district . . . were stealing water for which the DWP should be compensated."[9] Ellen Hardebeck responded to this accusation: "We don't view it as we're taking the City's water. We're saying that the City is going to have to put back 13 percent of the water they are taking from the lake."[10]

On July 1, 1997, when the Great Basin APCD's paycheck was supposed to come in, the Great Basin APCD was called to a meeting instead. Chair of the APCD's Governing Board Dave Watson explained, "At the eleventh hour, at the invitation of Michael Kenny of the Air Resource Board, Michael Dorame and I went over to Sacramento as part of a negotiating team . . . and during the course of that meeting, it was very clear that we were still not going to be able to use aqueduct water."[11] Los Angeles had offered two things instead: (1) 1.5 million dollars for the Great Basin APCD to continue its studies, and (2) a study looking into the "possibility" of using lower Owens River water for the project. In 1991, the Department of Water and Power had resolved another lawsuit with Owens Valley by agreeing to rewater parts of the lower Owens River that had been dried up by aqueduct diversions. Because the Department of Water and Power did not want to lose that water, however, it planned to redirect the water back to the aqueduct before it reached the lakebed. They had already designed an extensive piping system for just that purpose, so the Great Basin APCD had difficulty believing that this water would go to Owens Lake. Without more of a commitment from the Department of Water and Power, the Great Basin APCD did not know if it could trust the Department of Water and Power's qualified promise of water.

So on July 2, 1997, the APCD Governing Board was still in a pro- tracted "closed session" meeting when the public hearing was due to begin. The Great Basin APCD representatives were briefing the board on the previous day's proposal while the audience milled around outside. Fi- nally, the audience was handed a memo, called a Memorandum of Un- derstanding (MOU). This memo had been produced at the meeting in Sacramento, where the Great Basin APCD had tried to hammer out a compromise with the Department of Water and Power. The first num- bered paragraph authorized a "scientific advisory group" to be set up to study the Great Basin APCD's work and come up with its own sugges- tions about the dust. The second allowed for the possibility of 20,000 acre-feet of aqueduct water to be used "contingent upon the results of the study." That is, the water could be used only if the outside "advisory group" agreed it was necessary. Jerry Gewe had suggested to me earlier that "where we would like to take this is basically get back involved, but get involved through creating a scientific task force to conduct indepen- dent research."[12] He suggested that the State Air Resources Board, the EPA, the Department of Water and Power, and the Great Basin APCD select the members of the "independent" committee.

The chairman of the board, David Watson, opened the meeting with an ambiguous statement: "One of the reasons that we're late in getting started is that I'm struggling a great deal in my own mind to sort out what must remain confidential. I'm a little bit uncomfortable with the amount of material that has been discussed in closed session . . . and I'm trying to sort out where I can and where I can't go."[13] Ellen Hardebeck then proposed that the staff's recommended SIP be adopted, but Watson instead recommended that the board "utilize a ninety-day cooling off period" and go back into closed session. The two other members of the negotiating committee, Andrea Lawrence and Michael Dorame, opposed this. Then the board members, provoked by Hardebeck's opening comments, began to argue until it was agreed that the public hearing would commence. At this historic meeting in Independence, California, it looked as if the biggest standoff since the water wars of the 1920s was about to occur. Rather than proceeding with the adoption of the State Implementation Plan, David Watson, the Department of Water and Power, and the California Air Resources Board began by urging the APCD Board to adopt the proposed Memorandum of Understanding. Chris O'Donnell, a deputy mayor of Los Angeles, came forward and attempted to act as mediator. "We are here in part," he said, "because there has been a failure of department management to show leadership on this issue. What happened was that for ten years, the Department was very comfortable in spending four to five million dollars a year on research. It just went on and on and on, and there was never any conclusion."[14] O'Donnell urged adoption of the MOU. Edward Scholtman, an attorney for the City of Los Angeles, also urged adoption of the MOU, saying that it would require "putting aside the distrust" and engaging "in a process that will hopefully lead to potentially disinterested science." He concluded, "I wish you to know that the city does continue to have serious and substantial concerns. . . . They continue to include such matters as the use of such amount of water that would be sufficient for two hundred thousand people."[15] No one applauded when he finished speaking. The people were there in support of the Great Basin APCD, whose funding had been cut and who had to decide that day whether to pass the SIP or support the MOU.

The commanding officer of the Naval Air Weapons Station (NAWS), Capt. Stan Douglas, stood next to an elder of the Bishop Paiute tribe in a line for the microphone, waiting to support the Great Basin APCD. Political lines were drawn around dust and nothing else. The period of public comment finally opened; people seemed ready to rush the microphone, though they had waited in orderly fashion. Capt. Douglas was dressed in a white uniform and was there to speak of the problems of launching missiles in a dust storm. The Naval Air Weapons Station, which is as large as Vermont, is directly downwind from the Owens lakebed—and is the main industry for the city of Ridgecrest. Its specialty is air-launched weapons, and the facility was built in the Mojave desert specifically because of its pristine air quality, making it the "world's largest inland Navy station." Douglas complained that the 2,500 air-to-air tests per year, at a cost of $50,000 per test, were being compromised or continually canceled due to Owens Lake dust "events." The dust, he explained, affected the station's capacity to track the missiles by camera, which ultimately led to a "final increase in cost to the taxpayer if we're unable to do the mission." The base was trying to find ways around the problem, as he said: "We have developed infrared based systems that allow us to see through dust and clutter storms . . . the combined cost of that program so far is about five million dollars." But not only was the dust a risk for missile projects, it also continually put the lives of the pilots at risk. Douglas claimed, "Any reduction in visibility is a concern for flight safety to us. Because our pilots fly with VFR flight rules, meaning 'see and avoid'—and you have to be able to see to avoid."[16]

Because of the increasing problems with dust in the valley, the NAWS had started a tracking program of its own, this time focused on dust, not missiles. It had covered eleven "events" in the past year, beginning in April 1996, by Doppler radar, and Capt. Douglas had brought in some of the results of their findings. The lights went out, and the TV screen showed a yellow-colored plume of dust that picked up speed and volume and swept through the valley in the middle of the night. The plume shot out like an explosion, covering the whole Indian Wells Valley, and the audience let out an audible gasp. Indian Wells Valley, with the largest population downwind from the dust, had always been a point of controversy in the dust issue. The Department of Water and Power claimed that the valley wasn't affected, and the Great Basin APCD did not have jurisdiction over this valley. The morning after the "event," Douglas demonstrated that, though it was no longer visible on radar, dust was still in the valley. Instead, he had a photograph of Indian Wells Valley in which the mountains were missing, which he contrasted to a clear day with the mountains in view. As on any day of Owens Lake dust in the Valley, the mountains disappear, just as the San Gabriels do from the smog in Los Angeles.

Gina Marie Robinson, representing the mayor of Ridgecrest, also spoke up for the lives in that city. Although 85 percent of the jobs in Ridgecrest were on the U.S. Navy base, the city was aspiring to become a desert retirement and recreation community. Near Los Angeles and at the base of the Sierra Nevada Mountains, Ridgecrest's future appeared bright despite the recent downsizing of the Department of Defense. But the dust, it seemed, could bring an end to all of that. The dust was destroying the base's image as a place of pristine air quality, and it was becoming hard to imagine wealthy retirees coming to breathe the toxic dust of the valley. Robinson read a statement from the mayor claiming that the "events" had affected air quality and air visibility. She continued, "These impacts have resulted in poor health for the citizens of Ridgecrest and the surrounding Indian Wells Valley. . . . The city of Ridgecrest believes that its future economic diversification and recovery may well be impacted by the continuing degrading of the air quality of Indian Wells Valley."[17] A great recession in the city had already begun, with residents unable even to sell their houses in order to flee the dust. Many houses sat vacant instead.

Wilma Wheeler criticized the Department of Water and Power for being indifferent to the health of human beings: "To them money is all important over the health of the people of Owens Valley and surrounding areas. The Owens Lake dust travels far, thus threatening the health of the people in Los Angeles and Orange County as well."[18] A local from Death Valley described her drive in Owens Valley one day: "By the time I got to the Darwin exit . . . you needed to drive with lights on because the dust was so bad. By the time I turned around the corner towards Keeler, you couldn't see the lines on the highway any longer. They were gone. . . . I was wearing a bandanna over my mouth so I wouldn't cough so much."[19] Several more people came forward to talk about their respiratory problems or their fear of cancer. Sharon Rose, a public health educator for the prevention of respiratory diseases, commented: "I'm a little tired of hearing this called the 'dry lake,' or Owens Dry Lake. I think we should be referring to this as an environmental disaster, because that's what it is. If the DWP gets away with avoiding their responsibility, in my view, that's tantamount to Union Carbide walking away from the atrocity in Bhopal, India, with no restitution to those harmed. It would be comparable to Exxon walking away from the *Valdez* oil spill with no restitution. There has been compensation in those cases. I want to remind people of the cancers, leukemias, and the injuries of Three Mile Island, or Love Canal, or Chernobyl. These are environmental disasters, and we don't go around calling them nice words. They're not nice."[20] She concluded, "The philosophy of 'There it is, take it' can no longer be a guiding philosophy if the planet is to survive." "There it is, take it," are the words that William Mulholland uttered when the water first came over the San Gabriel Mountains into Los Angeles. But on July 2, 1997, the people of Owens Valley stood up—in solidarity—against the logic of that taking.

The Paiutes of Owens Valley revised the Department of Water and Power's rhetoric by claiming that one cannot take from the land without giving back. Michael Rogers, an elder from the Bishop tribe, claimed, "There will always be money and there will always be arguments over the money while the spirit of the land is killed. . . . The continued delays only add to the killing of the spirit of our land. In the Native American culture, if you take, you must give something back and we have yet to see that, in order to keep in balance with the environment. We cannot have balance if there is only take. . . . We must get started with the healing of the problem."[21] Harry Williams of the Bishop tribe concurred that the Department of Water and Power was destroying the land by not "giving back" anything to the ecosystem: "The balance of the world has been changing so much, there is out-of-control growth, and where is the fresh water going to come from? They are pumping us, and they want more. They don't want to give nothing back. I'm afraid for this world as a whole. I'm afraid for the survival of the human race. That's why I come here today. I come here to speak on behalf of the animals, the balance of power. You are one of the balances of power, and that is why I am here, and that is why I came here to say what I have to say, and I hope you come to the right decision. I almost hope that . . . the EPA comes in and fills the lake up. That is my hope, that the ecosystem will be recharged and things will become normal."[22] Dorothy Alther claimed that her clients, the Paiute tribes, would be "forced to take legal action" if the Great Basin APCD did not stand behind the proposed clean-up plan. If the APCD Board did not approve the SIP, the issue would eventually go to the EPA for the instigation of a federal dust control plan.

The APCD Governing Board listened in silence to the people who came to speak out against the Department of Water and Power. Board member Michael Dorame then moved that the State Implementation Plan be adopted. The board began to discuss the proposal. "Part of the healing that we heard about is for this board," board member Andrea Lawrence began. She urged that the board "implement the plan that we worked hard on and we know will mitigate this problem" and "not back off or be afraid of lawsuits." She concluded, "We're probably going to be in a lawsuit no matter which way we go, but if I have to get in a lawsuit, I want to get in a lawsuit for having done the right thing." Michael Dorame of the Great Basin APCD said the dry lake was "the black eye in the abusive relationship that we have had to suffer in this valley." He continued, "There comes a point where the abused spouse says, 'No more.' That's where we are today."[23] The APCD had decided that it was going to demand water, regardless of the consequences. Michael Dorame continued, "When the city of Los Angeles needed the water, they went for it. There weren't any delays, they went for it. We need clean air, and . . . how can you look out there [pointing at the audience] and say, 'We're going to put it off'? The people are crying out for this, and those of you who ignore the voice of the people are the fools, not those of us who are following that direction . . . and time will prove me correct." Another board member added, "As I look at this audience, and I see all these people that took the time off work—the distance they traveled here to express their opinion, it's remarkable. . . . The room is filled with people that want to see action. I commend you for standing up for what you feel is right." And yet another added, "I think we have not only a legal obligation to pass the SIP, but also a moral obligation—" and then he abruptly stopped, leaned back in his chair, and blinked back tears. "Short, but well-said," the woman next to him consoled.[24] Many attendees at this point were beginning to cry as the men from the Department of Water and Power stood in the hallway shaking their heads.

Michael Dorame concluded by shouting out: "Hear me, Los Angeles, 'There it is, fix it.'" Then the chairman said, "All in favor?" and the room filled with ayes. The chairman, who gave the only nay, looked confused as the audience broke out in cheers and applause. The executive officer of the

Great Basin APCD, Ellen Hardebeck, tried to fight back tears, as did other members of the board and the audience. The Great Basin APCD did not know what its future would be, as it was at the mercy of the Department of Water and Power. It did not know where salaries would come from and knew that its members may have voted themselves out of jobs. Hardebeck had known that the meeting might polarize the two parties and even end her own career. Seventy-five percent of the Great Basin APCD staff was paid by the City of Los Angeles, she claimed, and without that money people would have to start going home. "I believe that's their intent," she said, "to cripple us." Still, Hardebeck remained hopeful: "But twenty-five percent of the district will still be here, and we will say, 'I'm sorry. This is the SIP. We cannot change this, and all the people who could have done that are gone.'"[25] So it seemed that the SIP might live, even if the committee that had created it was dead. I asked Ellen afterward if the Department of Water and Power's plan might be to bring people in to challenge the SIP when there was no one left to defend it. She said, "I can defend this SIP. I know more about it than they do, and I'll still be here." With her job on the line, I asked, how this would be possible? She responded, "I've worked ten years for free, and then I was on the payroll for eleven years, so now I owe another ten years for free. . . . We won't go away."[26]

With all their jobs on the line, the meeting concluded. But although the Great Basin APCD was forced to begin firing employees right after that eventful meeting, it also quickly took the Department of Water and Power to the Court of Appeal.[27] There, the Department of Water and Power was forced to resume payment of salaries. In turn, the court asked the Great Basin APCD to defend the "reasonableness" of its mitigation measures before the State Air Resources Board (ARB). Don Mooney, a lawyer, claimed that since the City had filed the appeal, it should have had the "burden of proof" to defend its statement that the Great Basin APCD's actions were not reasonable. Instead, the "burden of proof" was shifted to the APCD to prove that its actions *were* reasonable before the ARB. The ARB had charged the APCD with failing to follow proper protocol in designing dust mitigation strategies because it had not followed the guidelines set for modeling ozone pollution as laid out in the state's Ozone Modeling Guidance Report. Most people saw this as a loophole that the state, in collusion with the Department of Water and Power, was using to shut down the dust mitigation program. Ellen Hardebeck complained to the ARB, "But we do not have an ozone problem. We know nothing about ozone, so don't ask me how to apply these things. We know nothing about it. Our PM–10 is wind-blown dust, so it is not photochemically formed. . . . This is all just dirt off the ground."[28] Dorothy Alther was also puzzled. "Why would ARB staff rely on ozone modeling guidance?" she said. She hired a consultant to the Paiute tribes to find an answer. But, she found, "This was an answer that my consultant could not give me."[29] Owens Lake was not emitting ozone. But the Great Basin APCD had been asked to prove that its actions were reasonable based upon an ozone model standard. "This is not the normal adjudicatory process," Don Mooney noted. "As someone who practices in administrative law, it has been an interesting process to watch."[30] The Great Basin APCD had received its funding, so it would not have to shut down, but it appeared that its project would nonetheless be killed. It would have to start over again, this time looking for ozone.

Just as things were looking dire, the leadership changed at the Department of Water and Power. David Freeman became the new head and, according to the *Daily News of Los Angeles,* began "unabashedly revealing 'dirty little secrets' about the sometimes Byzantine city utility."[31] For instance, he exposed plans by the Department of Water and Power for a $6 billion coal-power plant in Utah, even though this would significantly impact the air quality of Zion National Park. Freeman also acknowledged the DWP's responsibility, under the Clean Air Act, to fix the dust from Owens Lake. The DWP assistant director of water resources, Richard F. Harasick, finally claimed: "We're over the kicking and screaming. We want to be good stewards of the environment that's been given to us. It's a change in our way of thinking."[32] Around the same time, the ARB decided to relax the hard stance it had taken on ozone standards and instead required the Department of Water and Power and Great Basin APCD to reach an agreement. So after ten years of struggle over this very issue, the ARB gave the Department of Water and Power and Great Basin APCD one month to reach a compromise.

The health risk from Owens Lake dust set in motion a process by which the Department of Water and Power ultimately was forced to rethink itself. In July 1998, the Department of Water and Power and the Great Basin APCD reached an agreement in which the Department of Water and

Power would sacrifice water—though it did not say the water would come from the aqueduct. The Department of Water and Power, in turn, was given five years, until 2006, to sort out where this water would come from. It also gained the authority to "implement controls of [its] choice" on part of the lakebed but would have to begin developing the infrastructure for the mitigation measures immediately. The Department of Water and Power agreed to complete shallow flooding of 10 square miles of Owens Lake by the end of 2001 and another 3.5 square miles by the end of 2002. By the end of 2003, it agreed to cover three more square miles in vegetation. It also agreed to submit a revised SIP by 2003, which would outline how it planned to fix a total of 30 square miles by 2006.

The question remained as to where the water would come from. The Department of Water and Power still did not want to use aqueduct water. "That has a significant symbolism for us," said Harasick. "That's a real emotional issue, to put good, clean drinking water on the lakebed."[33] So the Department of Water and Power proposed pumping groundwater to irrigate Owens Lake, but Owens Valley residents insisted on an EIR to predict environmental damage to the area. An Owens Lake Groundwater Evaluation group was set up to show that additional studies were needed to determine the amount of pumping, if any, that could take place without causing undesirable environmental impacts at the lake. Then, in September 1999, the Department of Water and Power suddenly abandoned its plans for groundwater pumping. The Department of Water and Power decided to use aqueduct water, "for the time being," having been forced into this position as a default.[34] In the long run, however, Los Angeles stated that it had not given up on pumping from under Owens Lake and that there might have to be "some negative impacts" when and if future pumping did occur.[35] All of these issues may serve to complicate what already can seem like a comedy of errors . . . about choosing the best "negative impact." But on July 2, 1997, the "positive impact" of seeing the Great Basin APCD stand up to an institution as powerful as the DWP—at the cost of their own jobs—would stay with me forever.

CONCLUSION

On a cold November day in 2001, an unprecedented event occurred in Owens Valley. Water was released *voluntarily* from the Los Angeles Aqueduct back into Owens Lake. It was the first time the aqueduct had been cut open by something other than dynamite, allowing water to flow back into Owens Lake to implement shallow flooding on twelve square miles of lakebed. A crowd gathered to watch this symbolic event, which occurred almost ninety years after Owens River had been diverted to Los Angeles in November 1913. David Freeman said, "We had a big ceremony when we broke the hole in the aqueduct. People there never dreamed they would see the day when a drop of water would come out of that aqueduct and go to Owens Lake."[1] Now water is being returned to Owens Lake through a breach in the Los Angeles Aqueduct below Lone Pine. Currently the Department of Water and Power is sending 7 percent of its aqueduct water to flood portions of Owens Lake, having completed the first phase of the dust mitigation plan. By the end of 2006, the project will be entirely completed. At that time, the DWP estimates that it will have lost 30 percent of its aqueduct water. The aqueduct water is now being sprayed over 13.5 square miles of the lakebed from 5,000 "bubblers," or large sprinkler heads, during the windy season of September to June (see figure C.1). Thirty million saltgrass seedlings have been planted, and more are being planted every day (see figure C.2). Owens Lake is now a living experiment in what returning water will do to a decimated ecosystem. It is also an experiment in what losing water will do to Los Angeles.

I toured the lakebed again in April 2004 and saw brine flies, snowy plovers, Western phalanthropes, and California gulls. I had never seen any of these at the lake before. Even from the air, Owens Lake is now a different sight. Instead of a landscape that looks like snow, you can now see shal-

C.1. Shallow Flooding Bubbler on Owens Lake. Courtesy of Great Basin Air Pollution Control District, Bishop, CA.

C.2. Saltgrass fields on Owens Lake. Photo by Karen Piper. Used with permission.

low water glistening over a portion of the surface of the lake. Snowy plovers are returning, the salt grasses are growing, and the ecosystem is rapidly changing. It has yet to be seen what other plants will grow there and what animals will come back—or arrive for the first time. Owens Lake is in some ways a living work of art set in motion by the Great Basin APCD.

But Owens Lake has also become a developed landscape of roadways, tractors, piping, water filtering stations, and portable toilets. Plastic spikes cover the toilets, as well as any other stationary equipment, to keep ravens from landing there and preying on snowy plovers. There is also a new mining operation on the lakebed, by U.S. Borax, which hauls off the salty surface to processing plants elsewhere. The materials are used in cattle feed and in glass production. Pits filled with bright pink water surround mounds of drying soda at the mining site. The pink is caused by a unique kind of algae growth at Owens Lake, making the lake look like a Dr. Seuss landscape (see figure C.3). Owens Lake now appears to be a highly managed environment. It is certainly no longer forgotten. There are places on the lakebed where the grass is green and pools of water and bugs flow around the sprinkler heads. It is, for those who have breathed dust, a beautiful sight. For many, anything is better than the ninety years of dust they have endured.

On the lakebed today, a new landscape is emerging that is also changing the landscape of Los Angeles. The return of Owens River water not only has symbolic value for the Department of Water and Power. It also has a huge financial impact on the City. The DWP's accounting firm, Deloitte & Touche, has reported that the Department of Water and Power will be broke by 2006, the year that the restoration project must be complete.[2] The Department of Water and Power has already borrowed hundreds of millions of dollars for projects in Owens Valley for dust mitigation. Estimated payments to the contracting firm, CH2M Hill, have also doubled from $42 to $106 million. Today, the debt-to-revenue ratio of the DWP is precarious. "It would have been cheaper to cover the lake in dollar bills," DWP representative Pat Brown commented.[3] Deloitte & Touche have recommended that the DWP raise water rates 37 percent over the next five years simply to meet payroll costs.

Seven years ago, the Department of Water and Power talked about spending $50 to 60 million on dust mitigation measures. Today it is estimated that $521 million—or half a billion dollars—will be spent on the

C.3. U.S. Borax Mining Company. Photo by Karen Piper. Used with permission.

project.[4] This added expense has been due primarily to unexpected difficulties encountered in developing the project. According to Keeler resident and owner of the Cerro Gordo mine, Mike Patterson, managed vegetation has been put in the wrong areas, flooding is a "waste of water," and the flooding is drawing insects in droves—including no-seeums, horseflies, deer flies, and mosquitoes. Another problem is the muddy surface of the lakebed itself. "Tractors get stuck, bulldozers, excavators . . . everything gets stuck," Pat Brown complained. "We're making mud out of the lakebed."[5] In 2001, a DWP representative explained the progress of the project: "This year, they're just pulling their equipment out of the mud."[6] The DWP promotional video for the project explained that "standard tires sank and became hopelessly mired," so new tires had to be developed and placed on a special footing to keep them from sinking. Every time the equipment was moved, the footing had to be moved along with it. In 2004, DWP employee Pat Brown complained of the difficulty in fixing broken bubbler heads: "Not easy to sludge out through the quicksand and fix these things. . . ." He said that bubblers had to be repaired before the rains started, when the ground would be impossible to traverse. There are stories of DWP men being sucked up to their thighs in the mud and having to struggle to save their lives. Besides the mud, the wind has presented endless problems. Brown described a day during which twenty people were paid to sit in a hotel room all day because of the winds, which were blowing at sixty miles per hour.

In the areas where shallow flooding is being practiced, there have also been numerous problems to date. One problem is drainage. The water released onto the lake wants to flow to the lowest spot, the center, and pool there. So the Department of Water and Power has had to build a system of berms and breaks to keep water distributed around the lakebed rather than migrating to the center. Also, the bubblers that distribute the water immediately started clogging from silt carried down from the aqueduct because the mesh at the aqueduct opening was not fine enough. Because of this, a filtration system had to be built for the aqueduct water to filter out the silt. Today, on the lakebed, you can see filtration stations set up all over the lake, representing an additional cost to the DWP. Another, larger problem may be the growing insect population on the lake. "Last year," Mike Patterson said, "I killed three hundred or four hundred of them [mosquitoes]. . . .

We're trading one environmental problem for another. You'll be creating a
health threat for the whole western United States."[7] A report by the University of California, Davis, found that a rewatered Owens Lake created a
habitat suitable for four different encephalitis factors. To the south, West
Nile virus has already been discovered at the Salton Sea, and Owens Lake
is a becoming a perfect mosquito habitat at its delta. When asked about the
West Nile problem, Pat Brown of the Department of Water and Power
shrugged his shoulders and said it was "inevitable." "We're expecting to see
it here," he explained. Brown also agreed that shallow flooding was waste-
ful, especially when most irrigators were currently switching to drip systems. "Shallow flooding," he said, "utilizes, uses up, or wastes" more water
than managed vegetation does.

Saltgrass areas are also experiencing complications. Currently, 19.5
square miles of the lake bed have been covered with saltgrass, which is irrigated with a drip system. But, according to Pat Brown, four hundred acres
of saltgrass have to be replanted because they fell on land that was "too wet,
too dry, or too salty." The drip irrigation systems are also clogging because
of the brackish water, so they have to be flushed periodically with bleach
and sodium chloride. Finally, much of the saltier areas have to be flushed
with freshwater to leech out the salt before saltgrass will tolerate the soil.
Currently, 4 to 5 acre-feet of water are being used per acre to flush out the
soils. In other areas, the salty surface is being tilled into rows that line the
saltgrass seedlings on either side. But when it rains, rainfall pushes the salt
back down into the root zone. Therefore, the Department of Water and
Power has to irrigate *during* a rainstorm to maintain a positive pressure that
pushes the salty rainwater away from the saltgrass stands. Also, pooling
water alongside the main road had been killing saltgrass plugs. Because of
this, new drainage pipes had to be installed alongside the road.

Gravel, one of the proposed solutions, has been found to be insur-
mountably expensive, so an alternate solution for gravel-designated areas
has to be implemented. Pat Brown claimed that getting a permit for gravel
was impossible since there are simply no gravel operations in Owens Valley. Then the Department of Water and Power worried that winds would
blow sand over the gravel, eventually covering it. The DWP is also worried
about the effect of an earthquake on any of the solutions. Mike Patterson
explained, "If there's an earthquake, liquefaction would happen and swallow

the whole project." The Department of Water and Power may even potentially create an earthquake by pumping groundwater. Brown complained, "If you start taking pressure off this lake and cause an earthquake, who you gonna call? L.A., I guess." Besides that risk, there are already multiple earthquakes in this area. Gravel has been dropped as an alternative because of these problems, as well as the expense. "Gravel," Brown simply said, "is not going to fly." Currently, the Department of Water and Power is looking at the possibility of using native shrubs to cover the remaining section of the lakebed, since there is a mandate to use only native species on the lakebed. But this requires further study and further expense.

Another problem is managing wildlife. The Department of Water and Power is required to maintain 1,000 acres of the lakebed as bird habitat. Snowy plovers, California gulls, and other birds have been returning in droves to eat the flies on the muddy lakebed surface. The problem is that these birds are not staying in their allotted 1,000 acres of protected habitat. When they land in areas that are too salty, they die of toxic shock from drinking the briny water. In protected areas, a low salinity must be maintained so that brine flies can survive. The DWP is currently mixing water from Owens Lake's shallow brine pool with aqueduct water in an attempt to create the right salinity—but the lower the salinity, the higher the rate of evaporation. For this reason, the DWP does not want to maintain a low salinity on other sections of the lake. Also, the flood control system is turned off from June 30 to September 30, when dust storms do not occur. This may also lead to excessive bird kill as the water dries up, leaving birds to starve to death. Birds are also drawn to trenches following the main road, which provides a perfect windbreak for their nests, and then are run over by tractors and trucks. Finally, burrowing owls started to nest in the drainage pipes, forcing the DWP to cap all the drainage pipes on the lakebed.

All of these additional expenses and problems—mud, bird kill, wind, evaporation—are leading directly to increased water rates in Los Angeles. In addition to the infrastructure expenditures on the project, the Department of Water and Power will be required to spend $20 million a year to operate the project in perpetuity, primarily for replacement water for Los Angeles. When all the Owens Valley projects are completed, Los Angeles will be returning one-third of the aqueduct water to Owens Valley or

Mono Lake. This water must be replaced through conservation practices or purchased from California's water wholesaler, the Metropolitan Water District (MWD), which gets its water from the Colorado River and Northern California. The cost of this purchase is estimated to be $15 million a year for the 50,000 acre-feet a year of water needed when the project is fully finished. Because it is not as clean as Owens River water, MWD water requires extra expenses for purification. One Sierra Club activist suggested that the Department of Water and Power had actively tried to stall the dust mitigation project for so long simply because it was saving millions of dollars that would have gone to replacement water costs.[8]

Financial pressures within the Department of Water and Power have led to discussions of privatization. In 2001, the city hired the RAND Corporation to look into restructuring the DWP on a corporate model. RAND recommended turning the Department of Water and Power into a City-owned corporation, in which the City would be the sole shareholder.[9] Purportedly this would allow for greater flexibility in hiring and firing employees, as well as an ability to attract higher-waged corporate executives. In the meantime, private desalination plants are also looking into replenishing California's depleted water supply. Poseidon, a privately held company, has proposed building two of the biggest ocean-desalination plants in the Western Hemisphere—one in Huntington Beach and one in Carlsbad. Each would be capable of producing 50 million gallons of drinking water a day. The DWP is also planning to build its first desalination plant at Scattergood Generating Station in Playa del Rey, at an estimated cost of $69.5 million. Whether desalination will become a public or private industry in California is yet to be seen. It is, however, currently regarded as the only feasible answer to the upcoming water shortages. Interestingly, Owens Lake may be pushing forward new technologies in water reclamation as well as privatization of the water. Water privatization would finally make explicit the connection between the amount of money one has and the amount of water one receives. Huntington Beach Councilwoman Debbie Cook voted against private desalination projects, saying, "I think the public is very uncomfortable with the privatization of something as essential as water, especially after the energy crisis, and we saw the manipulation of energy."[10]

Ironically, the Department of Water and Power itself may be swallowed up in the trend to privatize public utilities. Besides the expense of cleaning up Owens Lake, there are large infrastructure repairs necessary for Los Angeles's water system. Large dams or irrigation systems that were built a century ago are now starting to crumble, desperately in need of upgrading, and public utilities in many cases are simply unable to fund the new infrastructure or repairs necessary for these old systems. The Los Angeles Aqueduct has been known to fail on several occasions, at one point sending 228 million gallons of water flowing into Owens Lake before the leak could be stopped.[11] The piping system for supplying Owens River water to the city has become corroded and needs to be replaced. There have also been problems with the reservoirs used to store the water. In 1963, the Baldwin Hills Reservoir failed, killing several people. In 1971, the Van Norman Dam cracked during an earthquake, and nearby residents had to be evacuated.[12] Most infamously, the St. Francis Dam, which was built by William Mulholland in 1926, failed in 1928, killing over five hundred people. Mulholland, who was never formally trained as an engineer, had placed the dam at a site where the soils were unstable. He had been called to look at the dam just hours before its collapse and declared that the leaks were safe. Today, the number of unsafe dams is increasing, particularly those that are susceptible to failure during hurricanes, earthquakes, or floods. Reservoirs are being filled with silt that is washed down rivers or off the mountains; the lifespan of dams is therefore automatically limited. But if all the environmental hazards created by urbanization were addressed and solved, including the potential for dam and levee failures, major public utilities could potentially be bankrupted.

Once Theodore Roosevelt argued that it "ought not to be within the power of private individuals to control such a necessary of life" as water. Today private companies are taking over water and electric systems across the country, as well as around the world. With water increasingly seen as a commodity, its very scarcity is making it an attractive investment for those who hope to market it in the future. Megacorporations such as Bechtel and Vivendi are now buying up public water utilities around the world and raising water prices. In 1997, United Water's Kinnaird Company was sold to Halliburton, at the time headed by Dick Cheney. For a time, Enron was also in the water business and eyeing California's water market. Now,

Cadiz, Inc. is proposing to mine the water beneath the Mojave Desert for sale to Los Angeles. In Bolivia, the corporate takeover of water supplies has already led to drastic water rate hikes. Maude Barlow commented, "This meant that water would now cost more than food; for those on minimum wage or unemployed, water bills suddenly accounted for close to half their monthly budgets."[13] Similarly, electricity shortages make money for corporations, as was seen in the recent deregulation crisis in California. In the late 1990s, deregulation forced the two top power companies, Southern California Edison and PG&E, to sell off their generators to the highest bidders, which included Duke, Reliant, Dynergy, and Enron of Texas. These companies then created artificial power shortages by making false announcements, shutting down power plants, and otherwise manufacturing an electricity "crisis" in order to raise prices and make millions of dollars.[14] Shortages led to blackouts throughout California, requiring the state ultimately to bail out the electricity distributors to get the lights turned back on. Enron executives manipulated the energy market to the point of nearly bankrupting the state, and some even joked about ruining California's economy. In tape-recorded phone conversations, one Enron employee said to another, "What we need to do is help in the cause of, ah, downfall of California." Another employee added, "This is where California breaks."[15]

The Department of Water and Power maintains its own generating systems, and so was unaffected by deregulation. After the deregulation of electricity in California, the DWP seemed to be the standard-bearer for the continuing value of public utilities. Roosevelt, it seemed, had been proven right about public power—areas served by the DWP were the only areas in Los Angeles that still had their lights on by 2001. Rolling blackouts shocked the city as power plants sat idle and flashlights were passed around the Huntington Library in Pasadena where I was working on this book. In some ways, the Department of Water and Power was lauded for being better than Southern California Edison and PG&E simply because as a municipal enterprise it was protected from deregulation laws. But today, despite the DWP's brief moment of glory, the forces of deregulation have not been stopped. Water, electricity, and pollution are being taken over daily by market forces, and the Department of Water and Power is still aware that it may have to privatize—or at least continue streamlining its operations—to keep up with current market trends.

Privatization, in true California fashion, thrives on disaster and shortages. For instance, the U.S. Global Water Corporation brochure advertises that it will "harvest the accelerating opportunity . . . as traditional sources of water around the world become progressively depleted and degraded."[16] Confiscated tapes from Enron traders recently revealed that even *faking* a shortage was good for business. Enron traders discussed shutting down power plants to increase demand and joked about the financial benefits of cutting off California's electricity—or even having disasters occur in the state. One trader, talking to a businessman who complained that his electricity rates had gone from $100 to $500 in a single month, advised him simply "MOVE." Later he described this conversation to another trader: "The guy was like horrified. I go, look, don't take it the wrong way. Move, it isn't getting fixed anytime soon." The conversation continued:

> BOB: That's so beautiful.
> KEVIN: Oh, the best thing that could happen is fuckin' an earthquake,
>   let that thing float out to the Pacific and let 'em use fuckin' candles.
> BOB: I know. Those guys—just cut 'em off.
> KEVIN: They're so fucked and they're so, like totally.
> BOB: They are so fucked. . . . They should just bring back fuckin' horses
>   and carriages, fuckin' lamps.[17]

These conversations, which were on tapes recently confiscated by the federal government, convey the idea that cutting people's electricity and water is good for business.[18] The traders even joke about starting a recession and watching the U.S. economy collapse. "We should all die," one employee said, and his colleague responded: "So we all just drink the fuckin' cool-aid [*sic*] and stick a fork in us. We're the Roman Empire. We're goin' fuckin' down."[19] For Enron traders, there was an almost suicidal pleasure in destruction, which was seen as bringing in money.

We are now living in a risk society where the consequences of modernization are beginning to overtake the benefits. How these consequences will be distributed—and who might benefit from them—is the question of this century. In the United States, it is generally the law that makes the ultimate decisions about the distribution of these risks. Litigation is the predominant lingua franca spoken in a risk society. Industry instigates risk, while science mitigates risk. But it is the law that arbitrates between industry and science in the course of mitigation negotiations. The problem emerges if the law serves or defends certain economic interests. Risk definition is a power-making business because it plays upon the public's fear. In the case of Owens Valley, the dust problem only reinforces outside control over the area, whether by the EPA, the State, or the City. As Jerry Gewe once said of Owens Valley, "When they have a problem, who do they turn to to solve the problem? It's always our equipment that bails them out."[20]

Those who see themselves at risk become the objects of concern in a risk society. The question is how much their fear will change the structure of society. Even if the risk is indeterminate, the fear of risk is overwhelming in many parts of the United States. This has significant impact on the economy and the actions of individuals. A culture living in fear of unknown or unaccounted-for risks, both political and environmental, is quickly growing in the United States. Terrorists are simply another unknown risk to which people fear they could be exposed. The world breaks down over time into those who have been exposed and those who have not. But does any of us know with any certainty the extent of our exposure?

By making people feel they have a choice in the extent to which they are exposed, the fear of risk is mitigated somewhat. You are given the illusion that a good duct-taping job will solve the problem. You're told that if you don't like it, you can always leave. Or as Gewe explained of people who moved into Ridgecrest, "They're making choices. They like the isolation of that location." But of course, only those who can afford to move away or know about the danger really have a choice. Those who remain and are exposed can always file a class action suit, but even this turns physical pain into an often very small per-capita gain while allowing industry to continue functioning. Sick individuals are hidden behind hospital walls with only their bodies to reveal the history of toxicity. These bodies are seen as individual units with individual histories of sickness, rather than cultural histories. Instead, there needs to be a new kind of history—what I would call a *cluster history*—that follows clusters of disease throughout the United States. Cluster histories would rewrite narratives of development as narratives of illness; they would read development in reverse, based upon its consequences and the impact on individual bodies.

In studying Owens Lake, I have tried to demonstrate that the notion of the "public good" has been flawed from the start. Large-scale state projects from the early twentieth century were often based in error and corruption—they were not the monuments to genius that they purported to be. At the same time, privatization as a solution today promises only larger mistakes and more corruption. Large-scale corporate enterprises often re-create many of the earlier mistakes of large-scale government enterprises, which often served private interests. A century ago, large-scale government "fixes" were often simply extensions of private interests, such as that of the real estate speculators in the San Fernando Valley. Today these same "fixes" are often mere extensions of government interests. For instance, energy deregulation directly benefited Dick Cheney, who also benefited from the water privation business with Halliburton. Cadiz, Inc. has also been charged with public-private collusion. In 2002, the watchdog group "Public Citizen" noticed that many California water board members and politicians were also employees of or investors in Cadiz. Deregulation, in the case of energy, was a way to regulate for more profit in an economy where profits seemed to be dwindling and thus hurting the current administration.

It is yet to be seen whether bringing water back to Owens Lake will be a first step in regulating for fairness—or whether risk will simply be shifted to another poor community. It is important to watch, in a cluster history, where risk *moves*. If Owens Lake is "cleaned up" by withholding water from border towns in Mexico, for instance, the burden of risk will have simply shifted. If the lakebed is pumped, leading to an earthquake or further environmental degradation, the burden of risk will also have shifted. If, however, the lawns of Beverly Hills finally go dry in order to protect the health of Owens Valley residents, we will know that equity is growing. But if the lawns of Beverly Hills are still green when people are sick from lack of clean water, we will recognize that corruption exists somewhere. In the West, lawns are monuments to corruption. On average, 50 to 70 percent of home water is used outdoors for watering lawns and gardens . . . and water use in the West, just as it was a century ago, is still almost double that in the East.[21] While the use of water was once lauded as a sign of progress and civilization in the West, it is now seen as an environmental irresponsibility.

While water is wasted in Los Angeles, those who have breathed the dust from Owens Lake still do not have any compensation for their suffering. In 1998, Sen. Pete Knight introduced a bill that would set up a trust fund to "compensate victims of the pollution . . . for their medical expenses and pain."[22] Though the State Senate passed Pete Knight's bill by a narrow margin, the bill died in the State Assembly. Now there is no mechanism set up to compensate those who have become sick or died because of dust exposure. Providing compensation in this case would mean admitting a direct connection between dust and illness, and even many residents do not want to believe that there has ever been any risk. It would have been better for all of us if the dust were simply safe to breathe.

Meanwhile, as we get sick, or don't get sick, Owens Lake is shifting again. Today, ironically, Owens Lake sports a giant "Think Safety" sign for contractors working on dust mitigation (see figure C.4). After eighty years of danger, this sign raises chuckles among Owens Valley residents in its bizarre juxtaposition of meanings. The City of Los Angeles tries to ignore the serious health risk of Owens Lake dust but worries about a contractor dropping something on his foot. But Owens Lake has always boasted a strange conglomeration of conflicting meanings and interpretations. An employee from the Ridgecrest Bureau of Land Management once told me, "Owens Lake is a moving target." He explained that there are so many different groups invested in defining the lakebed that you can never really get a handle on what it means. You thought you knew what would happen, he said, and then all the definitions shifted. As I wrote this book, I experienced the shifting borders of Owens Lake. At times it seemed to encapsulate Los Angeles's history; at other times, it did not even seem to exist. There were times when I would stand in the middle of Owens Lake and see nothing but heat waves mimicking water. There were other times when the lake looked full and I couldn't even walk on the surface without being sucked into its mud. Deciphering Owens Lake is a tricky business. It will cost hundreds of millions of dollars to build a piping and irrigation system that will have to be maintained in perpetuity—or as long as the City can afford to do so. In *The Control of Nature*, John McPhee suggests that attempts to control the natural world often lead to the need for escalating expenses and infrastructure as the world reacts to every action imposed upon it.[23] In the case of Owens Lake, the deputy mayor of Los Angeles,

C.4. "Think Safety." Photo by Shane Bradley. Used with permission.

Chris O'Donnell, stated that accepting responsibility for the dust will "place a significant burden—economic and otherwise—on Los Angeles."[24] The ultimate price tag for this burden is not yet calculable.

My body is similarly a tricky business now. It is just as hard to get a handle on sometimes. I live with the fear of cancer and autoimmune disorders. I know these diseases are just *risks*. I know my risk has been increased so many times per million people. It is hard to know what that means. My lungs have permanent scar tissue and my sinuses have been damaged. This at least seems *real*. Doctors look at my X-rays and see something they can explain to me. I don't want to admit, however, that X-rays and MRIs are the only honest language left. I don't want to admit that tumors are the last common language of a risk society . . . or that hospitals are our new scientific hope, our new engineering wonders, and our new homes. So for now, I will watch the water bubbling out onto Owens Lake and wait to see what it will bring. I know that it cannot remove the heavy metals from my lungs . . . but I also know that watching it trickle across the dry land feels like a soothing balm.

EPILOGUE

The idea for this book came from my father, who told me stories of "better days" when steamships sailed across Owens Lake. At the time, he was losing his own memories to Alzheimer's, so the memories he gave me seemed even more precious. My father's stories set me on a ten-year quest to try to reimagine the lake even as I watched him disappear. This book was motivated initially by nostalgia and a desire to hang on. But in the course of writing it, my father has died and my nostalgia has waned. I cannot say that I would go so far as Ted Schade in saying, "We'd layer it with tires if we could." But I can understand the frustration in such a statement when the immediacy of illness is everywhere. I ended this book simply by expressing the wish to breathe well and not develop cancer.

Today, Owens Lake dust is dissipating, though what may happen to the lake over the long run is unknown. In 2001, the Department of Water and Power placed a commemorative plaque beside the lakebed that reads, "Owens Lake was once 300 feet deep and part of a large ancient freshwater lake. As the climate changed over centuries, the lake began to dry up. . . . By 1905, diversion of water by farmers in the Owens Valley, coupled with drought in the region, had shrunk the lake even further. . . ." The roadside plaque was meant to commemorate the beginning of the dust control program in 2001. The inscription ends, "This program is part of a series of actions in which the City of Los Angeles and the Department of Water and Power have taken positive steps to protect the environment." This is all most passing motorists will ever know about Owens Lake—that the farmers and climate dried it up and the City of Los Angeles stepped in to protect it. But in reality, the City drained the lake and the people of Owens Valley fought for decades to save it. Finally they won a small battle, a victory for which the Department of Water and Power now takes credit.

The irony of that plaque couldn't be more perfect, a monument to lost history. The words register the defeat of a people whose story was silenced, and the bleak landscape behind the plaque betrays its optimism. While the plaque attempts to solidify and circumscribe history, making one version permanent, the story has not ended for Los Angeles.

To the south, the Salton Sea, which is California's largest inland sea, is now exhibiting the same tendency to evaporate and blow dust. Some say it will be an even bigger problem than Owens Lake, because it is an even bigger lake. The Salton Sea is thirty-two miles southeast of Riverside, a suburb of Los Angeles, and ninety miles east of San Diego. It extends all the way down to the Mexican border. It was created in 1905, when an irrigation canal from the Colorado River to the Imperial Valley (called the All American Canal because it was meant to keep water from Mexico) broke and sent water pouring into the Imperial Valley. This created one of the largest salt seas, 376 square miles, in the world. Two years later, the leak was stopped after a special train rail line and depot had been constructed to haul in supplies for an earthen dam to be built. Afterward, irrigation fields were maintained around the south end of the lake. Real estate speculators, touting the new lake as a tourist destination, subdivided and sold plots on the north shore, creating a new town, Salton City. Fish were introduced to the lake in order to try to turn the area into a resort fishing destination. This worked for a while, and Salton City drew a decent tourist crowd.

But the Salton Sea, like much of California, never quite lived up to its advertisements. There was no beach, the water smelled, and the salty earth made it impossible to grow trees for shade. The main problem was the instability of the lake itself. One year it flooded, destroying Salton City, which was never rebuilt. Then it started shrinking, becoming more and more saline as it disappeared. The lake had no outlet and, like the Owens Lake, evaporated very quickly. It was maintained only by the surrounding farms' irrigation runoff, which was also salty and so raised the salt levels in the lake. Eventually the saline conditions killed massive numbers of fish. Today the lake is dying, surrounded by piles of dead fish and birds and the smell of sulphur. When Owens Lake dried up, the migrating birds began flying south to the next lake they could find, Salton Sea, so the lake is environmentally crucial as well as essential for human health. Without this last remaining flyway stopover, the birds would have nowhere to go. But as the lake shrinks, dust with a similar composition to that of Owens Lake—with some pesticides added—is blowing around the Salton Sea.

In the Imperial Valley, corporate and absentee farmers grow produce, mainly alfalfa, which feeds the largest cattle feedlots in California. The feedlots are largely owned by Brawley Beef, whose grain is grown by El Toro Export LLC. Sixty percent of the land is owned by absentee landlords, and the majority of workers are bussed across the border from Mexico.[1] Some Mexicans return home after work, and some remain in *colonias*, informal groups of people sleeping in tents, mobile homes, or cardboard boxes, and lacking adequate water or plumbing services. There are currently fifteen registered *colonias* around the Salton Sea. In Imperial County, between 1990 and 2002, the unemployment ranged between 20 to 30 percent, three to five times the national average. Seventy-three percent of Imperial County residents are Hispanic, and in 2000, 29 percent of its children lived in poverty.[2] These are the people the dust will hit when it blows.

As the Salton Sea dries up, however, the dust from its surface threatens to cover all of Los Angeles, San Diego, Palm Springs, and other cities in Arizona and Mexico. For this reason, Sonny Bono, who was the mayor of Palm Springs before his election to Congress, was also a strong advocate of saving the lake. Today, his widow, Mary Bono, is pushing for the same thing. The problem with the Salton Sea is that it was never a natural lake. It was always a mistake, and many environmentalists still wish that this mistake could just be erased.

The reason the Salton Sea is shrinking rapidly now is that urban growth in Southern California has put a high demand on water that previously flowed into the lake. In this case, the city of San Diego is diverting water away from the farms surrounding the Salton Sea in order to fuel its growth, which then frees up water for the Metropolitan Water District to sell to Los Angeles. Since other sources are disappearing, Los Angeles has to rely more on the MWD for its water. But to replace the Owens Lake problem with a Salton Sea problem could be catastrophic in terms of the immensity of the dust it would create as well as the number of people who would be affected. On the other hand, simply keeping the water in the Imperial Valley will not solve the problem, either. Since the irrigation runoff water is already salty, the salinity of the lake would continue to increase if the water goes to farmers first. Also, pesticides, nutrients, and selenium are running into the lake from agricultural runoff. The only way to keep the dust from blowing without endangering the bird and fish life would be to maintain the lake with an enormous supply of fresh water or to build a desalination plant to remove salt from the irrigation runoff. Proponents of lake restoration are advocating the latter—but this is another huge expense that no one wants to pay, with start-up costs estimated at $2.3 billion.[3] Even then, the lake will have to be monitored in perpetuity to maintain a precise saline-freshwater balance. The selenium and pesticide problem remains unsolved. A third alternative is currently being developed: it involves building a dam in the middle of the lake and maintaining half of it while turning the rest into saline wetlands or dry land. The problem is still the selenium runoff, as well as the dust problem that will be created. But in this model, money will be generated by the sale of excess water to urban areas. The issue in the long run will be the amount of money required to maintain this semi-disaster.

The Salton Sea ultimately destroyed my faith in restoration simply because it is impossible to restore without requiring the whole Southwest to relocate for a few hundred years until the dust settles. Even then, the landscape would be irrevocably changed. The Salton Sea is a lake that never should have been, but the area can never go back to a better time. The myth of restoration is the myth of undoing what has been done, of using science to simulate a precolonial landscape in a small pocket of that colonial world. But without undoing the whole system, this simulation will remain only that—a photograph in miniature of what we believe was once a better time.

In *Faking Nature,* Robert Elliott makes a similar argument, suggesting that all we can do by our attempts to restore the natural environment is to make a bad copy. Elliott compares this to reproductions of paintings, which can never be worth the same as the originals.[4] I would go beyond this and argue that what restoration provides is an outlet for nostalgia. In colonial societies, it is not uncommon to have a concomitant sense of loss about what is being settled—and therefore destroyed. "Pristine," in this sense, is the memory of first contact. Restoration is a method of assuaging colonial guilt or undoing what was done. It is the metaphorical equivalent of the media manufacturing the peaceful, nature-loving "Indian" while at the same time massacring or ignoring real Indians. "Nature" is similarly resurrected as the simulation of what once was—beautiful, whole, clean—as urbanization proceeds unchecked and the industries that destroyed this environment are not called into question. But scientists are not good forgers. The environment cannot be changed without the help of industry. The damage cannot be undone without honestly confronting the source of the damage.

In this case, a great part of the damage is being caused by agricultural runoff that is polluted. And so a simple solution would be to eliminate the farms and feedlots that contribute to both the salinity and the chemical pollution of the lake. In essence, by continuing to support the beef industry in this area, the U.S. Government is also being forced to support an enormous clean-up effort in its wake. Maybe the desert is not the best place to grow alfalfa or keep cows. But our devotion to maintaining things as they are may ultimately prove our undoing in this war against natural processes.

The case of the Salton Sea will reveal, I believe, the limits of our ability to fix what has been broken. Yet the sea will nonetheless demand to be fixed. It will most likely remain an irritant and permanent fiasco. But if nothing else, it will stand as a reminder of the need for humility rather than bravado in our dialogue with the natural world. It will force us to keep talking. It will remind us that mistakes or abusive behavior cannot be erased any more than abusive behavior toward another human being is easily forgotten. If it is forgotten for a while, the memory usually returns—along with anger and the desire for revenge. I do not want to anthropomorphize the natural world, but it is, indeed, extracting its revenge now. The Salton Sea will have to be maintained, and millions or billions of dollars spent to maintain it. Otherwise, the dust will begin gradually drifting once again into the City of Los Angeles.

NOTES

Introduction

1. M. C. Reheis, "Dust Deposition Downwind of Owens (Dry) Lake, 1991–1994: Preliminary Findings," *Journal of Geophysical Research,* v. 102 (1997), pp. 25–26.
2. Quoted in Marla Cone, "Owens Valley Plan Seeks L.A. Water to Curb Pollution," *Los Angeles Times,* December 17, 1996.
3. "Visiting Owens Dry Lake with Huell Howser," #943, Huell Howser Productions, 2001.
4. See Michael Castleman, "'Tiny Particles, Big Problems," *Sierra,* November/December (1995): 26–27. In 1994, this study was repeated with 552,000 people in 151 cities, and the results were the same.
5. M. C. Reheis, "Dust Deposition Downwind of Owens (Dry) Lake, 1991–1994: Preliminary Findings," pp. 25–26.
6. Information about cadmium is from the "Toxicological Profile for Cadmium" by the U.S. Department of Health and Human Services, as well as *Cadmium in the Environment* by Hans Mislin and Oscar Ravera (Boston: Birkhauser, 1986). Information about nickel is from the same series of reports, entitled, "Toxicological Profile for Nickel." Information on selenium is from the medical data sheet in *Heavy Metal Hazards.* See also "State of Knowledge Report: Air Toxics and Indoor Air Quality in Australia 2001," *Environment Australia 2001,* <www.deh.gov.au/atmosphere/air-toxics/sok/profiles/respirable.html> (May 21, 2004).
7. Testimony of Theodore D. Schade, Great Basin Air Pollution Control District, "California State Water Resources Control Board Hearing Regarding Salton Sea," 2002.

8. T. E. Gill and D. A. Gillette, "Owens Lake: A Natural Laboratory for Aridification, Playa Desiccation and Desert Dust," *Geological Society of America: Abstracts with Programs,* v. 23, no. 5, 1991.

9. "Meeting Before the California Air Resources Board," Board Hearing Room, Sacramento, California, May 22, 1998, p. 186.

10. Quoted in Michael Fleeman, "Thirsty Town Fights L.A. for its Water," *Detroit News,* September 4, 1997.

11. "Meeting to Adopt the PM-10 Demonstration of Attainment SIP (PM-10 Attainment Plan)" at the Inyo County Courthouse, July 2, 1997.

12. Ibid.

13. Ibid.

14. Reheis, pp. 25–26.

15. "Meeting to Adopt the PM-10 Demonstration of Attainment SIP (PM-10 Attainment Plan)" at the Inyo County Courthouse, July 2, 1997.

16. David Babb, *101 Moments in Eastern Sierra History* (Bishop, CA: Community Printing and Publishing, 1999), pp. 100–101.

17. Harvey O. Banks and Edmund Brown, "Reconnaissance Investigation of Water Resources of Mono and Owens Basins, Mono and Inyo Counties," State of California, Department of Water Resources, August 1960, p. 62.

18. County of Inyo, Grand Jury, "Grand Jury Report for 1974–75," 1974.

19. U.S. Environmental Protection Agency, "Owens Valley Particulate Matter Plan: History of Particulate Matter (PM-10) Planning Efforts." <http://www.epa.gov/region09/air/owens/history.html> (September 29, 1999.)

20. Great Basin Air Pollution Control District, *Owens Valley PM10 Planning Area Demonstration of Attainment State Implementation Plan,* May 1997, pp. 2–7.

21. Ibid., p. ES-1.

22. Andrew Sasz, *EcoPopulism: Toxic Waste and the Movement for Environmental Justice* (Minneapolis: University of Minnesota Press, 1994), p. 31.

23. "Meeting Before the California Air Resources Board," p. 197.

24. J. J. Johnston, "Owens Lake: More than Air Problem," *Daily Independent,* November 11, 1977.

25. Linda Saholt, "Restoration and Advisory Board to Meet Dec. 13," *Daily Independent,* December 12, 2000.

26. Andrew Walters, "Study Backs Concerns Over Owens Lake Dust, Health," *Daily Independent,* January 28, 1998. See also Julian Lukins, "Air Base, Tribes Nix Dust Pact," *Daily Independent,* December 16, 1997.

27. Interview with Lou Paracchia in his home on July 6, 1999.

28. Quoted in William Overend, "Inyo County: Land of the New Colonials?" *Los Angeles Times,* January 4, 1981.

29. Ulrich Beck, *Ecological Enlightenment* (Atlantic Highlands, NJ: Humanities Press International, 1995), p. 2. See also Ulrich Beck, "Risk Society Revisited: Theory, Politics, and Research Programmes," *The Risk Society and Beyond: Critical Issues for Social Theory,* ed. Barbara Adam, Ulrich Beck, and Joost Van Loon (London: Sage, 2000).

30. David Babb, p. 73.

31. Quoted in Joan Brooks, *Desert Padre: The Life and Writings of Father John J. Crowley, 1891–1940* (Desert Hot Springs, CA: Mesquite Press, 1997), p. 103.

32. *Annual Report of the Board of Water Commissioners of the Domestic Water Works System of the City of Los Angeles,* p. 79. "Tenth Annual Report of the Board of Public Service Commissioners of the City of Los Angeles," Bureau of Water Works and Supply, Los Angeles, June 30, 1911, Department of Water and Power Library, p. 63.

33. Joseph McBride, ed., *Filmmakers on Filmmaking,* Vol. 2 (Los Angeles: J. P. Tarcher, 1983).

34. Quoted in Michael London, "Watered-Down Drama," *Los Angeles Times,* April 3, 1983.

35. Quoted in "Cadillac Desert: Water and the Transformation of Nature," PBS Series, 1996.

36. The quotes from this paragraph are all from Michael London.

37. Ibid.

38. Hall Daily, "David-Goliath Fight Continues Over Water from Owens Valley," *Bakersfield Californian,* October 26, 1980.

39. Thomas E. Gill and Thomas A. Cahill, "Playa-Generated Dust Storms from Owens Lake," *The History of Water: Eastern Sierra Nevada, Owens Valley, White-Inyo Mountains* (Los Angeles: White Mountain Research Station, 1992), p. 65.

40. "Meeting of the California Air Resources Board," pp. 204–205.

41. Interview with Jerry Gewe at his office on June 25, 1997.

42. See also Page Stegner, "Water and Power," *Harper's*, March 1981, p. 65.

43. Norris Hundley, Jr., *The Great Thirst: Californians and Water, 1770s–1990s* (Berkeley: University of California Press, 1992), pp. 296, 385.

44. Interview with Jerry Gewe at his office on June 25, 1997.

45. Janet Allen, "The Real Erin Brockovich: Deadly Chromium 6 in L.A.'s Water," *Whole Life Times*, April 2001, p. 27.

46. Interview with Jerry Gewe at his office on June 25, 1997.

47. B. Wynne, "Risk and Social Learning: Reification to Engagement," in *Social Theories of Risk*, ed. S. Krimsky and D. Golding (Westport, CT: Praeger, 1992).

48. "Political Difficulties Facing Waste-to-Energy Conversion Plant Siting, Report for the California Waste Management Board," Technical Information Series, Los Angeles: Cerrell Associates, Inc., 1984. See Andrew Sasz, *Ecopopulism: Toxic Waste and the Movement for Environmental Justice* (Minneapolis: University of Minnesota Press, 1995), pp. 105–108.

49. "Meeting Before the California Air Resources Board," p. 135.

50. Janet Allen, "The Real Erin Brockovich: Deadly Chromium 6 in L.A.'s Water," *Whole Life Times*, April 2001, pp. 27, 63.

51. From an unpublished paper by Andrew Hurley, University of Missouri–St. Louis, entitled, "Rethinking Urban Environmental History through Comparative Analysis: A Look at Los Angeles and Mexico City" (2002).

52. Memo from Lawrence H. Summers to "Distribution" at the World Bank, December 12, 1991 <http://www.whirledbank.org/ourwords/summers.html> (August 25, 2002)

53. Norris Hundley, Jr., p. 152.

54. Note from Lawrence Summers to Kenneth Lay, May 25, 1999. Quoted in "Enron Lobbying Correction: $2.5 Million for Six Months of Pressing its Agenda on Bush Administration, Congress," *News-Star*, March 8, 2002.

55. Christopher Schwarzen, "Enron Tapes Back Case for Refunds, Local Utility Contends," *The Seattle* Times, June 3, 2004.

56. Testimony by Lynn Scarlett before U.S. Senate Environment and Public Works Committee State Environmental Innovations, May 2, 2000.

57. "Meeting to Adopt the PM-10 Demonstration of Attainment SIP (PM-10 Attainment Plan)" at the Inyo County Courthouse, July 2, 1997.

Chapter One

1. This is from a personal interview at the Los Angeles Aqueduct Intake, Owens Valley, in May of 1997.

2. Los Angeles Department of Water and Power, "A Hundred or a Thousand Fold More Important," <web.ladwp.com/~wsoweb/Aqueduct/historyoflaa/hundred.htm> (August 1, 2002).

3. Quoted in John Walton, *Western Times and Water Wars: State, Culture, and Rebellion in California* (Berkeley: University of California Press, 1992), p. 132.

4. Abraham Hoffman, *Vision or Villainy: Origins of the Owens Valley–Los Angeles Water Controversy* (College Station: Texas A&M University Press, 1981), p. xv.

5. Quoted in Catherine Mulholland, *William Mulholland and the Rise of Los Angeles* (Berkeley: University of California Press, 2000), p. 133.

6. Los Angeles Department of Water and Power, "A Hundred or a Thousand Fold More Important," <http://wsoweb.ladwp.com/Aqueduct/historyoflaa/hundred/htm> (August 1, 2002).

7. Theodore Roosevelt, "The Expansion of the White Races," Address at the Celebration of the African Diamond Jubilee of the Methodist Episcopal Church, Washington, D. C., January 18, 1909. Quoted in Theodore Roosevelt, *American Problems* (New York: Charles Scribner's Sons, 1926).

8. Quoted in Neil Smith, *Uneven Development* (New York: Basil Blackwell, 1984), p. 60.

9. Theodore Roosevelt, "The Administration of the Island Possessions," Address at the Coliseum, Hartford, Conn., August 22, 1902. Quoted in Theodore Roosevelt, *American Problems* (New York: Charles Scribner's Sons, 1926).

10. Theodore Roosevelt, "Expansion and Peace," *Independent,* December 21, 1899.

11. Quoted in Kevin Starr, *Material Dreams: Southern California through the 1920s* (Oxford: Oxford University Press, 1990), p. 137.

12. As Arundhati Roy complained, large-scale water development projects are simply a way of gaining authority by taking water from the poor and gifting it to the rich. A. Roy, "The Greater Common Good," *The Cost of Living* (New York: Modern Library, 1999), p. 16.

13. W. M. Mulholland, "Water Commissioners' Report, Including Report on Water Supply, for the Year Ending November 30, 1905," Los Angeles, 1906, Department of Water and Power Library, p. 25.

14. *Annual Report of the Board of Water Commissioners of the Domestic Water Works System of the City of Los Angeles* (Los Angeles: Press of the Out West Company, 1902), p. 79.

15. Morrow Mayo, *Los Angeles* (New York: Knopf, 1933).

16. Catherine Mulholland, *William Mulholland and the Rise of Los Angeles* (Berkeley: University of California Press, 2000), p. 262.

17. Quoted in W. A. Chalfant, *Story of Inyo* (Bishop, CA: Chalfant Press, 1933), p. 408.

18. Quoted in Mark Pahuta, "Sand Canyon Station," 1998.

19. "Vigilance," *The Intake*, June/July 1930.

20. Edwin F. L. Nevin, "Esprit de Corps," *The Intake*, Vol. 1, No. 1, March, 1924, p. 4.

21. Catherine Mulholland, *William Mulholland and the Rise of Los Angeles* (Berkeley: University of California Press, 2000), p. 159.

22. City of Los Angeles, "Second Annual Report of the Bureau of the Los Angeles Aqueduct," December 5, 1907, Department of Water and Power Library, p. 14.

23. *The Intake*, December 1928 (advertisement).

24. "On Guard," *The Intake*, April/May 1934.

25. Mulholland, xv.

26. Quoted in Mulholland, p. 244.

27. K. Starr, *Material Dreams* (New York: Oxford University Press, 1990), p. 59.

28. Norman Smith, *A History of Dams* (Secaucus, NJ: The Citadel Press, 1972), p. 217.

29. Donald Worster, *Rivers of Empire: Water, Aridity, and the Growth of the American West* (Oxford: Oxford University Press, 1985), p. 143.

30. Worster, pp. 148–149.

31. Starr, p. 13.

32. Starr, p. 17.

33. Los Angeles Department of Water and Power, *Sharing the Vision: The Story of the Los Angeles Aqueduct,* 1988.

34. Los Angeles Department of Water and Power, "William Mulholland: The Man Who Built the Los Angeles–Owens River Aqueduct." (September 2, 2002) <http://www.ladwp.com/aboutdwp/history/mulholl/mulholl.htm>

35. Mulholland, p. 245.

36. Los Angeles Department of Water and Power, *Sharing the Vision: The Story of the Los Angeles Aqueduct,* 1988.

37. *The Intake,* December 1928 (advertisement).

38. *The Intake,* December 1939 (advertisement).

39. *The Intake,* December 1940 (advertisement).

40. Starr, *Material Dreams,* p. 57.

41. Mulholland, p. 156.

42. Raymond G. Taylor, *Men, Medicine, and Water: The Building of the Los Angeles Aqueduct, 1908–1913* (Los Angeles: Friends of the LACMA Library), 1982, p. 56.

43. Ibid., p. 117.

44. Abraham Hoffman, *Vision or Villainy: Origins of the Owens Valley–Los Angeles Water Controversy* (College Station: Texas A&M University Press, 1981), p. 150.

45. Remi A. Nadeau, *The Water Seekers,* 4th edition (Santa Barbara: Crest Publishers, 1997), p. 43.

46. Quoted in ibid., p. 43.

47. Jane Thomann, *Zig-Zag Post Office and its Neighbors, 1885 to 1971* (Ridgecrest, CA: Historical Society of the Upper Mojave Desert, 1996), p. 75.

48. Ibid., p. 102.

49. Quoted in Pahuta, "Sand Canyon Station," 1998.

50. *How It Was: Some Memories by Early Settlers of the Indian Wells Valley and Vicinity* (Ridgecrest, CA: Historical Society of the Upper Mojave Desert, 1994), p. 2.

51. Quoted in Pahuta.

52. Quoted in Nadeau, p. 43.

53. Wilma R. Olson, *Olancha Remembered* (Sacramento, CA: W. R. Olson, 1997), p. 65.

54. "Fourteenth Annual Report of the Board of Public Service Commissioners of the City of Los Angeles," Bureau of Water Works and

Supply, Bureau of Power and Light, June 30, 1915, Department of Water and Power Library, p. 33.

55. Mulholland, p. 262.

56. W. A. Chalfant, *The Story of Inyo* (Bishop, CA: Chalfant Press, 1933), p. 396.

57. *How It Was: Some Memories by Early Settlers of the Indian Wells Valley and Vicinity*, p. 53.

58. Ibid., pp. 28–29.

59. Ken Wortley, *Adventures with the Misfits* (Pub. by Author: 1984), p. 105.

60. Ibid., p. 105.

61. Michael Sayer and Albert E. Kahn, *Sabotage! The Secret War Against America* (New York; London: Harper and Brothers, 1942), p. 62.

62. Ibid., p. 62.

63. Quoted in Pahuta.

64. *Los Angeles Times*, August 28, 1942.

65. "To All Employees of the Department of Water and Power," *Los Angeles Times*, August 21, 1942.

66. "Troops Ready to Take Over City Utilities," *Los Angeles Times*, February 23, 1944.

67. "Strike Three," *The Intake*, November-December 1993, p. 3.

68. "Healing Relationships: The Strike Revisited," *The Intake*, November-December 1993, p. 6.

69. Ibid, p. 6.

70. "A Grim Diagnosis: But the Prognosis for a Healthy Recovery is Good," *The Intake*, June-July 1994, p. 8.

71. Los Angeles City Civil Service Department. "Basic Space Survey Guided Basic Building Plan," *The Newsletter*, Vol. 5, No. 12 (June 1965), p. 3.

72. "A Grim Diagnosis: But the Prognosis for a Healthy Recovery is Good," *The Intake*, June-July 1994, p. 8.

73. Richard Knox, "Remarks Before the Great Basin Air Pollution Control District," July 2, 1997, p. 1.

74. Richard Knox, "Riordan's Remark Insensitive to Valley's History," *Inyo Register*, August 26, 1997.

75. Ibid.

76. "Jawbone Canyon," *Antelope Valley Press*, October 1, 1998. See also Stacy Matros, "Jawbone Canyon Store Reduced to Ashes," *Antelope Valley Press*, December 16, 1998.

77. Quoted in William Overend, "Inyo Counties: Land of the New Colonials?" *Los Angeles Times,* January 4, 1981.

78. Ibid.

79. Ibid.

80. Interview with Jerry Gewe at his office on June 25, 1997.

81. David Isenberg, "Less Talk, More Walk: Strengthening Homeland Security Now," Center for Defense Information, January 15, 2003.

82. Office of Mayor James K. Hahn, Memo for Immediate Release, "Mayor Hahn, LADWP Announce Increased Security Measures for LA's Water and Power System: Enhanced Protection of City's Utility Comes as War Begins," March 20, 2003.

83. Los Angeles Department of Water and Power, "William Mulholland: The Man Who Built the Los Angeles–Owens River Aqueduct," <http://www.ladwp.com/aboutdwp/history/mulholl/mulholl.htm> (September 2, 2002).

84. David Babb, p. 103.

85. Michael Hardt and Antonio Negri, *Empire* (Cambridge, MA: Harvard University Press, 2001), p. 135.

Chapter Two

1. The Los Angeles Department of Water and Power, "Annual Water Quality Report for 1999."

2. D. J. Waldie, "The Myth of the L.A. River," *Buzz* 7 (4): 80–85, April 1996.

3. Quoted in Catherine Mulholland, *William Mulholland and the Rise of Los Angeles* (Berkeley: University of California Press, 2000), p. 206.

4. "Tenth Annual Report of the Board of Public Service Commissioners of the City of Los Angeles," Bureau of Water Works and Supply, Los Angeles, June 30, 1911, Department of Water and Power Library, p. 49.

5. Ibid., p. 63.

6. Blake Gumprecht, *The Los Angeles River: Its Life, Death, and Possible Rebirth* (Baltimore: The Johns Hopkins University Press, 1999), p. 118.

7. Marc Reisner, *Overtapped Oasis: Reform or Revolution for Western Water* (Washington, D.C.: Island Press, 1990), p. 70.

8. John and Laree Caughey, *Los Angeles: Biography of a City* (Berkeley: University of California Press, 1977), p. 138.

9. Quoted in Gumprecht, p. 113.

10. Quoted in Mulholland, p. 27.

11. Quoted in ibid., p. 27.

12. Quoted in ibid., p. 27.

13. John and Laree Caughey, *Los Angeles: Biography of a City,* p. 174.

14. Ibid., p. 174.

15. Quoted in Mulholland, p. 14.

16. Ibid., p. 33.

17. Charles Houser, "The Story of Our City and Its Environments," *The Intake,* January 1926, p. 15.

18. P. B. Hardesty, "Genesis, or In the Beginning," *The Intake,* April 1924, p. 6.

19. Kevin Starr, *Material Dreams* (New York: Oxford University Press, 1990), p. 3.

20. Norman Smith, *A History of Dams* (Secaucus, NJ: The Citadel Press), 1972, p. 117.

21. Ibid., pp. 121, 128.

22. *Annual Report of the Board of Water Commissioners of the Domestic Water Works System of the City of Los Angeles* (Los Angeles: Press of the Out West Company, 1902), p. 29.

23. Ibid., p. 29.

24. Theodore Roosevelt, *On Race, Riots, Reds, Crime,* ed. Archibald Roosevelt (Metairie, LA: Sons of Liberty, 1968), p. 15.

25. Raphael J. Sonenshein, *Politics in Black and White* (Princeton, NJ: Princeton University Press, 1994), p. 27.

26. Mike Davis, *Ecology of Fear: Los Angeles and the Imagination of Disaster* (New York: Vintage, 1999), p. 162.

27. Quoted in Starr, p. 120.

28. Ibid., p. 10. In 1948, race restrictive covenants were outlawed in Los Angeles, and Anglos began to move outside the city limits, where they could create municipalities with new race-restrictive regulations. By 1950, Los Angeles contained 78 percent of the blacks in the county—suburbs outside the city boundaries, in contrast, were predominantly white. Keith E. Collins, *Black Los Angeles: The Maturing of the Ghetto, 1940–1950* (Saratoga, CA: Century Twenty One Publishing, 1980), p. 19.

29. Sonenshein, p. 28.

30. Gumprecht, p. 26.

31. Quoted in Collins, p. 70.

32. Gumprecht, pp. 28–29.

33. Daryl F. Gates, *My Life in the LAPD* (New York: Bantam Books, 1992), p. 39.

34. Ibid., p. 39.

35. Ibid., p. 109.

36. Ibid., p. 117.

37. Ibid., p. 222.

38. Michael Finnegan, Patrick McGreevy, and Sue Fox, "Valley Could Split from L.A., but at a Price, Study Says," *Los Angeles Times,* March 29, 2001.

39. Nancy Peterson Walter, "The Land Exchange Act of 1937: Creation of the Indian Reservations at Bishop, Big Pine, and Lone Pine, California, through a Land Trade between the United States of America and the City of Los Angeles," Ph.D. dissertation, Union Institute and University, 1986, p. 93.

40. Quoted in William Overend, "Inyo County: Land of the New Colonials?" *Los Angeles Times,* January 4, 1981.

41. John Steven McGroarty, "High Sierras Offer Fine Playground," *The Intake,* August 1928.

42. Richard Coke Wood, *The Owens Valley and the Los Angeles Water Controversy: Owens Valley as I Knew It* (Stockton, CA: Pacific Center for Western Studies, 1973), p. 64.

43. "Owens Valley Park Plans Recited: Writer Points Out Possibilities of Playground in High Sierra Country," *The Intake,* April 1933: 21–22.

44. P. B. Hardesty, "Unveiling the American Alps," *The Intake,* August 1928.

45. David Babb, *101 Moments in Eastern Sierra History* (Bishop, CA: Community Printing and Publishing, 1999), p. 44.

46. John Steven McGroarty, "High Sierras Offer Fine Playground," *The Intake,* August 1928, p. 21.

47. Babb, p. 66.

48. *The Intake,* April 1933.

49. Theodore Roosevelt, *Ranch Life and the Hunting Trail* (New York: Century Co., 1902).

50. John Muir, *My First Summer in the Sierra* (New York: Houghton Mifflin Co., 1998), pp. 278, 304.

51. Quoted in Diana Meyers Bahr, *Viola Martinez: California Paiute* (Norman: University of Oklahoma Press, 2003), p. 40.

52. Quoted in Bahr, p. 27.

53. Ibid., p. 14.

54. Michelle Boorsten, "Whiteness of National Parks: Flaw or Harmless Social Reality?" *Los Angeles Sentinel*, Sept. 24, 1997, p. A–9.

55. Quoted in Gumprecht, p. 117.

56. Grady Clay, *Close-Up: How to Read the American City* (Chicago: University of Chicago Press, 1980), p. 49.

57. Davis, *Ecology of Fear*, p. 234.

58. Starr, p. 229.

59. "Burning All Illusions: LA Insurrection 1965/1992," *Do or Die*, No. 9 (2000), pp. 99–100.

60. Caughey, p. 174.

61. See John McPhee, The *Control of Nature* (New York: The Noonday Press, 1999), p. 222.

62. The Friends of the Los Angeles River are the most active opponents to this proposal, and information on their reasons for resistance can be found on their web page. Other involved groups are the Sierra Club, Heal the Bay, and the Chinese Yard Alliance.

63. D. J. Waldie, "The Myth of the L.A. River," *Buzz* 7(4): 80–85, April 1996.

64. Janet G. Hering, "Chinatown Revisited: Arsenic and the Los Angeles Water Supply," *Engineering and Science*, No. 3 (1997), pp. 35–40.

Chapter Three

1. John Walton, *Western Times and Water Wars: State, Culture, and Rebellion in California* (Berkeley: University of California Press, 1992), p. 21.

2. Quoted in D. Clora Cragen, *The Boys in the Sky Blue Pants: The Men and Events at Camp Independence and Forts of Eastern California, Nevada, and Utah, 1862–1877* (Fresno, CA: Pioneer Publishing Company, 1975), p. 51.

3. Ibid., p. 51.

4. Wilma R. Olson, *Olancha Remembered* (Sacramento, CA: W. R. Olson, 1997), p. 55.

5. "The Indian at Home," *Sierra Magazine Club Bulletin*, January 1909, n.p.

6. David Spurr, *The Rhetoric of Empire: Colonial Discourse in Journalism, Travel Writing, and Imperial Administration* (Durham, NC: Duke University Press, 1993), pp. 92–93.

7. David Babb, *101 Moments in Eastern Sierra History* (Bishop, CA: Community Printing and Publishing, 1999), p. 1.

8. Philip J. Wilke and Harry W. Lawton, ed., *The Expedition of Capt. J. W. Davidson from Fort Tejon to the Owens Valley in 1859* (Socorro, NM: Balena Press, 1976), p. 36.

9. Mary Austin, *The Land of Little Rain* (New York: Penguin Books, 1988), p. 91.

10. Wilke and Lawton, pp. 20, 27.

11. Ibid., p. 26

12. Ibid., p. 19.

13. Ibid., p. 29.

14. Ibid., p. 48

15. Ibid., p. 19.

16. Ibid., p. 19.

17. Walton, p. 17.

18. Robert A. Sauder, *The Lost Frontier: Water Diversion in the Growth and Destruction of Owens Valley Agriculture* (Tucson: The University of Arizona Press, 1994), p. 30

19. Quoted in ibid., p. 31.

20. Walton, p. 18.

21. Cragen, p. 8.

22. Ibid., p. 8.

23. Walton, p. 19.

24. Cragen, p. 56.

25. Quoted in Walton, p. 21.

26. Quoted in Cragen, p. 60.

27. Cragen, p. 60.

28. Quoted in Cragen, p. 70.

29. Cragen, p. 16.

30. Rebecca Fish Ewan, *A Land Between: Owens Valley, California* (Baltimore: The Johns Hopkins University Press, 2000), p. 94.

31. W. A. Chalfant, *The Story of Inyo* (Bishop, CA: Chalfant Press, 1933), p. 138.

32. Quoted in Cragen, p. 81.
33. The going rate in the Central Valley was about $1 a day. See Walton, p. 25.
34. Cragen, p. 122.
35. Ibid., p. 30.
36. Quoted in ibid., p. 71.
37. Quoted in ibid., p. 85.
38. Quoted in Walton, p. 33.
39. N. Walter, p. 174.
40. This was an Executive Order issued May 9, 1912, by President Taft.
41. Quoted in Walter, p. 243.
42. A. J. Ford, E. A. Porter, and C. D. Carl, "Report on the Condition of the Indians in Owens Valley California," Department of Water and Power, June 30, 1932, p. 6.
43. Ibid., p. 11.
44. Ibid., p. 10.
45. Ibid., p. 4.
46. Ibid., p. 15.
47. Ibid., p. 11.
48. E. A. Porter, "Final Report on the Owens Valley Indian Situation, Including a Suggested Plan for Adjustment of Same," Department of Water and Power, January 9, 1936, p. 15.
49. Ibid., p. 15.
50. Michel Foucault, The *Order of Things: An Archaeology of the Human Sciences* (New York: Vintage Books, 1994), p. 143.
51. Harry W. Lawton, Philip J. Wilke, Mary DeDeker, and William M. Mason, "Agriculture Among the Paiute of Owens Valley," *Before the Wilderness: Environmental Management by Native Californians*, ed. Thomas C. Blackburn and Kat Anderson (Menlo Park, CA: Ballena Press, 1993), p. 333.
52. Roy Harvey Pearce, *Savagism and Civilization: A Study of the Indian and the American Mind* (Berkeley: University of California Press, 1988), p. 70.
53. Wilke and Lawton, p. 28.
54. Theodore Roosevelt, *On Race, Riots, Reds, Crime*, ed. Archibald Roosevelt (Metairie, LA: Sons of Liberty, 1968), p. 30.
55. Quoted in Walter, p. 115.
56. Porter, pp. 7–8.

57. Nancy Walter attempted to locate this ballot during her research by checking both the National Archives and the Archives of the Department of Water and Power.

58. This is from a letter dated August 16, 1937, from the Assistant Commissioner of Indian Affairs, William Zimmerman, to Douglas Clark, the Assistant Land Field Agent of the Bureau of Indian Affairs.

59. Walter, p. 76.

60. Ibid., p. 378.

61. Ibid., p. 372.

62. "Exchanging of Certain Land and Water Rights in California," *Congressional Record—House,* March 10, 1937, p. 2077.

63. Ibid., p. 2077.

64. Ibid., p. 2077.

65. Although their consent may have been given, there is no proof to substantiate this fact. Also, their consent was sought after the proposed project was already in progress. Nancy Walter wrote, "Their role in the land exchange turns out to be minimal for they were governed by circumstances beyond their control" (365).

66. Quoted in Walter, p. 327.

67. Quoted in Diana Meyers Bahr, *Viola Martinez: California Paiute* (Norman: University of Oklahoma Press, 2003), p. 84.

68. Quoted in ibid., p. 84.

69. Quoted in ibid., p. 52.

70. A. J. Ford, E. A. Porter, and C. D. Carl, "Report on the Condition of the Indians in Owens Valley California," Department of Water and Power, June 30, 1932. [DWP-A-MC 1]

71. Walter, p. 292.

72. Ibid., p. 310–311.

73. Jessie A. Garrett and Ronald C. Larson, *Camp and Community: Manzanar and the Owens Valley,* Fullerton Oral History Program (Fullerton: California State University, 1977), p. 18.

74. *Inyo Register,* November 10, 1985.

75. Sauder, p. 150.

76. In the 1980 census, the population of Owens Valley Indians living on reservations was 1,853.

77. Interview with Allen Spoonhunter at the Bishop Paiute Reservation in May 1998.

78. Walter, p. 90.

79. Ibid., p. 379.
80. Ibid., p. 115.
81. Quoted in Bahr, p. 89.
82. Quoted in Walter, p. 353.
83. Walter, p. 353.
84. Quoted in Walter, p. 110.
85. Walter, p. 380.
86. Interview with Jerry Gewe at his office on June 25, 1997.
87. Raymond Williams, *Key Words: A Vocabulary of Culture and Society* (New York: Oxford University Press, 1985).
88. This is from an interview with Dorothy Alther, who represents the Toyabie Indian Health Project.
89. Mark Hill and William S. Platts, "Technical Memorandum #9, Management of Tules and Organic Sediments," Los Angeles: Ecosystem Sciences, 2000. <www.inyowater.org/LORP/tech-memo9.html>
90. "Pulverizing Pests," *Inyo Register,* June 21–22, 1997.
91. Susan Hill, "Technical Memorandum #6, Results of User Group Interviews," Los Angeles: Ecosystems Sciences, 2000. <www.inyowater.org/LORP/techmemo6.html>
92. Charlotte Bacoch, "Basketweaver Profile," *California Indian Basketweavers Association,* Newsletter #31 Summer 2000. <www.ciba.org/archive/news31.htm>
93. This estimate of ten thousand years is based upon anthropological findings and is part of the "land bridge" theory of travel from Asia. Native Americans who claim to have lived there "forever" have, however, disputed this theory. The Lone Pine tribe is a mixture of Paiute and Shoshone, whereas further up the valley, everyone is Paiute. The Western Shoshone, in Nevada and Death Valley, traditionally came over the hills to the Owens River to camp in the summer, thus having considerable contact with the Lone Pine Paiutes and ultimately intermarrying. Just north of Owens Valley, in the Bridgeport area, live the Washoe Indians, who have also intermarried with Paiutes.

Chapter Four

1. Jeanne Wakatsuki Houston and James D. Houston, *Farewell to Manzanar* (New York: Bantam Books, 1973), p. 186.

2. Harlan D. Unrau, *The Evacuation and Relocation of Persons of Japanese Ancestry During World War II: A Historical Study of the Manzanar War Relocation Center,* Vols. 1 and 2 (Washington, D.C.: United States Department of the Interior, 1996). <http://www.nps.gov/manz/hrs/hrs.htm>

3. Quoted in ibid.

4. Paul Rogers, "WWII Internment Camp Survivors Upset by Lack of Progress on Memorial," *San Jose Mercury News,* March 10, 1997.

5. Quoted in Rogers, "WWII Internment Camp Survivors Upset by Lack of Progress on Memorial."

6. Quoted in Donald Worster, *Rivers of Empire: Water, Aridity, and the Growth of the American West* (Oxford: Oxford University Press, 1985), p. 155.

7. Kevin Starr, *Material Dreams: Southern California through the 1920s* (Oxford: Oxford University Press, 1990), p. 25.

8. Starr, p. 29.

9. Larry Van Horn, "American Indian Links to Manzanar," *Cultural Resource Management,* No. 5 (2001), pp. 16–18.

10. Ibid.

11. W. A. Chalfant, *The Story of Inyo* (Bishop, CA: Chalfant Press, 1933), p. 407.

12. Quoted in Harlan D. Unrau, p. 6–1.

13. Linda Thomas, "Desert Pears," *Tapestry,* <www.wowwomen.com/tapestry/arch-rambles/desertpears.html>

14. Arthur A. Hansen and Betty E. Mitson, eds., *Voices Long Silent,* Fullerton Oral History Program (Fullerton: California State University, 1974), p. 62.

15. Jessie A. Garrett and Ronald C. Larson, *Camp and Community: Manzanar and the Owens Valley,* Fullerton Oral History Program (Fullerton, CA: California State University, 1977), p. 19.

16. Quoted in Diana Meyers Bahr, *Viola Martinez: California Paiute* (Norman: University of Oklahoma Press, 2003), p. 101.

17. Quoted in ibid., p. 103

18. Quoted in ibid., p. 99.

19. John Armor and Peter Wright, *Manzanar* (New York: Times Books, 1988), p. 92.

20. Jeanne Wakatsuki Houston and James D. Houston, *Farewell to Manzanar* (New York: Bantam Books, 1973), p. 99.

21. Garrett and Larson, p. 39.
22. J. Burton, M. Farrell, F. Lord, and R. Lord, *Confinement and Ethnicity: An Overview of World War II Japanese-American Relocation Sites,* Report 74, Tucson, Arizona: Western Archaeological and Conservation Center. <www.cr.nps.gov/history/online_books/anthropology74/ce0.htm>
23. Garrett and Larson, p. 98.
24. Ibid., p. 38.
25. Ibid., p. 38, 66.
26. Ibid., p. 81.
27. Ibid., p. 107.
28. Ibid., p. 52.
29. Ibid., p. 66.
30. Ibid., p. 109.
31. Ibid., p. 48.
32. Ibid., p. 99.
33. Ibid., p. 60.
34. Ibid., p. 110.
35. Hall Daily, "David-Goliath Fight Continues Over Water from Owens Valley," *Bakersfield Californian,* October 26, 1980.
36. Robert A. Sauder, *The Lost Frontier: Water Diversion in the Growth and Destruction of Owens Valley Agriculture* (Tucson: University of Arizona Press, 1994), pp. 96–97.
37. "Ansel Adams' Manzanar War Relocation Center Photographs," Special Collections in the Library of Congress. <http://www.loc.gov/rr/print/coll/109_anse.html>
38. Ansel Adams, *Born Free and Equal: Photographs of the Loyal Japanese Americans at Manzanar Relocation Center* (New York: U.S. Camera, 1944), p. 35.
39. Larry Van Horn, "American Indian Links to Manzanar," *Cultural Resource Management,* No. 5 (2001), pp. 16–18.
40. Armor and Wright, xiii.
41. John Tateishi, *And Justice for All: An Oral History of the Japanese American Detention Camps* (New York: Random House), 1984, p. 95.
42. Interview with Helen Brill, "Voices from the Second World War Collection," Thomas J. Dodd Research Center, University of Connecticut.
43. Ibid.

44. These two quotes are from Arthur A. Hansen, ed., *Japanese American World War II Evacuation Oral History Project* (Westport, CT: Meckler Publishing, 1991), pp. 236, 206.

45. Dorothy Swaine Thomas and Richard S. Nishimoto, *The Spoilage* (Berkeley and Los Angeles: University of California Press, 1946), pp. 3, 69.

46. Ellen Levine, *A Fence Away from Freedom: Japanese Americans and World War II* (New York: G. P. Putnam's Sons, 1995), p. 51.

47. Aly Colon, "Bainbridge Residents Recall Confinement," *Seattle Times,* May 7, 1996.

48. Houston and Houston, p. 88.

49. M. C. Reheis, "Dust Deposition Downwind of Owens (Dry) Lake, 1991–1994: Preliminary Findings," *Journal of Geophysical Research,* v. 102 (1997), pp. 25–26.

50. Houston and Houston, pp. 23–24.

51. Eleanor Roosevelt, "To Undo a Mistake is Always Harder than to Not Create One Originally," Franklin D. Roosevelt Library (Hyde Park, New York). This essay was published in a revised form on October 10, 1943, in *Collier's Magazine.*

52. Appendix 25, "The Silverman Report: Project Director's Report," *Final Report, Manzanar,* Vol. I, pp. A 174–75, RG 210, Entry 4b, Box 71, File, "Manzanar Final Reports."

53. Joan Brooks, *Desert Padre: The Life and Writings of Father John J. Crowley, 1891–1940* (Desert Hot Springs, CA: Mesquite Press, 1997), p. 45.

54. Great Basin Air Pollution Control District, *Owens Valley PM–10 Planning Area Demonstration of Attainment State Implementation Plan,* Draft, May 1997, p. 4–1.

55. Ibid., pp. 3–8.

56. Quoted in Garrett and Larson, p. 65.

57. Rabin [*sic*] Merritt to Samuel B. Morris, General Manager and Chief Engineer, Department of Water and Power, Los Angeles, March 26, 1946, Correspondence—Removal of Buildings, November 1945–April 1946, Manzanar Relocation Center, Administrative and Executive Files, Water Executive Office, LADWP Historical Records.

58. Ibid.

59. Ibid.

60. Ibid.

61. Burton S. Grant, Assistant Chief Engineer of Water Works to Samuel B. Morris and Laurence E. Goit, May 9, 1946, Correspondence—Removal of Buildings, May-June 1946, Manzanar Relocation Center, Administrative and Executive Files, Water Executive Office, LADWP Historical Records.
62. Presentation by Andrew Freeman for the Center for Land Use Interpretation, Owens Valley Bus Tour, April 24, 2004.
63. Garrett and Larson, p. 91.
64. Ibid., p. 73.
65. Ibid., p. 102.
66. Robert Ito, "Concentration Camp or Summer Camp? A New Generation of Revisionists Tries to Put a Happy Face on the Japanese American Relocation Camps," *MoJo News*, September 15, 1998.
67. William Booth, "A Lonely Patch of History: Japanese-Americans Were Forced to Live Here, They Don't Want It to Be Forgotten," *Washington Post*, April 15, 1997.
68. Paul Rogers, "W.W. II Internment Camp Survivors Upset by Lack of Progress on Memorial," *San Jose Mercury News*, March 10, 1997.
69. Quoted in Rebecca Fish Ewan, *A Land Between: Owens Valley, California* (Baltimore: The Johns Hopkins University Press, 2000), p. 165.
70. "After Years of Effort, First Tours Will Be Given at Manzanar Site," *Boston Globe*, July 27, 1997.
71. Quoted in Ibid.
72. Kimberly Edds, "New Museum Revives Painful Memories for Internees," *Washington Post*, April 26, 2004.

Chapter Five

1. Quoted in Michael Fleeman, "Thirsty Town Fights L.A. for its Water," *Detroit News*, September 4, 1997.
2. "Los Angeles Will Fight Pollution Board's Order to Return Water to Owens Lake," *Daily Independent*, July 3, 1997.
3. Julian Lukins, "Sea Water Option Too Costly for Los Angeles," *Inyo Register*, July 15, 1997.
4. Ibid.
5. Letter from Ellen Hardebeck to Karen Piper, dated April 7, 2003.
6. Interview with Ellen Hardebeck at the Great Basin Unified Air Pollution Control District Office, Bishop, California, May 1997.

7. Letter from Ellen Hardebeck to Karen Piper, dated April 7, 2003.

8. Fen Montaigne, "Water Pressure," *National Geographic,* September 2002, p. 19.

9. "Meeting Before the California Air Resources Board," May 22, 1998, p. 145.

10. Laura Dobbins, "Winter Visitors," *Daily Independent,* February 15, 1998.

11. During my interview with him on June 25, 1997, Jerry Gewe gave me a newspaper clipping on the dust mitigation proposals that had been faxed to him from Kearney. He did not seem to remember the note from Kearney that had been written on the fax.

12. Quoted in Page Stegner, "Water and Power," *Harper's,* March 1981, p. 68.

13. Barbara Adam and Joost Van Loon, "Introduction: Repositioning Risk; the Challenge for Social Theory," *The Risk Society and Beyond: Critical Issues for Social Theory,* ed. Barbara Adam, Ulrich Beck, and Joost Van Loon (London: Sage, 2000), p. 6.

14. John Hart, *Storm Over Mono: The Mono Lake Battle and the California Water Future* (Berkeley: University of California Press, 1996), p. 60.

15. *National Audubon Society v. Superior Court of Alpine County* (1983) 33 Cal.3d 419, 189 Cal. Rptr. 346, 658 P.2d 1.

16. Ibid.

17. Great Basin Unified Air Pollution Control District, *Owens Valley PM10 Planning Area Best Available Control Measures State Implementation Plan,* June 29, 1994, p. 67.

18. Marla Cone, "Owens Valley Plan Seeks L.A. Water to Curb Pollution," *Los Angeles Times,* December 17, 1996.

19. This is from a personal interview on Owens Lake in May 1997.

20. Hart, p. 77.

21. Ibid., p. 77

22. Ibid., p. 80.

23. Aldo Leopold, *A Sand County Almanac* (New York: Oxford University Press, 1978), p. 96.

24. Hart, p. 81.

25. David Babb, *101 Moments in Eastern Sierra History* (Bishop, CA: Community Printing and Publishing, 1999), p. 96.

26. "Meeting to Adopt the PM–10 Demonstration of Attainment SIP (PM–10 Attainment Plan)" at the Inyo County Courthouse, July 2, 1997.

27. Ibid.

28. Quoted in Hart, p. 60.

29. Ibid., p. 66

30. Ibid., p. 74.

31. Ibid., p. 127

32. Charles Petit, "Just Add Water," *San Francisco Chronicle,* November 26, 1995.

33. "Meeting Before the California Air Resources Board," Board Hearing Room, Sacramento, California, May 22,1998, p. 85.

34. *Mono Lake Newsletter,* Special Issue, 1994, p. 7.

35. Ibid., p. 7.

36. Interview with Dorothy Alther at the Bishop Paiute Tribe Reservation, May 1997.

37. Marc Reisner, *Overtapped Oasis: Reform or Revolution for Western Water* (Washington, D.C.: Island Press, 1990), pp. 28, 31–33. See also Peter Gleick, "Demand Focus Drive a New Water Attitude," *Source* 22 (November 2002). <http://thesource.melbournewater.com.au/content/Issue/November2002>

38. "Purchase of Farms Studied—to Reap the Water," *Los Angeles Times,* December 16, 1985.

39. Interview with Jerry Gewe at his office on June 25, 1997.

40. Ibid.

41. Quoted in Janet Allen, "The Real Erin Brockovich: Deadly Chromium 6 in L.A.'s Water," *Whole Life Times,* April 2001, p. 27.

42. "Meeting to Adopt the PM–10 Demonstration of Attainment SIP (PM–10 Attainment Plan)" at the Inyo County Courthouse, July 2, 1997.

43. Gayatri Chakravorty Spivak, "Subaltern Studies: Deconstructing Historiography," *Selected Subaltern Studies,* ed. Ranajit Guha and Gayatri Spivak (New York: Oxford University Press, 1988).

44. Quoted in William Overend, "Inyo, County: Land of the New Colonials?" *Los Angeles Times,* January 4, 1981.

Chapter Six

1. Interview with Ellen Hardebeck at the Great Basin Unified Air Pollution Control District Office, Bishop, California, May 1997.

2. Interview with Dorothy Alther at the Bishop Paiute Tribe Reservation, May 1997.

3. Letter from Roberta S. Zinman, Deputy City Attorney, to Don Sorenson, Inyo County Auditor, dated June 5, 1997.

4. Julian Lukins, "Great Basin Endorses Knight Bill in Principle," *Inyo Register,* February 14–15, 1998.

5. Interview with Jerry Gewe at his office on June 25, 1997.

6. Interview with Ellen Hardebeck at the Great Basin Unified Air Pollution Control District Office, Bishop, California, May 1997.

7. Interview with Dorothy Alther at the Bishop Paiute Tribe Reservation, May 1997.

8. Julian Lukins, "Knight Rides to Dry Lake's Rescue," *Inyo Register,* February 7–8, 1998.

9. This is from a letter by Dr. Richard Karina read at the "Meeting to Adopt the PM–10 Demonstration of Attainment SIP (PM–10 Attainment Plan)" at the Inyo County Courthouse, July 2, 1997.

10. Meeting Before the California Air Resources Board," May 22, 1998, p. 140.

11. "Meeting to Adopt the PM–10 Demonstration of Attainment SIP (PM–10 Attainment Plan)" at the Inyo County Courthouse, July 2, 1997.

12. Interview with Jerry Gewe at his office on June 25, 1997.

13. "Meeting to Adopt the PM–10 Demonstration of Attainment SIP (PM–10 Attainment Plan)" at the Inyo County Courthouse, July 2, 1997. The following quotes are from a transcript of the meeting.

14. Ibid.

15. Ibid.

16. Ibid.

17. Ibid.

18. Ibid.

19. Ibid.

20. Ibid.

21. Ibid.

22. Ibid.

23. Julian Lukins, "MOU Rejected," *Inyo Register,* December 18, 1997.

24. "Meeting Before the California Air Resources Board," May 22, 1998, p. 217.

25.   "Meeting to Adopt the PM–10 Demonstration of Attainment SIP (PM–10 Attainment Plan)" at the Inyo County Courthouse, July 2, 1997.

26.   Interview with Ellen Hardebeck at the Great Basin Unified Air Pollution Control District Office, Bishop, California, May 1997.

27.   "Meeting Before the California Air Resources Board," p. 87.

28.   Ibid., p. 129.

29.   Ibid., p. 214.

30.   Ibid., p. 202.

31.   "DWP Chief Too Visionary? Freeman Should Focus More on Business than Social Engineering," *Daily News of Los Angeles,* May 17, 1999.

32.   Jane Braxton Little, "Dust settles in Owens Valley," *High Country News* 32.8 (April 24, 2000).

33.   Bettina Boxall, "New Era for Old Foes in Water Wars," *Los Angeles Times,* November 18, 2001.

34.   "Owens Lake Groundwater Evaluation," *The Owens Valley Monitor,* 1999–2000   <http://www.inyowater.org/Annual_Reports/ 1999–2000/olge.htm>.

35.   Quoted in Mike Prather, "Update on Owens Lake," *Mono Lake Newsletter* (Winter 2000), p. 13.

Conclusion

1.   Quoted in Laura Mecoy, "Springing to Life: L.A. Revives a Lake it Drained," *Sacramento Bee,* July 7, 2002.

2.   William J. Kelly, "Money in the Lake: You Will End Up Paying for Repairing Owens Valley," *LA Weekly,* April 30-May 6, 2004.

3.   Presentation by Pat Brown, Department of Water and Power, for the Center for Land Use Interpretation, Owens Valley Bus Tour, April 25, 2004.

4.   See Kelly, "Money in the Lake."

5.   Presentation by Pat Brown, Department of Water and Power, for the Center for Land Use Interpretation, Owens Valley Bus Tour, April 25, 2004.

6.   From a personal conversation at the Interagency Visitors Center, Owens Lake, California, December 2001.

7. Presentation by Mike Patterson for the Center for Land Use Interpretation, Owens Valley Bus Tour, April 24, 2004.

8. Quoted in William J. Kelly, "Money in the Lake."

9. Walter S. Baer, Edmund D. Edelman, James W. Ingram III, and Sergej Mahnovski, *Governance in a Changing Market: The Los Angeles Department of Water and Power* (Santa Monica, CA: RAND Publications, 2001).

10. Bettina Boxall, "Desalination Projects Raise Issues of Private Profit, Public Interest," *Los Angeles Times,* March 21, 2004.

11. Abraham Hoffman, *Vision or Villainy: Origins of the Owens Valley-Los Angeles Water Controversy* (College Station: Texas A&M University Press, 1981), p. 272.

12. Ibid., 250.

13. Maude Barlow, "Desperate Bolivians Fought Street Battles to Halt a Water-for-Profit Scheme," *Globe & Mail,* May 9, 2000.

14. See "Enron's Secret Role in Power Blackouts," *Mail & Guardian,* April 8, 2005. See also Timothy Egan, "Tapes Show Enron Arranged Plant Shutdown," *New York Times,* February 4, 2005.

15. "More Enron Tapes, More Gloating," *CBS News,* June 8, 2004.

16. Maude Barlow, "Blue Gold: The Global Water Crisis and The Commodification of the World's Water Supply," a Special Report Produced and Published by the International Forum on Globalization (IFG), June 1999. <www.ifg.org/bgsummary.html> (September 9, 2002).

17. "Enron Tapes Anger Lawmakers," *CBS Evening News,* June 2, 2004.

18. Richard A. Oppel, Jr., "Enron's Many Strands: The Strategies; How Enron Got California To Buy Power It Didn't Need," *New York Times,* May 8, 2002.

19. Christopher Schwarzen, "Enron Tapes Back Case for Refunds, Local Utility Contends," *Seattle Times,* June 3, 2004. The entire transcript of these tapes is available at this site: <http://seattletimes.nwsource.com/html/localnews/2001945474_webenronaudio02.html>

20. Interview with Jerry Gewe at his office on June 25, 1997.

21. Statistics provided by the American Water Works Association, <www.awwa.org>.

22. Julian Lukins, "Knight Rides to Dry Lake's Rescue," *Inyo Register,* February 7–8, 1998.

23. John McPhee, *The Control of Nature* (New York: The Noonday Press, 1989), p. 235.

24. Julian Lukins, "LA Set to Take Dry Lake Burden," *Daily Independent,* October 23, 1997.

Epilogue

1. Matt Jenkins, "The Royal Squeeze," *High Country News,* Vol. 34, No. 17, September 16, 2002.

2. "An Analysis of Imperial County's Unemployment Rate," *CCBRES Bulletin,* San Diego State University, Imperial Valley Campus, Vol. 4, No. 5, May 2003. See also "Economic Development and Education in the Imperial Valley," *CCBRES Bulletin,* San Diego State University, Imperial Valley Campus, Vol. 5, No. 7, July 2004.

3. Bettye Wells Miller, "Thirsty for Water Dollars," *Riverside Press Enterprise,* May 25, 2003.

4. Robert Elliot, "Faking Nature," in *Environmental Ethics,* ed. Robert Elliot (New York: Oxford University Press, 1995), pp. 76–88.

INDEX